A Methodist Minister in Paris

The Letters of Andrew Longacre
1860-1862

Edited by
Wanda Willard Smith

Center for Methodist Studies at Bridwell Library

BRIDWELL LIBRARY ❧ SOUTHERN METHODIST UNIVERSITY

DALLAS, TEXAS 2002

Copyright 2002 by Bridwell Library, Perkins School of Theology, Southern Methodist University.
All Rights Reserved.

A Methodist minister in Paris : the letters of Andrew Longacre, 1860-1862 / edited by Wanda Willard Smith.

p.   cm.

Includes bibliographical references.
ISBN 0-941881-28-8.

1. Longacre, Andrew, 1831-1906-Correspondence. 2. Methodists-France-Correspondence.
3. Bridwell Library-Exhibitions. I.Bridwell Library. Center for Methodist Studies. II. Smith, Wanda
Willard, 1923-

BX8495.L66 A3 2002

Original Photography by Jon Speck.
Design and typesetting by Bradley Hutchinson at Digital Letterpress in Austin, Texas. The typefaces
are Poetica Chancery and Minion. Printed on acid-free Mohawk Superfine by The Stinehour Press in
Lunenburg, Vermont. Bound by Acme Bookbinding in Charlestown, Massachusetts.

Table of Contents

List of Illustrations

[Unless otherwise attributed, all the illustrations below have been loaned by Dr. Andrew Longacre, Jr., of Skaneateles, New York, including the drawings, sketches, and watercolors by the Reverend Andrew Longacre which are mounted in a portfolio and are so identified.]

Foreword

ANDREW LONGACRE (1831–1906) is not a name that leaps off the pages of American or even Methodist history. Few will have heard of him, or, if the name sounds familiar, it is probably because of his more famous father, the American engraver John Barton Longacre. No, Andrew Longacre did not leave a lasting mark on history. He was a minister, a good minister, who led an interesting life, no more, no less. And yet, through his letters, preserved at Bridwell Library, and through his diaries and sketches generously lent by the Longacre family, we get a glimpse not just of Andrew Longacre, but also of his times.

Wanda Smith, Research Archivist at Bridwell Library, has edited Longacre's letters with scholarly care and a growing fondness for their author. As you read these letters by an eloquent young minister serving the American Church in Paris, you, too, may become smitten. At the very least, you will experience a small part of history through the very personal medium of the private letter. Whether writing about Parisian life, characters in his congregation, the Civil War, or his travels, Longacre brings the nineteenth century to life in his letters. The beauty of these letters is that they can be read as micro history or simply enjoyed as fine examples of epistolary art.

In the course of her research, Ms. Smith managed to locate the descendents of Andrew Longacre and has developed a warm friendship with several of them. We are grateful to the Longacre family for the loan of Andrew's diaries and portfolio that were so useful in the research for this catalogue, and for allowing us to display some wonderful family portraits in the exhibition.

Andrew Longacre writes in one of his letters: "As to my own life for the last four weeks, a great deal might be said. Whether I shall be able to say it or any part of it with interest remains to be seen." He needn't have worried; he succeeded in that letter and in others.

Valerie R. Hotchkiss
J.S. Bridwell Foundation Endowed Librarian
February 2002

Preface

ANDREW LONGACRE, a young Methodist minister of the Philadelphia Conference, wrote these letters between 1860-1862, while he was serving as assistant pastor at the (non-denominational) American Chapel in Paris. All of them save one were addressed to his younger brother back home in Philadelphia, James Madison Longacre, who is always affectionately referred to as "Jim."

This remarkable correspondence came to Bridwell Library in 1956 as a part of the Bishop Frederick D. Leete Methodist Historical Library. How and from whom Bishop Leete acquired these letters is not known. The recipient, James Madison Longacre, died in 1903; his widow, Augusta McClintock Longacre, in 1928. Their last surviving child, James Barton Longacre (named in honor of his grandfather), died in 1947. One assumes that the letters remained in the Longacre family until at least that time. When Bishop Leete issued the first number of *The Journal of the Methodist Historical Library* in March, 1952, the Andrew Longacre letters were listed as a part of the collection. However, two errors occur in this notice: (1) the number of letters was given as twenty-five when there are, in fact, seventy-two; and (2) the letters were said to be addressed to Andrew's brother, "J. B." Longacre (James Barton Longacre was Andrew's father).

Most of these letters were written with a gold pen (Andrew's experiments with a steel pen were not satisfactory) in black ink on both sides of slick, very thin, onionskin paper. The pages measure approximately 5 ¼ by 8 inches. Some of the letters are cross-written; that is, after completing a page, Andrew turned the stationery a quarter turn and wrote across the previous text, making reading and transcription a challenge. No envelopes survive.

In punctuating his letters, Andrew used many dashes—some in place of periods, commas, semi-colons, some for just a pause in thought. This makes for a very "busy" page. Therefore, most of the dashes have been omitted and, where necessary, periods, commas, etc., have been supplied, although the results are not always perfectly correct where the rules of punctuation are concerned. Andrew used British spelling for some words and, after he had been in Paris awhile, occasional French forms.

An added dimension to these letters has been provided by Andrew's personal diaries, journals, letters, sermon notes, sketches, paintings, and photographs preserved by his daughter, Lydia. This treasured archive was inherited by Andrew's great-grandson and namesake of Skaneateles, New York, who, with great generosity, has made it available to us to illustrate and illuminate the letters his ancestor wrote during his years abroad.

Not a great deal is known about the brother who received these letters. He was born May 18, 1833, and was named almost certainly for the fourth president of the United States, because his father, James Barton Longacre, had spent some time with James Madison at his home in Montpelier, Virginia, working on a presidential portrait.

In the United States census for 1850, James Madison Longacre was listed in his father's household, age seventeen, employed in "dry goods." In 1860, still living in his father's house, he was twenty-seven years old and working as an "accountant." At the time of this correspondence, Jim was employed by a Philadelphia insurance company.

Wanda Willard Smith, Methodist Archivist
Center for Methodist Studies, Bridwell Library
June 12, 2001

Acknowledgements

No work of this nature is ever accomplished alone, and I am particularly fortunate to have been assisted by a number of valued colleagues and friends at home and abroad whose gifts of time, expertise, and interest did much to bring this project to completion.

Valerie Hotchkiss, the director of Bridwell Library, has championed the work from its inception and has given unstinting encouragement and support to all my efforts. Page A. Thomas, the director of the Center for Methodist Studies at Bridwell Library and my supervisor, agreeably postponed some of my duties and responsibilities at the Center to enable me to give almost full attention to these letters and the exhibition.

Others at Bridwell to whom I am greatly indebted include Jon Speck, Exhibitions Manager, not only for his gifted and masterful work in mounting the exhibition, but also for his cheerful and steady disposition in dealing with and solving the myriad problems that surface regularly in a project such as this. Amber Sturgess, Assistant to the Director, vetted the manuscript and translated the French words and phrases. Eric White, Curator of Special Collections, and Charles Baker, Cataloger, read the manuscript and offered advice and assistance. Sally Key, Conservator, prepared some items for the exhibition. Ellen Frost, Acquisitions Librarian, Linda Umoh and Sandra Sherman, Cataloging, John Wadhams, Interlibrary Loans, and Leann Pace-Mahoney, Circulation, located and quickly made available rare and out-of-print sources. From the entire Bridwell staff came unfailing moral support and camaraderie.

I owe an enormous debt of gratitude and appreciation to Dr. Andrew Longacre, Jr., and his wife, Virginia, of Skaneateles, New York. Andy, the great-grandson and namesake of the author of these letters, made this project his own and became my collaborator from the beginning. He not only made available his ancestor's archive, he also went out of his way to locate other family records. He read the manuscript and made astute and helpful suggestions and comments for correction and improvement. And, he loaned valued family portraits and documents for the exhibition.

Breta Eleanor Del Mar Revill, the granddaughter of Andrew Longacre, and her husband, Peter, of Rocky Hill, Connecticut, read the manuscript and made many useful comments and corrections. Eleanor also graciously loaned the portrait of her ancestor, painted during his tenure at the American Chapel in Paris, to serve as the frontispiece of this edition of his letters as well as the centerpiece of the exhibition.

Gratitude is also expressed to Emily Muller, Asheville, North Carolina, another granddaughter of Andrew Longacre, and to his great-granddaughters, Harriette Longacre Phelps, Washington, D. C., Sally L. Frost, East Dorset, Vermont, and the Reverend Marian McCart, Rock Island, Illinois, who loaned portraits, photographs, and documents from their share of the Longacre archives.

Colleagues to whom I owe much appreciation and gratitude include Richard P. Heitzenrater, William Kellon Quick Professor of Church History and Wesley Studies, Duke University, for his expertise in all things Methodist; Victor P. Furnish, University Distinguished Professor Emeritus of New Testament, Perkins School of Theology, Southern Methodist University, for information and guidance on Andrew Longacre's travels in Egypt, Palestine, Syria, Lebanon, and Turkey; Charles Wood, Lehman Professor of Christian Doctrine, Perkins School of Theology, who made on-site observations and provided helpful information on the original location of the American Chapel in Paris; and Kenneth E. Rowe, Methodist Librarian and Professor of Church History, Drew University, who brought to light remote and little-known sources.

Appreciation is also expressed to Isaac Gewirtz, Ruth Carr, and Mimi Bowling, of the New York Public Library; Jane Schroeder, Archives and Special Collections, Dickinson College, Carlisle, Pennsylvania; Peter Harrington, Curator, Anne S. K. Brown Military Collection, Brown University Library, Providence, Rhode Island; Max Moeller, Pennsylvania Historical Society; the Reverend Carol M. Simpson, Associate Pastor of the American Church in Paris; and Roger Hewitt, Isle of Wight History Centre, Newport, Isle of Wight.

Others who read the manuscript for typographical and/or factual errors and offered suggestions for improvement were: Bishop John Wesley Hardt, James E. Kirby, Professor of Church History, Perkins School of Theology, the Reverend Ann Johnson, Mary Ann Marshall, and R. Russell Smith, IV, all of Dallas; Karen Heitzenrater, Durham, North Carolina; and Joan Little of New York City. For these vigilant eyes and nimble minds I am profoundly grateful.

Introduction

The Longacres

ANDREW LONGACRE was born June 12, 1831, into an old and prominent Philadelphia family. His ancestors had arrived in Pennsylvania from Sweden in 1634 and settled on the Delaware River below the site of Philadelphia.[1]

His father, James Barton Longacre, was born in Delaware County, Pennsylvania, August 11, 1794. At age fourteen, after his mother died and his father remarried, James left home and went to Philadelphia. Befriended by the Methodists there, he found employment in a brass foundry before going to work in the bookstore of John F. Watson. Watson soon recognized the talents of the boy, took him into his family as an apprentice, and later apprenticed him to George Murray to learn the art of engraving. The quality of his work was outstanding and James advanced rapidly. He remained with Murray until 1819 when he set up in business for himself. Regarded as one of the best engravers in the country, his numerous works were circulated widely. He engraved the portraits of George Washington, Thomas Jefferson, and John Hancock on the facsimile of the Declaration of Independence published by John Binns in 1820. Soon after going into business for himself, Longacre was commissioned to make engravings from original portraits for John Sanderson's *Biographies of the Signers of the Declaration of Independence* (Philadelphia, 1820-1827). Later, with James Herring, Longacre published *The National Portrait Gallery of Distinguished Americans* (Philadelphia, 1834-1839). On September 16, 1844, President John Tyler appointed him Chief Engraver of the U. S. Mint, a position he held until his death in 1869. One of his most memorable coin designs was the Indian Head penny.[2]

While still young, James became a member of St. George's Methodist Episcopal Church in Philadelphia where for many years he served variously as class leader, steward, and trustee. In 1855, along with others, he left St. George's to form Central church, serving in the same positions until his death. He was on the first board of Methodist trustees of Dickinson College, in Carlisle, Pennsylvania, on the first board of managers of the Philadelphia Conference Tract Society and Publishing House, and for thirty years was a vice-president of the American Sunday School Union.

Andrew's mother, Eliza Stiles Longacre, was born June 29, 1807, in Tuckerton, New Jersey, the youngest of nine children of Samuel and Eliza Chew Stiles. On May 22, 1827, at age nineteen, she married James Barton Longacre, thirteen years her senior. Eliza, like her new husband, was a staunch and devout Methodist. It was said of her that she was "an advocate of the highest attainable spiritual life." She espoused the Wesleyan doctrine of sanctification, and following the example of the well-known female evangelist, Phoebe Palmer, she established in her home a "Tuesday Meeting for the Promotion of Holiness."[3]

Eliza and James Barton Longacre were singularly devoted to their faith and to the care and upbringing of a growing family. Over the next twenty-three years, six children were born to them:

Sarah ("Sallie"), Andrew, James Madison, Eliza Huldah, Orleans ("Orly"), and Phoebe Palmer Longacre. The Longacre home was a place of religious instruction, family prayer, Bible reading, and hymn-singing. This religious home life flourished amidst a library of fine books, knowledge of and appreciation for art, literature, and music, lively conversation, an extended family, and a host of friends.

Then, in 1850, tragedy struck a double blow. Eliza Longacre had given birth to her sixth child on April 6 of that year. Three weeks later, on May 1, shortly before her forty-third birthday, Eliza died, probably from complications following childbirth. She left a husband and six children, age 22 to her newborn infant, who did not long survive her mother.[4] The early and untimely deaths of mother and child had a profound effect on the entire family. For Andrew, the death of his mother was a devastating loss. Yearly, for the rest of his life, he observed the anniversary and noted it in his diaries.

Andrew Longacre's Early Life

The earliest event of record in Andrew's life (other than his birth) is his religious conversion when he was twelve years old. He joined Union Methodist Episcopal Church where his sister, Sallie, was a member. But two pivotal events in Andrew's youth and early manhood cannot be dated precisely.

The first is his call to the ministry. The best answer seems to be sometime in the latter part of 1850, for in December of that year he announced to the Sunday School class he had been teaching at Union church that he would no longer be able to meet with them, because "God has called me to preach and I must obey."[5]

The second undated event was a serious illness that "threatened to make me a life-long invalid" and that occurred after he had consecrated himself to serve God as a minister.[6] Evidence points to sometime during the first nine or ten months of 1856: few entries were made in his diary until late in the year, and the *Minutes* of the Philadelphia Conference list him as a supernumerary from 1857-1860.[7]

Andrew's exact illness is never identified, but the symptoms that plagued him later in life, the fact that his health was never robust, and that (even though he lived to the age of seventy-four) the cause of his death was valvular heart disease suggest that his affliction may have been rheumatic fever. In any case, knowledge of these physical limitations is crucial to the understanding of Andrew Longacre, the man, and his career.

Andrew had inherited the artistic talents of his father, had studied with him, and intended to follow in his father's footsteps as an engraver. From an early age, he made sketches and painted. But little is known of Andrew's formal education. A brief biographical sketch reports that "he was educated in his native city, but prevented by successive failures in health from completing his studies."[8] Nevertheless, his was a well-furnished mind, gifted, sophisticated, erudite.

In 1851, the first year after Andrew had answered the call to the ministry, he traveled with the presiding elder of the South Philadelphia District, Thomas J. Thompson, a former pastor at Union church and family friend. In Methodist terms this meant that Andrew was afforded the opportunity to observe, study, and be educated in the duties and responsibilities of the pastoral office. Since no Methodist theological schools then existed in that part of the country, this was invaluable training for his life's work, although one can be reasonably certain that some such instruction had begun at his mother's knee.

In 1852 Andrew was admitted on trial in the Philadelphia Conference and appointed to Chestnut Hill in the Reading District. Over the next four years, he was admitted into full connection, ordained deacon, then elder, and appointed to various churches in the South Philadelphia District. Too frail to serve a church full time between 1857-60, he continued to preach on occasion when health permitted.

Thus matters stood at the end of January, 1860, when Andrew called on his physician "to consult him as to my taking an effective relation to the Conference in the spring. He did not approve it." Three weeks later, Andrew once again called on the doctor. "He thought I had better rest another year—or I must stipulate an easy appointment, which I am unwilling to do." [9]

The Philadelphia Conference convened at Union church on March 21, 1860. A week later, while attending conference, Andrew noted in his diary that Dr. John McClintock (who had been serving at St. Paul's Methodist Episcopal Church in New York City) "proposed my coming to Paris to assist him in the Fall from the first of November. He offers to board me and bear my expenses but feels unable to offer a salary. Postponed a definite reply till sometime in the future." [10]

On the last day of the conference, March 30, Andrew had a short conversation with his bishop "about Paris, etc." On April 11, a letter arrived from John McClintock saying there had been a change of plan and he "desires me to go either by April 28 or May 5." After further discussions with his bishop, his presiding elder, and family members, "all of whom heartily approved it," Andrew wrote to McClintock the following day, "accepting his proposition." [11]

This decision set off a flurry of preparations. Andrew purchased a French Grammar and arranged to take lessons. His old trunk could not be repaired so he bought a new one. On April 25, he took the train to Washington where he met his father. Together they went to the Department of State for a passport. They called on the Secretary of State, Lewis Cass, and received a letter of introduction to the United States Minister to France, Charles J. Faulkner. Next came a visit to the White House where they were received by President James Buchanan. Back home in Philadelphia, there was packing and shipping to do and travel plans to be made. On May 2, he bid farewell to friends and family and took the train to New York.

Andrew felt that his selection by McClintock was providential. "It has come to me as the rain and the sunshine come to the fields, without request or even the dreaming of such a possibility. . . . It seems simply 'the Lord's doing'. I am quite confident that in going I am only following the divine ordering." [12] Nevertheless, he had serious apprehensions. Five days before sailing Andrew wrote in his diary, "I felt sadly [about leaving] but confident in God's guidance and protection. It seemed right for me to go even if I should be lost [at sea]." [13]

While understanding the pitfalls, he was firmly aware of his mission and intent: "I go to a hard field, spiritually considered. I go alone, to a land of almost magical power to tempt & lead astray, at least to some extent, all sorts of men. I am sure I go to do good. This is the object, as far as motive is concerned the sole object of my going. (Perhaps I ought to include a desire for improved health.) I know I cannot do good without grace for my own preservation, & the baptism of the spirit of God upon my ministry." [14] The commitment made, he sailed from New York on May 5, 1860, destination Paris.

The McClintocks

John McClintock, Jr., was also a Philadelphian, born October 27, 1814.[15] Both his parents were emigrants from County Tyrone, Ireland. Like the Longacres, the McClintocks were devout Methodists and the two families had long known each other through church and community activities. John McClintock's father had also been a member of St. George's Methodist Episcopal Church where he served as a class leader and trustee.

When only fourteen years old, McClintock went to work at the Methodist Book Concern in New York City. He was converted there and seriously considered entering the ministry but, instead, returned to Philadelphia in 1832 and entered the University of Pennsylvania, graduating in three years. In spite of recurrent throat trouble and other physical disabilities that made preaching difficult, he was admitted on trial to the Philadelphia Conference of the Methodist Episcopal Church in 1835 and ordained elder in 1840.

McClintock thought the educational field offered him a more realistic opportunity for service than the itinerancy and, in 1837, he accepted a teaching post at Dickinson College in Carlisle, Pennsylvania. In 1848, he was elected editor of the *Methodist Quarterly Review*, a position perfectly suited to his scholarly tastes.

Shortly after he had taken up his position at Dickinson College, McClintock married Carolina Augusta Wakeman. Of their three children, only two survived: a son, Emory, and a daughter, Augusta. After his wife's death in 1850, McClintock married Catharine Emory, the widow of his best friend, Robert Emory, who had two young children of her own (John and Maria Emory). This was the family with whom Andrew Longacre would live during his years in Paris.

McClintock was appointed to St. Paul's Methodist Episcopal Church in New York City in 1858. Although his health was never robust and illness was often his companion, "he accepted sickness as a discipline and always said that he needed it for his own good."[16] He was an eloquent preacher, a cheerful and genial man, with a wide circle of friends.

In 1860, John McClintock was approached by the American Foreign and Christian Union (AFCU) in New York to go to Paris as pastor of the American Chapel. Not physically strong enough to take on the work alone, he knew he would need an assistant. He first offered the post to a fellow minister who was not able to accept. He then thought of Andrew Longacre. Having known Andrew and the Longacre family all of his life, McClintock thoroughly understood the physical limitations of his younger colleague. But he also knew well Andrew's gifts and graces, knew that he was a sincere Christian with an unwavering devotion to his ministerial calling, and therefore extended the invitation.

American and Foreign Christian Union and The American Chapel in Paris

The organization that invited John McClintock to go to Paris as minister of the American Chapel[17] was formed in New York City in 1849 when three U. S. based missionary societies merged. The American and Foreign Christian Union had no denominational affiliations, its members being drawn from various evangelical bodies—Congregational, Presbyterian, Baptist, Methodist, and

Dutch Reformed. Its goal was to provide American residents, businessmen, and travelers in Paris opportunities for and benefits of Protestant worship.

The AFCU was the governing body of the American Chapel, it participated in the selection of the senior pastor, and acted as the official employer. It raised money for endowments from which were funded the senior pastor position, insurance on the building, and assistance with major capital expenditures. And, it still functions as such today for the descendant of the Chapel, the American Church in Paris.

Although not officially founded until 1857, the American Chapel in Paris can, in some sense, trace its history back to 1814 when the first public worship services in English were held in Paris by a chaplain of the British military forces. These services took place in the French Protestant Temple of the Oratoire. In 1816 a few Americans then living in Paris were able to obtain the use of the Oratoire on Monday evenings. A separate room was constructed for their use (known as the "Upper Room"), and Americans held public worship there on Sundays until 1830.

At that time an unused school in the rue Taitbout was taken over by a group of French-Americans who maintained separate Sunday services and schools. This facility became known as "Chapelle Taitbout." In 1840 the congregation purchased property and built a chapel in the rue de Provence. It was known as the Église Réformée Evangélique, but the name "Chapelle Taitbout" was carried over from the old location. In the years following, it was supplied by a number of different ministers.

In 1857, the American and Foreign Christian Union in New York asked Dr. Edward Kirk to organize the congregation on a non-sectarian basis. Since a foreign entity was not permitted to own land in Paris at that time, Kirk purchased a building site in his own name at No. 21, rue de Berri, located in the newly developing western part of the city.

An elegant structure of neo-Gothic design, erected at a cost of $46,000, and seating approximately six hundred persons, was dedicated on May 2, 1858. The first sermon in the Chapel was preached by the Reverend R. H. Seeley, a congregational minister of Springfield, Massachusetts. His pastorate was brief, lasting only until September 1859. In December of that year, Dr. George L. Prentiss was appointed to fill the pulpit until a permanent pastor could be named—i.e., until John McClintock arrived.[18]

Arrangements for the worship services at the Chapel were a compromise in order to accommodate a large number of loyal supporters of the Chapel who preferred the Episcopal form of liturgy and a more evangelical group who preferred informal extemporary prayers. Therefore, on Sundays at 11:15 a.m. the Morning Prayer of the Protestant Episcopal Church was read; at 12 o'clock extemporary prayer introduced the sermon; the afternoon service at 3 o'clock was non-liturgical.[19] Prayer Meetings were held on Thursdays at 7:30 p.m.

Paris

Andrew Longacre was twenty-eight years old when he arrived in Paris on May 17, 1860. From his diary, we know that part of the crossing from New York had been rough, and seasickness and homesickness were his companions for much of the twelve-day voyage. By the time the ship docked at Le Havre, however, he was in better spirits.

A fellow passenger from Philadelphia and a seasoned traveler, Dr. John Maris, kindly assisted Andrew in landing and getting his luggage through customs. They stayed overnight at Le Havre and then took the train to Paris. There, Dr. Maris again befriended the young clergyman. He helped find hotel accommodations and the next day accompanied Andrew when he presented his credentials to J. W. Tucker, the Secretary and Treasurer of the Executive Committee of the American Chapel. Andrew met with other members of the congregation and then called on Dr. George L. Prentiss, the acting pastor at the Chapel.

Finding a place to live was an immediate concern since he had arrived before the McClintocks had established their residence. A week passed before he found satisfactory rooms, during which time Andrew "suffered very much from low spirits."[20] Never before had he been so far away from home and family for such an extended period of time. He sorely missed the "home-life" he had always known and felt acutely the pain of separation. He missed sharing in the "religious privileges of home."[21] And, in particular, he missed the love and support of his younger brother, Jim.

Andrew's homesickness revealed in these letters is often palpable. Writing to Jim and other family members was one way of alleviating the pangs of separation while at the same time sharing his new experiences in a foreign country. And their letters to him were lifelines to all that was familiar and cherished. They could never write often enough to keep his homesickness totally at bay.

Realizing his French would not carry him far, Andrew arranged for more lessons, he purchased an easel and art supplies, and he explored the newly expanding city north of the Champs Élysées and west to the Bois de Boulogne. He went to the Louvre to study the Italian schools of painting as well as the French and German.[22] He met many of his parishioners, some of whom were to play important roles in his life.

The Chapel families befriended their young minister, and he became especially close to several of them, notably, the J. D. B. Curtises, the Woodbury Langdons, the banker John Munroe and his family, the Thomas N. Dales, Alexander Van Rensselaer, and, when the Henry J. Bakers arrived in Paris, an old friendship from Baltimore and New York days was happily renewed. We meet all of these and many others in Andrew's letters. He visited in their homes and dined at their tables, accompanied them on walks and drives about the city and its environs, attended exhibitions, went to galleries, museums, churches, and military parades.

Emperor Louis Napoleon and the Second Empire

The Paris that Andrew found in 1860 was undergoing a massive program of demolition and reconstruction begun nine years earlier. In an 1851 *coup d'etât* Louis Napoleon became Emperor of France and began immediately to transform the medieval capital, long ruled by king, pope, and church, into a modern commercial and industrial metropolis under his imperial rule.

Dark, filthy slums that fostered crime, disease, and despair were destroyed. Narrow, twisting, congested, polluted streets were straightened, widened, and lengthened into grand boulevards. Ancient structures were torn down and elegant new buildings went up in their places. A chaos of debris was everywhere while builders, architects, and decorators swarmed over all.

 Public parks and gardens, newly planted with trees and flowers, squares, fountains, and monuments were constructed. Canals and artesian wells increased the Paris water supply.

Left:
James Madison Longacre.
Philadelphia, November 7, 1860.
Loaned by Sally L. Frost, East Dorset, Vermont.

Bottom Left:
Eliza Stiles Longacre, 1839.
Painted by Emanuel Leutze.

Bottom Right:
James Barton Longacre, 1839.
Painted by Emanuel Leutze.

Right:
Longacre Family: Eliza Huldah, James Madison,
Sarah Longacre Keen, and Andrew.
Philadelphia, ca. 1851.
Loaned by Sally L. Frost, East Dorset, Vermont.

Bottom Left:
Andrew Longacre in "cassock, gown, and bands."
Paris, July 10, 1860.

Bottom Right:
James Barton Longacre (father)
and James Madison Longacre (son). Philadelphia, 1860.
Loaned by Sally L. Frost, East Dorset, Vermont.

18

Underground, a sewer system (for which Paris is renowned to this day) and gas lines were being built. Brilliant, exquisitely designed street lamps replaced dim, flickering lanterns. Many of the accomplishments were due in large part to Louis' prefect of the Seine, Georges Eugène Haussmann, who in total dedication to his emperor worked tirelessly to perform these miracles. The energy and magnificence of all this activity were evident to all observers.

Paris streets were crowded with every form of humanity. Elegantly dressed pedestrians strolled along the new boulevards and in the parks and gardens. Mingling in the crowds were musicians, singers, organ-grinders with pet monkeys, jugglers, sword-swallowers, peddlers. Carriages, omnibuses, and riders on horseback jockeyed for space. Movement, noise, color were everywhere.

And, there were Louis Napoleon's soldiers. The Second Empire had begun under a military dictatorship. Over time the harshness had diminished, but the whole régime was still cast in a military mode. Soldiers in colorful uniforms, resplendent in their richness and variety, were seen at all hours. Military bands played in the gardens, and parades were mounted on any occasion.[23]

Andrew later recalled that Paris was just then "robing itself in the unparalleled splendor of the Second Empire."[24] His letters to his brother back in Philadelphia open a window onto this magical world. Through his eyes, we stroll down the Champs Élysées ("the most grand promenade"), see the Emperor, Empress Eugénie, and the Prince Imperial review the troops on the Champs-de-Mars, walk through the Bois de Boulogne ("that paradise of Paris"), listen to music in the Tuileries Gardens, attend exhibitions at the Palais de l'Industrie, explore the streets, buildings, and monuments on the Left Bank.

To enable his family to follow him on his walks, Andrew sent them a map. Since the layout of the city that Andrew knew is much the same today, we can follow him still. To preserve a visual record of these times, Andrew's sketchbook was always near at hand, and his paintings reveal some of the scenes that caught his attention.

The Assistant Pastor

Andrew preached his first sermon at the American Chapel on Sunday afternoon, May 27, 1860, on John 12:21, "We would see Jesus." The congregation, he noted in his diary, was "better than I expected to see."[25] He continued to assist Dr. Prentiss at the Chapel until Prentiss's departure. Bidding him goodbye on Thursday morning, June 7, Andrew then conducted his first Thursday evening prayer meeting at the Chapel. Fourteen were present.[26]

He found that the congregation at the Chapel was made up of all denominations, all classes of society, and all shades of politics. Many were Americans of wealth and leisure, others were of more moderate means. Often accompanied by wives, children, and extended families, entrepreneurs with business interests in England, France, Italy, and other parts of Europe, flocked to Paris and made it their overseas base of operations. These, along with professional men, government officials, artists, and an ever present stream of travelers also made their way to the American Chapel.

The McClintocks arrived on June 28th. It took several days to make living arrangements for their large family. McClintock rented the first and second floors of a large "hôtel" previously leased by Dr. Prentiss at No. 42, rue des Ecuries d'Artois, located near the Chapel and the Arc de Triomphe. Much to Andrew's delight he found the new place very satisfactory. Not only were the physical surroundings and furnishings comfortable and pleasing but being once again part of a warm and friendly family buoyed his spirits.

Andrew acknowledged that it was "a delicate thing to attempt to live in any man's family,"[27] but he immediately felt at home. He found his host to be kind and considerate, and the relationship that developed between them was like that of an older brother to a younger.

Soon after he arrived in Paris, McClintock adopted the custom of opening his home one evening every week to the reception of all who chose to call. Andrew recalled years afterward, "These little, free, cheery reunions he greatly enjoyed; as did all who shared in them. His house was common ground, where all who came laid aside the real or fancied distinctions insisted upon elsewhere. The passing traveler here met the American Parisian, who seldom visited his native land; active men of business, ministers on their vacation, students of art, of medicine, or of theology, men of leisure, mingled together. . . . All were delightful to him."[28]

"I am too much a Methodist"

Andrew quickly learned that serving a non-denominational church in the French capital was not the same as serving small Methodist churches in Philadelphia. Sometimes this gave him pause and more than once in his letters to Jim he remarked on the differences. He found that the "sympathies and kindnesses" afforded a Methodist minister back home were not always forthcoming from his Paris congregation. "As a field of ministerial labor Paris is not attractive; there are many and great drawbacks to one's usefulness."[29] With few exceptions, the earnest, praying, pastoral visits that were expected by American Methodist church members were not acceptable to the Chapel congregation. Andrew sorely missed this aspect of the ministry and longed for what he believed to be an integral part of the pastoral office. "I fancy, I am too much a Methodist," he wrote. "I grow hungry for real warmhearted Methodist communion."[30]

There were rewards, of course. Most Americans in the congregation welcomed their fellow countrymen as old friends. Andrew found that he could preach shorter sermons at the Chapel than in Philadelphia. And when, seven months after his arrival, Woodbury Langdon came forward at the close of the service on Christmas Day, 1860, to receive his first communion, Andrew was overjoyed. McClintock was quick to give all the credit to Andrew: "A great change has been going on in him [Langdon] for some months; . . . this blessed result is due largely to Mr. Longacre, who has been greatly useful to him and his family. A work of grace is going on in the hearts of other persons here—some men of mark."[31]

In addition to his responsibilities as assistant pastor at the American Chapel, Andrew had to deal with two ongoing problems: lack of money and the uncertainties of his tenure. The financial arrangements between Andrew and McClintock, which went back to the initial agreement that McClintock would "board me and bear expenses" but offer no salary, are difficult to follow and even more difficult to balance. McClintock himself was often in financial straits. At times he was late in reimbursing Andrew for expenses incurred in Chapel duties; on other occasions he would borrow small sums from Andrew's depleted resources.

Living in Paris was costly, and Andrew was often hard-pressed to meet his own financial obligations. Many of his letters to Jim speak of the perennial problem of money, of borrowing, and repayment of loans. Without an occasional wedding or infant baptism or the sale of a painting now and then, Andrew would have been in dire circumstances indeed.

Andrew's other concern was the ill-defined and constantly fluctuating arrangements of his tenure at the Chapel. As the months went by, the situation kept shifting like desert sand, keeping him in a continual state of uncertainty. McClintock himself seemed ambivalent about his own plans, sometimes thinking *he* would return home and Andrew would take over the Chapel responsibilities.[32]

Through it all, however, the relationship between the two men remained strong. Before finally sailing for home in May, 1862, Andrew wrote his former colleague a letter of appreciation. McClintock replied: "The last part of your letter has affected my feelings very much. My own fear always has been, with reference to you, as to all others that come under my influence, that the flagrant weaknesses of my character must do more harm than any virtues I possess could do good. If it be otherwise, I thank God for *overruling mercies*, as Cromwell would say. It may be a comfort to you to know that your presence with us has had a most excellent effect upon our entire household, and that you leave us bearing the affection of each and all away with you."[33]

After two long years abroad, Andrew was finally going home—but to a country at war with itself.

"God save our unhappy country"

In the midst of Andrew's tenure in Paris, the American Civil War erupted. The outbreak had an immediate impact on the congregation of the American Chapel. Every scrap of information about the situation back home was eagerly sought after, the distance adding anxiety to an already tense situation. News from America did not always arrive in timely fashion, a cause of great concern for families and friends whose loved ones were nearer the conflict.

Most Chapel members thought it impossible that "madmen" would go so far as to "break up the Government."[34] But South Carolina seceded from the Union on December 20, 1860, and on February 9, 1861, the Confederate States of America was formed with Jefferson Davis as president.[35]

In May 1861, Andrew received word that the war had come to the Longacre household in Philadelphia: his younger brother, Orly, had joined the United States Navy. Andrew felt that, at twenty-one, Orly was old enough not to be led astray and that serving aboard a navy ship was safer than army duty. But for Andrew, separated from home by a wide ocean, he could only write, "My heart bleeds for my country, and I know not what to fear nor what to expect. . . . It seems more like a fearful vision or a wild tale. . . . God save our unhappy country."[36]

"Time went by on golden wheels"

From the moment of his arrival in France, Andrew had hoped to see more of Europe, but two obstacles stood in his way: he was financially strapped and he was reluctant to travel alone. He disliked having to map out transportation schedules and make hotel reservations, and he was not confident in dealing with customs agents in countries where he did not know the language. Initially, he wanted to go to Germany, especially to see Baden and the Rhine, but no opportunity presented itself.

When Francis Lycett, a wealthy English Wesleyan layman, invited him to visit, Andrew was overjoyed at the prospect and, in the fall of 1860, he spent ten days in London as a guest in the Lycett home. They took him about the city and its points of interest and introduced him to prominent English Methodists. As was often his custom when traveling, Andrew preached—on this occasion in the chapel at Highbury Grove.

In the spring of 1861, a trip to Italy was arranged for him as chaperone to Nelson Dale, the fifteen-year-old son of Mr. and Mrs. Thomas N. Dale, who were prominent members of the American Chapel. Nelson spoke French, German, and some Italian, which facilitated communications enormously. He was an intelligent and well-read youth who had traveled a great deal and enjoyed it. Financial assistance was provided by Andrew's brother, Jim, and Mr. Dale worked out details of the trip before they departed.

With John McClintock's encouragement and blessing, Andrew and Nelson left Paris on February 25, not returning until March 31. They visited Turin, Florence, Pisa, Rome, and other points in between. They went to cathedrals and museums where Andrew was able to see firsthand many of the world's masterpieces he had only read about heretofore. Some members of the congregation of the American Chapel in Paris were also in Rome, and their presence added much to Andrew's pleasure and happiness. As he wrote to Jim, "Surrounded by friends, in the midst of things of beauty and association and most deeply interesting, the time went by on golden wheels."[37]

In July, 1861, Andrew had an unexpected but welcome opportunity to travel to Ireland. Mr. and Mrs. Henry J. Baker, his old friends from New York, had been living in Paris for several months. Andrew had hoped to sail back to America with them on their return voyage. But when John McClintock asked him to remain at the Chapel awhile longer, Andrew agreed to do so. Henry Baker had already been called back home for both personal and business reasons brought about by the outbreak of the Civil War. It was, therefore, decided that Andrew would accompany Mrs. Baker and her household as far as Liverpool, her port of departure. Before sailing, she wanted to see something of Ireland. Andrew was invited along for the trip, and he gladly accepted. He spent eleven days touring Ireland, eleven more in London with the Francis Lycetts, and three on the Isle of Wight, before returning to Paris in early August.

The Eastern Tour

In September, 1861, Andrew's tenure at the Chapel was finished and he was making plans to sail for home when a letter arrived from Alexander Van Rensselaer inviting Andrew to travel with him the coming winter. Andrew replied that he was free to go but had no financial resources for such an excursion.

Andrew had met Van Rensselaer soon after his arrival in Paris in the spring of 1860. Not long afterward Van Rensselaer had asked Andrew to accompany him on a trip to Russia, but Andrew's responsibilities at the Chapel and lack of funds prevented his accepting. In the months that followed Andrew found that Van Rensselaer's friendship was "one of the cheering things in my life on this side of the ocean." He was a cultivated, refined, even-tempered gentleman, kind and very pious.[38]

Receiving Andrew's qualified letter of acceptance, Van Rensselaer replied immediately, expressing his pleasure at the prospect of their traveling together with Andrew as his guest. Thus began the preparations for the great "Eastern Tour" which would take the travelers (by train, boat, donkey cart, carriage, and caravan) through France, Spain, the Mediterranean, Egypt, the Middle East, Turkey, and back through Europe, along the way visiting great cathedrals, mosques, museums, monuments, and historical sites. The tour lasted more than seven months. Leaving Paris on September 10, 1861, they did not return until late April, 1862. As with all things in his life, Andrew felt this golden opportunity was providential, another sign of God's watchful care of him, an unexpected gift of which he could never have dreamed.

Andrew Longacre, the Man, the Artist, the Minister

Photographs and contemporary firsthand accounts testify that Andrew Longacre was a tall, elegant, and remarkably handsome man. His physical beauty was inherited primarily from his mother—and also much of his spiritual nature. In addition, he had many extraordinary qualities. He was talented, articulate, kindhearted, gentle, conscientious, with an inordinate love of his family and friends. This last "great part of my nature" he recognized as "a positive weakness."[39]

He was a gentleman in the highest and best sense of the word, cultivated and refined, with a sensitive regard for everyone. His politeness was from the heart. His sense of honor had no room for deceit or duplicity. A winning smile and melodious voice drew everyone to him. Withal, he had a keen sense of humor and a quick appreciation of genuine wit.

He had implicit trust in the love and providence of God, fully assured that he was continually guided by a benevolent, omnipotent Being. "I walk by the grace of God according to the light I have."[40] He was often heard to say, "I am doing my best, God knows I am; I come short, yes, I know that; but He knows my frame, and remembers that I am dust. He does not expect anything from me except to be a loyal, loving child."[41] With this self-understanding, he lived and died a loving, dutiful, obedient child of God.

Andrew Longacre was also an artist. He viewed the world and everything in it with an artist's eye. Attention to line, form, color, and composition was inherent in his nature. Throughout his life he sketched and painted portraits, landscapes, and miniatures in pencil, pen, and watercolor. Often, he painted what was before his eyes: the rooms in which he lived (including views from his windows), hotel rooms during his travels, ships' cabins when at sea. Therefore, we have a visual record of some of these places which, at that time, could not be easily photographed. For years, proceeds from his art were Andrew's basic source of income, and meticulous accounts of these works were faithfully recorded in his diaries.

His artistic orientation was classical. Most modern art did not impress him overmuch, although he admired the "cattle pieces" of Rosa Bonheur. While visiting London in the fall of 1860, he went to the National Gallery to see, among other things, the landscapes of J. M. W. Turner, "but was very disappointed."[42] However, when he made another visit the following year, he pronounced Turner's, *Sun Rising in the Mist [Vapour]*, "good." He found "Landseer's horse with a gay lady very beautiful—that is, the horse," and concluded there were "some good landscapes but [with] evident ill effect of the pre-Raphaelite teaching."[43]

During his years in Paris, Andrew made frequent trips to the Louvre and other galleries to study the paintings, but there is no evidence in his letters or diaries that Andrew met any of the contemporary French artists who were soon to be known as the Impressionists. He did, however, meet two American painters then working in Paris who, with their wives, attended the American Chapel: William P. Dana and Edward Harrison May. Numerous entries in Andrew's diaries record his associations with these men. Eventually, Edward May asked Andrew to pose for a portrait, and over several months in the fall and spring of 1860-61, Andrew spent a number of hours in May's studio for this purpose. Although unsigned, the portrait that serves as the frontispiece of this edition of Andrew's letters is almost certainly the one painted by Edward Harrison May.[44]

Andrew was also a poet, a writer, and something of a mystic. The whole bent and focus of his mind was meditative, prayerful, devotional. Fénelon, Mme. Guyon, and Lacordaire were read frequently and many of Andrew's writings, prayers, and spiritual self-examinations are reminiscent of these authors. It was said of him that he was more like the saintly John Fletcher, John Wesley's "designated successor," than the vigorous and peripatetic Wesley.[45]

"I have not to choose my own path"

Andrew's dedication to his ministerial calling was unwavering. An entry in his *MS Journal* reveals his self-understanding: "I have not to choose my own path. God appoints it and fits me for it, just as he sees best. It is my vocation to sink into and perfectly conform to his perfect will. If he wills for me . . . a ministry unremarkable and even without much apparent fruit, it is for me to accept the dispensation, not struggle against it. This shall be my glory in his sight, that I have fulfilled his will, finished the work he gave me to do. . . . I can only wait—diligently doing what my hands find to do, careful in the faithful discharge of every duty. . . . I must wait and watch for God's divine appointing, ever counting it my highest glory, to 'please God'."[46]

Even with this strong sense of his purpose in life, the ministry was not an easy field for him. From the beginning, he had found the "painfulness of preaching" to be a particular burden, and years of practice gave little relief. "For some time before every service there has always been a burden of soul—almost insufferable. . . . How to describe it I scarcely know. It is a burden of sorrow and responsibility, a weight upon my soul, my mind, and my affections and sympathies, so that free and unrestrained weeping would be a great relief, tho' it is never given me. . . . [This] may be attributable to timidity, partly to an intense desire to do good—and a fear of speaking so as not to do so; but the great part seems some undefined weight of sorrow, a bearing the cross up the hill of Calvary. . . . I think that it is not presumption for me to conclude that this sorrow is my form of fellowship with the suffering of my Lord. To others, that fellowship may exist in a different and equally solemn form; to me it is in the ministration of the Word."[47]

His goal in preaching was to set before those who heard him "the higher Christian life, not insisting on names or forms or schemes of doctrine but upon a holy heart and life before God." He did not "feel free to press upon people the state of entire sanctification as a present attainment as an immediate thing." Instead, he "felt it better to let the truth go home that they might have time understandingly to decide what to do and then by the Spirit's help to do it."[48]

For Andrew, administering the sacrament of Holy Communion was a high privilege in which he "never felt more solemnly my duty, my peculiar office." As he gave the bread and wine to his people, he "longed to impart with the outward form the hidden grace, so to present the Crucified to every soul, as to awaken all the affections and unite them to him. I saw the deep necessity upon me, favored with such an office, to show forth in all my life 'the Lord's death till he come'."[49]

His was a pastor's heart. He had a tender regard for souls, all souls, and their salvation. Visiting his flock from "house to house" was a duty and responsibility with which he felt particularly at ease. Counseling, speaking "seriously" about things eternal, praying were almost second nature to him. A much larger and more detailed picture of Andrew's activities and self-understanding as a pastor is far more evident in his manuscript diaries and journals than in his letters. But the following excerpt from one letter says everything about his lifelong dedication to his divine calling: "I thank God that the monitor within is more exacting than friends without. I am tortured half the time with the thought of the littleness, the variableness, the inconsistency of my efforts to do good. It is painful, but I am thankful, oh how thankful, that it is so. Lately these feelings have arisen upon me with renewed force. I must do more for God. My life must be a more faithful witness and testimony for him. The world has a right to demand it of me, and I know God expects it of me."[50]

Andrew Longacre was a man shaped by his times, his home, and his church, and all of these influences are reflected in his letters. Written one hundred and forty years ago in a world that no longer exists, these letters were intended only for the eyes of his beloved brother, though perhaps to be shared with his father and siblings. Andrew could never have imagined his letters would be read by anyone outside his family, but his words and the images they evoke are as fresh and vibrant today as when first put on paper, pointing always to "a more excellent way" and revealing the kind, gentle, loving spirit of a truly remarkable man.

A Methodist Minister in Paris
The Letters of Andrew Longacre 1860-1862

My dear Jim,

Having written to Eliza[1] on the steamer,[2] I feel as if I really wanted to address this "gem of epistolary correspondence" to you. To perpetrate even this feeble attempt at a joke, you may be sure I am getting out of the heavier shadows that seemed to overwhelm me for a day or two after my arrival in this European village.

I was sick enough on the steamer to have gone to the bottom of the sea without a sigh, and I have been deep enough in the "blues" within the last two or three days to understand why there are so many suicides in Paris.[3] Do not be alarmed. I do not mean to insinuate that I felt at all suicidal but it would have been a great release to have gone off to a better country just at that time.

To come to facts instead of feelings. The sail along the Isle of Wight, by Cowes, with the whole country glowing in the wonderful loveliness of an English spring, was entrancing to travelers, sea-sick (in two senses). [p. 2] We saw the ivy covered castle of the author of "Bell's Life" which alone is a gem of beauty beyond anything I ever saw.[4] Next to it was the Queen's house, Osborne,[5] a real palace with a wide rolling park stretching down from its stately walls to the sea. All around these, or rather all on one side of them, were the beautiful humbler summer houses where people come to have the best climate England can afford. But I had no great idea even of the best after we were compelled [to] lie still for some three or four hours befogged before coming up to all this vision [of] British beauty.

On the other side of us, some miles of water spreading between, was Southampton, whither a small steamboat conveyed our English travellers, some 30 or more. Away in the distance we saw quite plainly the immense proportions of the *Great Eastern* with its six or eight masts.[6]

Turning away from this we sailed soon out [of] sight of land and toward the latter part of the afternoon we came in view of the French coast. [p. 3] How eagerly we gathered on the deck as our long looked for "harbor" Havre came to sight. Nothing could be more novel than the appearance of the town as we approached. It was the living reality of what we had only known before in pictures. Old high houses, narrow streets, crooked & shooting out in all directions. The great stone "quais" between which the long winding docks, like canals, ran far into the town, filled with vessels from many quarters. All these were so new and quite in keeping with the crowds of people who gathered to see our huge vessel land her six hundred souls.

The landing was very tedious. After waiting out from the quai sometime, a boat pushed off from shore with two officers in uniform. As they came near, a party of gentlemen were putting off from the steamer in a hired boat. But these were stopped until all had given up their passports. The officers then came on board and taking their places, after a long delay on the gang-way, took one by one the open passports from our hands as we [p. 4] pushed by them, escaping at last from our floating prison. Taking a hack, or a voiture,[7] as we have to call them here, Dr. Maris,[8] his friend and travelling companion, Mr. Chas. B. Stockwell, and I reached after nightfall the Hotel de l'Europe. There we lodged. The next morning we went together to the *douane* (Anglicé, Custom House) where we were obliged by reason of the crowd to wait some three hours before we were allowed to rescue our beaten and battered baggage from the officers of the law. Free at last, we took tickets (paying for our baggage by weight) for the train to Paris which left Havre at 2 P.M. The price of my ticket was 60 ½ francs. Everything about the R. Road & cars was quiet and orderly and clean in striking contrast to our noisy and dirty depots. Birds were flying about and picking up grains close by the feet of the employees who were all in a uniform. The ride, which was by daylight as far as Mayence,[9] was all new and strange. The landscape, the fields without fences, the cattle tethered, the cottages with immense thatched roofs, the rare, grand houses, the absence of middle-class farms, the trees trimmed up into tall green poles, [p. 5] were continual surprises to our unaccustomed eyes. At Rouen some of our fellow travelers stopped for the night to spend some part of the following day there in looking at its Cathedral & antiquities. We had three grand views of the town & the Cathedral as we rode on. We were struck with the freeness of the track of the R.R. from dust, the spaces being filled with broken stone, and the sides covered with grass, while no roads cross it on the same level. We reached the large depot in Paris[10] at 10 ½ at night. Again our baggage was examined by Government officials, the *octroi*, and after a great deal of bother & delay, & feeing of porters, we took, that is Dr. Maris, Mr. S[tockwell], and I, two voitures & rode to the Hotel du Louvre. Here we found no room, tho' it is called the largest hotel in the world, so we drove up a square further along the rue Rivoli to the "Hotel des Trois Empereurs" and here we were comfortably located.

The next day I delivered my letter to three persons, Mr. Tucker,[11] Mr. Curtis[12] (to whom Mr. Keen[13] had got me some letters besides my official one) and the Reverend Mr. Prentiss.[14] Dr. Maris [p. 6] kindly accompanied me, as my French could not carry me very far.

With the exception of the first visit to Mr. Tucker, my introduction to my new work was most pleasant. Mr. Curtis especially is a most excellent & loveable man. Of great wealth, extensive business, living splendidly, he is yet a sincere, intelligent, and I hope spiritual Christian. He invited me to dine with him the next day, which I did in company with a Mr. G. F. Dale of Phila[delphia], to whom I had a letter from our friend Crowell, and a young gentleman touring Paris. The dinner was singular, only one dish being served at a time. That was set in the middle of the round table then taken off by a waiter and carved, then carried to each person who helped himself. In this way were served first soup, fish, fowl, beef, and then one by one two kinds of vegetables & afterwards dessert. Three kinds of wine were before us. My drink is, as all say it ought to be, the simple plain Bordeaux, or red wine, mixed with the water which without it is not wholesome.

But I need not attempt to carry out this journalizing [p. 7] or I am afraid my letter will be like something rather more known to fame, which was commenced on too grand a scale, so the author died & left it unfinished—Macauley's History.

Our Chapel is beautiful, but must be seen to be enjoyed. A written description would be of no account.

The people are very kind. There seemed a great deal of hearty good fellowship among the Americans here. They welcome a fellow-countryman as tho' he were an old friend. Oh, you cannot imagine how sweet it sounds to hear our dear English sounds in this nasal Babel of French. Yet it is astonishing how one can get on with a little bit of French and a good use of motions. I enquire my way, bargain with the drivers and porters, buy what articles I want, with a success that amazes me.

Today I went with Mrs. Curtis and her mother to the Palais de l'Industrie[15] to see a flower show, now open. It did not so greatly surpass ours, except in the skill & taste in the arrangement of the objects which [p. 8] comprised everything that could be linked with flowers or their culture and some which could not. Of course the place alone is splendid. But I must stop. I fear now a little that my letters may miss the Wednesday steamer.

I should have written more letters but have been too unsettled to do so. In a few days I expect to be in a comfortable home somewhere. Write by every steamer or by those which come to Havre at all events. Love to all. No language can express the longing I have had for some face I have loved & known. How are all? How is Sallie? Tell me all that is going on.

Love again to all. Oh if only I had wings, or if that poor old Atlantic Telegraph had not been a failure.[16] Instead of writing Good bye.

Your affectionate Brother,
Andrew

My dear Jim,

Though on Saturdays generally I don't feel much like writing letters, yet as it is possible I may have an opportunity of sending this by private hands[1] to America on Monday morning, I must write now or not at all. Besides, contrary as it is to my ordinary practice, I do feel like it now. All day, I have had a good deal of home-feeling and I do not know but it has only grown stronger toward evening. The near approach of my second official Sunday here when I must try to preach under such difficult circumstances from those which are around me at home seems to intensify my desires & longings for a little at least of home sympathy and interest. But I make do without it. I must nerve my single self to bear my responsibility without the aid of near and dear friends ready with their earnest prayers and expressions and looks of interest to lighten the heavy burden. It goes hard. I do so long to know how I make out whether the impression made is all it should be and whether I have made any mistakes or not. However I am certainly growing old enough to stand alone. My twenty-ninth year ended on Tuesday, and I suppose I must conclude that "childhood and youth" are passed. The childish things must be pushed out by the greater more solemn things of maturing manhood, and as a man I must go forward to do the man's work. Yet I have a haunting fear that something of the child will always remain with me. Some of the mental & affectional bones will never harden. However, I am content to submit to the apparent weakness if I may preserve these avenues of pleasure keen and sensitive.

But I did not intend to take up so much room with this sentimentality. I fear you will think a little too much of the soft remains. Two things I have to say by way of replies. First, never withhold a long letter & send a short one because the first (I find I had mistaken the side of the sheet and I cannot afford to re-write so please excuse[2]) [p. 2] seems old. By the time it comes to me the date will be of little account. Second, on sending papers, and I shall be very glad to have them, send me rather some weekly, even if it be not the very latest date, and it is better not to send two

Paris
June 16, 1860
[LETTER 2]

The Letters of Andrew Longacre ⋆ 29

of the same date, as of course a good deal of matter will be common to both. I do not mean to suggest that you send papers continually but only occasionally. With a little trouble I can get the American papers, that is many of them. I have now a borrowed copy of the New York semi-weekly Times. On another point I wish to make a suggestion. You desire me to send at least one letter home by every steamer. I have done so. But neither of the last two have brought me one line from home. I confidently expected letters by the *Adriatic*[3] which comes to Havre, but none came. I felt the disappointment keenly. It came on one of my sick days, and I am not sure I have got over the pain yet. At least one letter a week I ought to have from the many hands at home. You may not know that there is no difference in cost between the English & Havre mails.

Now to such news as I have. Thursday was the grand fête of the annexation of Savoy to France.[4] I did not attempt to go [to] the high mass at Notre Dame for fear of the crowd. But tho' quite unwell I walked out to the Champ de Mars to see the emperor review some fifty- to seventy-five thousand troops. The day was fine, and the scene to the last degree imposing. The great field of the Champ de Mars is a large expanse of ground without a tree and free from grass. On the sides it rises into elevations along the entire length from which perhaps two hundred thousand people I think can survey the scene. Half that number I should suppose were out on Thursday. These long rising hills are nicely shaded with trees and make very good places from which to enjoy the grand scenes that are not infrequently displayed on the field between. The plain extends from the Seine to the grand line of buildings used for the Military School. In the middle one of these buildings was a place prepared, canopied, &c, for the Imperial family. I saw quite distinctly the Emperor mounted & the Empress & Prince in an open carriage with six horses, attended by a large body of officers and guards, tho' they were [p. 3] at considerable distance from me. The movements of the cavalry were particularly fine. In various costumes & in full parade trim, the whole made a brilliant display. The affair was very simple. After sundry evolutions, the field was arranged, the cavalry on one side & the infantry on the other. The Emperor arrived and rode up the line slowly attended by a numerous staff. Then he rode down again to receive the Empress who was attended by quite a body of cavalry. Then they formed a sort of procession, a body of cavalry preceding the carriage for the Empress & closing with more cavalry. This procession made the tour of the field down & up. Then stopping at the place prepared, the whole body in the field formed gradually into broad lines & passed before them, leaving the field by different streets. At one time I observed, while on the grand tour of the field, the Emperor left his place & rode by the side of the carriage. I could see him raising his chapeau in acknowledgement of the cries of "*Vive l'Empereur*" tho' I was too distant to hear the voices.[5]

In the evening the city was illuminated. I say the city but in fact it was only the public buildings & some few private houses. It was optional with the people to do it, so the majority did not. On some fêtes I hear that the people are especially requested (not to say required) to take part at least such as live in conspicuous positions.

The French enjoy a fête. Men, women, and children give up the day to a quiet, good-humored, orderly enjoyment. The unchanging good-humor of the people is one of the most striking things in France. They are not what we would call polite, but of perfect equanimity, never put out, never grumbling. I mean of course in the general public affairs of life.

Yet what is singular, they never seem to laugh. They will stand with open eyes gazing at the most comical things, listening apparently (for I don't understand their tongue) to the funniest speeches, yet with only a very sedate smile. If you ever hear a laugh, you may be sure it is American or [p. 4] English. Their universal order is a feature I have noticed particularly. Everything is neat and regular. It would amuse you to go along the shop windows & see candies, cakes, cherries, strawberries and in fact almost everything arrayed in regular geometrical figures. Even in the market the better qualities of fruit, strawberries & cherries are arranged by regular rows and boxes. The same principle is carried into all things public & private.

Last evening I dined with the Ambassador's family[6] in a quiet way, only one gentleman & lady being guests beside myself. They were very kind & scolded me for not coming oftener. You can imagine why I had not done so when I tell you that they had a dancing party the night before till three o'clock in the morning. "Oh you should have been here, Mr. Longacre," said one of the young ladies & Mrs. F[aulkner]. "I think I was better away," I replied, "Why," said Miss F[aulkner], "you don't disapprove of dancing, do you?" "Of course, I don't dance," I said. "No, but you might look on." "It is not very pleasant simply to look on an amusement in which one has no part," I answered. The young lady said, "I suppose not" and so the matter ended. Very important was it not? Only this. It shows how the pious folks behave here. Mrs. F[aulkner] quite piques herself upon her devotions & the church. But they are all of the same sort; or if not quite, near enough to make me feel there is an immense distance between my ideas of right and theirs. When I can, without sacrificing something even more important, I talk with them pretty plainly, but I don't flatter myself with great hopes of success. I am gradually finding some pleasant people, some who are quite friendly. A Mr. Van Rensselaer[7] I like very much. He is brother to a Mrs. John Cruger[8] to whom I brought a letter from Mrs. [Stephen] Olin.[9] He quite surprised me yesterday in riding with him by a very delicate sort of invitation to travel with him in Russia this summer, visiting Stockholm, Copenhagen, &c. I was pleased with the compliment, or kindness rather, tho' of course it will be impossible for me to leave Dr. McClintock. But it is bed-time & I must say goodnight. Love to all, Father, Eliza, & Cline.[10]

Your affct brother, Andrew Longacre

Dear Jim,

I enclose with the letter I wrote on Saturday, this, with a map of Paris. It is somewhat damaged by the taking out of its shell, yet all that is important is tolerably fair. It is one I used myself for some time here, and I like it better than one I have got since.[1] It will have an interest to you folks at home—having little views, tho' very imperfect ones, of some of the public buildings. As to the scale I can give you a sort of rule: the distance from the Arc de Triomph[e] to the Palace of the Tuileries is about two miles. My home at present is in the rue de l'Arcade which is just to the left of the church of the Madeleine, and a door or two above the rue Chauveau Lagarde which runs directly back of that church. My church is on the rue de Berri[2]—the fourth street on the North side of the Avenue Champs Élysées from the Arc de Triumph. [p. 2] I wish I had time to write a great deal more, but I have not. Occasionally in writing I shall refer to Parisian localities, and thus it will be a comfort to me to know you can follow me in your thoughts.

I hope you will see hereafter that no steamer sails without some missive for me. If it comes rather heavily on your purses, I will settle it when I come home.

I have a shirt & pair of stockings of yours which I will send if I ever find one going to America who is enough of a friend to ask to carry such a package. As I do not use them, they will be of use, even if not in your hands till I come home.

Write often & long.

Yours affectionately

Andrew

Paris
June 25, 1860

[LETTER 4]

My dear Jim,

Imagine my surprise on last Saturday, the day before yesterday, about five o'clock in the afternoon, just as I had completed my preparations for Sunday, to see my room-door open and Dr. Palmer[1] walk in. But I hardly think you can fairly enter into the surprise and pleasure of that moment with all your imagining. He had got into Paris that day after a flying trip with Walter[2] and some English gentlemen to Switzerland and part of Germany. The jaunt was undertaken chiefly on Walter's account who goes home the fourth of July—next Wednesday a week—and who, not knowing whether he should ever visit Europe again did not wish to return without seeing a little of the continent. He kindly consents to carry with him your shirt and stockings, although I am hardly willing to bother him with them. I shall write to you, as before this comes to hand you will know, of course, to have someone call for [p. 2] them in New York.

You spoke of sending me papers sometimes. An occasional <u>Christian Advocate</u> would be very welcome. The first of these I have seen is one Dr. Palmer has lent me. Indeed I would rather you should send me that paper than any other—as the secular papers all come to Munroe's[3] and tho' I have not gone there much, for want of time, yet I could go and sit there and read all I wished, particularly since the members of the firm are attendants upon my church.

Things are looking more brightly here. Yesterday was the best Sunday, indeed, the only comfortable one I have had. I think some actual good was done, and perhaps even more general impression. Some of the official men looked very brightly and seemed confident they were going to have crowded congregations. Before leaving church in the afternoon I saw some people selecting a pew. And one pleasant thing I must not forget. After the afternoon service, [p. 3] a Mr. Lycett from London, who I learn is a prominent Wesleyan there, came up to me, introduced himself, spoke of his having attended both services & of his enjoyment of them and gave me a particular invitation if I came to London to come to his house.[4]

Other things I need not mention. Altogether as you can well imagine I feel better than I have done. I ought to say that during the last week I had a special spirit of prayer for the aid of the Holy Spirit, and I felt better satisfied that God would help me than I have done for a long time.

It is very hard work to get time for prayer here. There are so many demands upon my time. Hitherto I am ashamed that I have not been as faithful in this particular as I ought to have been. I have yielded too much to the "outside pressure." But I think the experience of the past week has been of great use to me. If God will so mercifully and bountifully own my first meagre efforts to be more faithful, surely if I give myself [p. 4] yet more to him in this way, I may expect at least, the continuance of his favor. One thing, I am glad for: I find I am able to preach shorter sermons than in Philadelphia. I don't think I have yet exceeded three quarters of an hour in any one of six sermons.

Of course now I am on tip-toe of expectations, looking for Dr. McClintock's arrival. He was to sail on the 16th and will be due in Paris by Thursday if not before.[5] I sincerely hope he brings word from home with him. My letters from that unforgotten region have not been very full or very abundant.

I should like to send a whole pile of letters in this package but do not think I shall have time to write them as Walter must leave Paris this afternoon.

Yours faithfully

Andrew Longacre

Love to all.

⸙

My dear Jim,

Although it is Friday and I am but partially prepared for my sermon on Sunday and so perhaps according to the strictest ideas of duty ought to be at work, especially as I shall have but little time for it tomorrow, yet I feel like writing to you, and do not feel like writing sermons and after considerable effort to "go against the grain," I give up to enjoy myself. However, I ought to say in extenuation of my conduct that I am not well, and therefore really unfit for hard work.

I shall not attempt to say how glad I was to get a good long letter from you. You will have learned before this from letters written during a few weeks past, that I was beginning to think it a little strange you did not write oftener and more fully. You will find the best way to do is to keep writing without reference to the mails, just when you can, and when you feel like it. Then when the time for the mail comes, just bundle up what you have written and send it.

Several things occur to me to say, and so I will waste no time in generalities. As to your very kind Italian suggestions, asking cost &c of a trip in that direction, I cannot answer now. I have some idea but too vague for use. Besides my own course is not yet plain, [p. 2] neither can I tell how far my present means will go, or what may turn up on this side. Tomorrow I leave my bachelor-room at No. 11, rue de l'Arcade and go to live with Dr. McClintock who moves today from the hotel[1] to 42 rue des Ecuries d'Artois. Of course my expenses will be very greatly lessened in living with him. My whole expenses since landing have been about $100.00, rather under than over, I think. This exceeds considerably my calculations, but it has seemed inevitable.

You will receive a letter from me before this reaches you as to a loan &c thro' Dr. Maris. I do not know that it will be best. Were the sum larger it would be better to do it directly thro' a banker. You will reply—and there will be ample time to think over it—before any action is necessary. Since receiving so kind an invitation to stay with a gentleman in London, should I visit that city, I quite incline to make a little trip there. It would seem strange to be here so long and not see the wonders of London. I may go in September if all is convenient.

You suggest my making photographic purchases for you. I will do it with pleasure but need some guide from you in regard to subjects & amount. Several things have struck me in this line. Those card portraits are to be had in considerable numbers & of all the great personages of the day a[t] 1 f[ranc] 50 c[entimes, or] (30 c[en]ts) apiece. All the Imperial family & branches, the Marshalls of France, titled people, divines, actors, foreign celeb- [p. 3] rities. Would you like any of them and of whom? There is made for them a sort of Album, very prettily got up and varying in size & price, from 10 francs upward. There are also little carved stands for them: that is, made to hold one or several which make very real ornaments for an étagère. I mean to get some of these on my own account to send home as gifts. Besides them are views of Paris, plain photographs of good size @ 2 f[rancs] 50 [centimes] (50 c[ents]) which I like very much. Some of them I mean to get on my own account. There are very excellent photographic views in good numbers of many places of interest, copies of celebrated paintings &c, at all sorts of prices. Lastly, stereoscopic views on card, "ad infinitum." I think the choice of glass ones is as good at home as it is here, and they are about the same price or but little higher, hardly enough to pay for the risks of transporting. Stereoscopes are very cheap. You can get one in wood, with 12 card views, for 6 francs. Let me have an idea of what you would like and I can readily get it. It will be a pleasure. Very small things are easily sent over, but people generally carry so much that a package of any size is a burden, and there are few whom I could make such a request of. As the fall approaches, there will be more people going home, so such opportunities will be multiplied.

I have not been very well. My room, on the ground floor, is unfavorable for one of my rheu- [p. 4] matic tendencies. But tomorrow I bid a final adieu to this affliction. Dr. McClintock's rooms are very pleasant. Dr. [George L.] Prentiss resided in the same house, so I shall feel quite like going home to be there. They are pretty well up town. You can find the place on the map. It is near the Arc of Triomphe, to the north of the Avenue des Champs Élysées. Our home will be between the rue de l'Oratoire and the rue de Berri. If you choose you can send my letters there, tho' it is no trouble to call at Munroe's for them.

I get quite in a disposition to fly home every once in a while. The life here is so outside of me. It does not seem to enter in, to touch my deeper feelings & sympathies at all.

I enclose a long letter to Eliza—which you will please hand to her.

I hope the good people don't forget the needy one far far away. I hope they pray for me. I need all they can allow me of that.

The summer is here at last, tho' not like ours even now. Warm & mild, but not oppressively hot. I almost long for a right hot American day, to burn up all the bad feelings, aches & pains. I suppose I must wait till next summer for that.

Love to all. Yours faithfully,

Andy

Excuse the tone of languor. I have had a diarrhoea & Sunday is at hand.

My dear Jim,

Your very welcome letter of June 22nd was handed me, together with one from Father, yesterday morning at church. The mail had just come in, and Mr. Munroe very kindly brought them up. It's kind of you to write by every opportunity. Letters from home cannot come too often for me. Hitherto they have seemed to come so slowly that I have been half discouraged about writing myself. Now since things seem fairly understood and the stream of regular correspondence is opened, I hope there will be no breaking off.

In my last letter to you, my desire to say several things made me give fewer words to one matter than I had intended. In answer to your very kind suggestions as to an Italian tour, I felt very deeply in my heart what, if I do not forget, I did not give one word to express: my very sincere thanks for the suggested kindness. It was an appeal that I felt almost too much to be able to respond to. I had not at all expected such a thing and felt a kind of overwhelming sense of the kindness of it. I am as unable now, as then, to say anything definite about it. Before long perhaps, or possibly not for some months, if I should consent to remain here next winter with Dr. McClintock, I shall let you know all I can find out on the whole affair. Today I have been making up a very little package for home which Mr. Charles Dunlap, the brother-in-law of Mr. Henry Day (formerly a partner of Mr. Keen's), has promised to take to New York for [p. 2] there he will give it to Mr. Keen & so it will find its way home. He leaves England for New York the latter part of this month. The things I send are not of much value, but it is a sort of comfort to me to send even little things. They are some of those stands for photographs of which I spoke in my last letter to you. These cost about eight francs for the three; there are others more finely carved that cost double and treble the price. I expect to go tomorrow to have a photograph taken in my church dress, cassock, gown & bands, and will send on copies of it by the earliest opportunity.[1]

I was glad to get the letter from George West. I have been anxious for some word about his mother,[2] and besides it is a pleasure to hear from him. I shall reply soon. Let me hear from you of Ed. & Maria whenever you learn anything. I fear he does not get on very well in his efforts at business on his own account. Very possibly he may have been too hasty in leaving the oppressive but safe protection of his father's name and credit. I was glad you acted as you did in regard to the tents for the pic-nic at Eastwick's, yet it is not best to be too entirely involved with the West side of the case. It may turn out a favor, even to them, for you not to be too reserved in your intercourse with that family. Of course, however, circumstances must guide you. George and Maria have private wrongs which are not at all yours.

How I should like it, tho' it is almost [p. 3] foolish to speak of such a thing, if you could drop in upon me and pay me ever so little a visit one of these fine days. Yet it would be worse afterward. I have a very nice room, indeed, quite fine in fact and, as to location in the city and in the house, all I could wish. This part of Paris is high and new. The streets are wide and kept clean and there is nothing offensively old or ugly anywhere near.[3] We are just around the corner from the church, not more than two minutes' walk. Dr. McClintock has taken for a month or two (it is uncertain whether he will hold them longer) two "appartements"—one the premier étage & the other next above it, the deuxiéme. My room is a front one on the upper floor, and the only bed-room which is entered from the ante-chambre. From the ante-chambre, the door opens into a little dressing-room, very small, but large enough, with wash-stand & places to hang clothes, & set books, &c. From that another door leads into my room. A very neat French bed-stead with chintz curtains falling from a sort of canopy stands in one corner, with a little table-au-lit near the head. A sort of marble top bureau, or set of drawers, rather, stands on one side facing the marble mantel-piece. There the mantel rises to the ceiling, the omnipresent mirror, of such size as would be thought fine enough for quite an elegant parlor in Phila[delphia]. A gilt clock (also omnipresent) & candlesticks, finish the mantel furniture. By the side of this between [p. 4] the fire-place & the window stands the escritoire at which I am now writing, precisely similar to the one I had in the rue de l'Arcade. Two diverse stuffed back chairs—and two lighter ones—are covered with chintz to match the curtains of the bed & of the window. The window itself opens in the middle and reaches to the floor or nearly, with a little ornamental iron railing across the lower part outside. This grand window seems to me a special luxury. Long before I wake the sun streams thro' it, in rays reflected from the opposite side of the street, and when I rise and draw back the curtains & open the sash, the tide of light and pure air that pours in is a perfect delight to me, after my *rez-de-chaussée*[4] room whose front window caught about two hours sunshine out of each day. The sun is a great institution in Paris, especially this season, when the summer has been so backward that people scarcely knew if it was coming at all. It has come at last. Not with the grand wash and flood of our American sunshine, but with a gentle heat, refined, delicate, Parisian, and after illuminating the streets from a cloudless sky from half past three in the A.M. till almost nine in the evening or "thereabouts" leaves them only pleasantly warm or hardly that. On Saturday I rode with Mrs. [Richard] Ray in the Bois de Boulogne (that paradise of Paris)[5] and tho' I wore an overcoat, I was compelled to borrow her veil to tie around my neck for fear [p. 5] of sore throat. If the summers are such cool affairs as this has been, I shall certainly not be able to endure the winter. Why it has not been over a week since I went down to dinner about half past five in the afternoon with my thick winter overcoat on and kept it buttoned up too.[6] I hope tho' that is all over. At any rate it would be sheer ingratitude to think of such things in the delightful weather of yesterday and today.

I like the McClintocks very much. They are open and above-board, talk out all they feel or think, which of course puts one at once at his ease with them. Dr. M[cClintock] is fussy. He notices little things in the children & even in Mrs. M[cClintock] and quite "takes on" about them for a moment or two. But they all seem to understand it and show no symptoms of breaking their hearts. I think he is generous and liberal in all senses of the words. He treats me very kindly. I was out quite late on Saturday evening with Mrs. Ray and found him sitting up alone for me, but he was as kind as possible, made me sit down and tell about my visit and did not seem the least annoyed that I had not come in sooner. As my room is on the other floor, and I am to have a key of my own,[7] I shall avoid hereafter the possibility of annoying any one by accidental lateness of hours. Another thing illustrates his kindness of manner toward me. After sermon yesterday afternoon I went to dine, as has been my habit, with Mr. Curtis and did not get home till after ten in the evening. He [p. 6] was in the parlor with Mrs. M[cClintock] when I came in and immediately told me that they had all been very much pleased with my sermon. He had had a funeral service which kept him from church so he spoke for the family. It is not so much in what is said at such times as the spirit to say anything and the manner that makes it seem a special kindness.

I know very well it is a delicate thing to attempt to live in any man's family, but <u>so far</u> things seem all I could ask. Should a "change come o'er the spirit of my dream,"[8] you will doubtless hear of it. But I prefer now to anticipate nothing of the kind. Dr. M[cClintock] seems to wish me to take a special interest in Emory,[9] who is so clever a fellow every way that it is no difficult thing to do.

But I shall weary you with my interminable epistles. I cannot repress the desire that you at home should know all about me and feel as if the distance between us were not so much a fact as a display of geographical figures.

This afternoon I am to dine with Dr. M[cClintock] at Mr. Munroe's, the Banker's. Mrs. Munroe apologized to me the other day for not having asked me before, saying it had been on account of illness in the family. She is a very nice lady, quite pretty with nice looking little boys, one is a namesake of mine, Andrew. Of course, they live in grand style. But the "finis" must come. Love to all. Good bye for a day or two. Yours faithfully,

Andrew Longacre

My dear Jim,

Several letters of yours have arrived since I wrote to you last. One last evening acknowledging the receipt of the map I sent some time ago. While on the subject of the map I may as well answer your questions about localities. Our chapel is on the upper side of the rue de Berry [Berri] (the west side), just to the north of the entrance of the rue de Ponthieu. My home now at Dr. McClintock's is quite near, the rue des Ecuries d'Artois, being the first street north of the chapel and our house, the third or fourth one below the rue de l'Oratoire on the north side of the street. I say north and south, east and west, not speaking accurately because the streets do not run in these directions but only inclining that way.

It is a great comfort and satisfaction to hear from home so regularly as I have done for a week or two past. I am very glad you intend to keep your good habits. Little things at home seem trifling to you, and because you have nothing out of the way to write you may think it is not worthwhile to write at all. There cannot be a greater mistake. The letters that most interest me are those which come nearest daguerreotyping every-day home life that tell me all the little things, who comes and goes, what is projected and what is done, the last jokes that have stirred the quiet family waters. It is these hourly and daily items that really make up the life you are [p. 2] living and the recital of them therefore best reproduces that life before me.

Since my last homewards, I have had an opportunity of sending a small package containing several card-portraits, with one or two of myself. I suppose they will come to hand at the same time with this letter, or a day or two afterwards. I could not send to all, so you will not feel slighted to find nothing for yourself in the package. I await with some interest your replies to several of my late letters, which I suppose will arrive in due time.

Paris is much like home in one respect—everybody that is anybody must go somewhere in the summer. Though the weather again (after a week or two of fine warm temperature) is strangely cool and there is therefore no need to go away for comfort, the good folks are going in troops. Our congregation has thus lost many of its familiar faces, but the arrival of others keeps up pretty well the general size of our audiences.

I am thinking myself of making a little journey to see the Rhine, with Cologne & perhaps Baden Baden and Switzerland, sometime while our congregations are small. If I can accomplish this, and have a week or two in London in September, I shall be very glad. The latter point seems quite feasible since I have so kind an invitation to stay [p. 3] while there with Mr. Lycett of which I have written before. The chief expense of the trip would have been the board in London. Now that that is out of the way, I can hope to go.

Mr. & Mrs. Curtis go this week to Versailles where they have taken an apartment, with room for a visitor, and they kindly invited me to spend some time with them. It is not far, not more than an hour from the city, and it is on that account they go as Mr. Curtis this season is quite busy and cannot leave his business.

The matter which as yet prevents my coming to a conclusion about the Rhine, &c, is the want of a travelling companion. I do not want to go alone and so unless I can find some pleasant and agreeable fellow, I shall hardly feel like attempting it.

I continue to enjoy my residence with Dr. McClintock very much. He is remarkably kind and considerate, willing to allow me all the relaxation I desire and treating me altogether with a degree of consideration I do not look for. Yesterday, he opened the service & read the chapter for me in the afternoon, which hitherto I have done for myself, and I thought he seemed only to have waited for me to ask him to do it. As I read the service in the morning, it seems only fair that he should open my service in the afternoon.[1] He preached a fine, very fine sermon yesterday, and for the first time, seemed fairly and fully to impress the audience favorably. [p. 4]

Hitherto, I think my sermons have been more <u>effective</u> than his, tho' of course in thought, in elaborate study & learned illustration, there is no comparison. One comforting sign, the afternoon congregations have steadily increased until now they are perhaps about half as large as the morning. This is a very great advance, altho' it is not saying much. Compared with the congregations at home, our small numbers here are nothing. Yesterday, which was not a favorable day, however—rainy, &c—besides many being out of town, we had only 210 in the morning and 100 in the afternoon. One gets used to it here, tho' it would be rather discouraging to one not knowing anything of the habit here upon his first coming.

Things seem coming to a very pleasant state in church matters. There is an evident rallying around the pastor and more of the church life and church character manifested as at home than I have seen. Our prayer-meeting[2] comes on very encouragingly. Altogether things look brighter and better than they have done at all. Oh, if there only could be a coming down of the Holy Ghost, a real baptising of the people into the spirit and power of living, ardent, piety. But we can only work on, patiently, trustfully, leaving special blessings to the will of him who only can dispense them.

Don't let them forget to pray for me. Love to all.

Yours faithfully,

Andrew Longacre

My dear Jim,

I was quite sorry to have to send off my last letters without one to you, but after writing to Father and Eliza I had time for no more. As I feel like writing and have leisure today, I take this opportunity tho' it is sometime before my letter will go. I have leisure on a Saturday by the consent of Rev. Dr. [William] Adams of New York to preach in the morning tomorrow which allows me to be free, Dr. McC[lintock] taking my afternoon service. This is the third Sunday I had no preaching. However, it is probable that the Sunday after I may have to preach twice as Dr. McClintock will be away at Brussels. After closing my letter to Eliza at Versailles, I went with Mrs. Curtis to see the palaces of the Grand & Petit Trianons. Not having my passport, I could not get into the latter, so we spent our time in the first and a long while more in the beautiful park of the latter palace.

There is nothing very remarkable about the palace of the Grand Trianon. It is a small sized palace—all on one floor. The difference between the large state appartments [sic] and the retired private rooms is very striking. All was redolent of Marie Antoinette, tho' her special palace was the other one, the Petit Trianon. In one room was a very elegant bed prepared in 1846 for the royal repose of Queen Victoria, who [p. 2] however disappointed king Louis Philippe & made her visit some years later.[1]

The Petit Trianon, judged externally, is quite a handsome mansion, such as many private persons could afford to keep, perhaps as large tho' hardly I think as the President's house at Washington. The park is most beautiful, sloping lawns, and hills, with beautiful pebble walks and a lake with a winding stream. All thro' it are very fine trees, not in rows but set about as in the best parks at home. Then there is a pretty open circular marble temple on an island approached by two bridges, and far out of sight of that you come across, on the borders of the lake, a little hamlet of quaint & odd cottages. In one of these was the dairy where Marie Antoinette made butter. It is a very cottage looking place outside, but within the floor is of tessellated marble, with tables of marble on sculptured legs, & the water falls thro' a marble figure into a shell-shaped marble basin. I gathered some pebbles from the walks and one or two I will enclose in this for Eliza with a little shell from the same place. The afternoon was lovely after a rainy morning and the walk altogether was very delightful. Coming home we came out on the "*Tapis Vert*" in front of the great palace and found in contrast to our quiet ramble some thousands of people [p. 3] gathered together listening to a military band which plays two afternoons a week. After enjoying the music for a little while we went home to dinner.

The next morning early I came into town with Mr. Curtis and arrived just in time to join a party—Dr. Mc[Clintock] and family, Mr. & Mrs. Wright,[2] & Mr. Roland and a friend of his[3] (Mr. R. brought letters of introduction to me from Father & Mr. Neill[4])—on a day's excursion to Fontainebleau.

This is one of the favorite resorts of the present Emperor. It is a large palace with a grand park, fountains &c, & all in the midst of a forest of some 60 miles in circumference. We lunched at the hotel & then walked, rather too rapidly for me, thro' the palace, rich with the oldest historical associations. Part of the building was put up by St. Louis, a great deal by Francis II [i.e., Francis I], Henry II, Henry IV, &c, &c. Here we saw the nuptial couch of the young duchess of Orleans, mother of the Count of Paris, the bed-room & bath-room of Napoleon I, the grand saloon made by Henry II or III for his mistress, Diane de Poitiers. The long library is very beautiful as also the chapel of the Holy Trinity and another one dedicated to Thomas à Becket. We rode for hours thro' the forest, walking among rocks said to have been inhabited once by hermits with all sorts of holes and caves [p. 4] for their resting places. At some points we had superb views stretching miles and miles away. We rode beneath oaks said to be [planted between?] 1300–1400—300 & 400 years old, one of the oldest, having been witness to the ancient Druidical rites in the time of King Pharamond.[5]

I broke off a little twig from a tree said to be either planted by or a favorite of Madame de Maintenon.[6] I shall put that in my letter also for Eliza. She will value such trifles more than you. If she will take the trouble to write on a slip of paper to be put with them from whence they came, by & by, if I travel much, she may have quite a collection of odds & ends, with some interest from association.

Now to reply to some things in your letters. First as to the draft in connection with a loan from Dr. Maris, I do not know that I shall need it, or if I do that it would not be better to get the money in some other way. If I conclude to draw on you in that way, it shall be as you suggest—a week or two after sight. Since writing to you about it, I have thought that I could get all the money thro' Dr. M[cClintock] as well as in any other way. I cannot decide about it now.

Miss Grosholz was mistaken in saying I was at Baden. Dr. Maris & Mr. Stockwell went but I remained in Paris. I hope to get to the Rhine before very long, tho' whether [p. 5] Baden will come in my way or not, I can't say now. If I can, I should like to go over to London in September.

As to purchases for you, I will do as you say, use discretion. Sometime I may send you a list of portraits which are exposed for sale, and let you make your selection. As to selling others, if you can get orders for anything of the kind I will pay what you send out for and you can make what charges you please for my profit if you care to. I am afraid I am not very well fitted for this business. The price of those card portraits here is 30 cts (1 ½ francs) apiece. Perhaps before I close this letter I can get a list, more or less complete & send with it.

I must close now for the present to resume soon again.

Monday, August 13th

As a conclusion to the whole matter of money, you need give yourself no care until you hear further from me. I am not at all certain or settled in regard to it. If I should not go to Italy I do not think that I shall need any more than I have. If I should go, I shall have to think of your kind proposition [made] some [p. 6] time ago.

Paris is very full of strangers just now. People are coming in crowds to be present at the festivities of the Emperor's fête which comes off in grand style next Wednesday the fifteenth.[7] There will be a solemn high mass in the morning, and all sorts of games and amusements in the afternoon and all the theatres & circuses will give gratuitous exhibitions. At night a grand illumination.

I received the "Weekly Herald" and am much obliged for it. Could you ever send me a copy of the <u>Christian Advocate</u> I should be obliged. It does not come to Dr. McClintock as I had supposed it would. <u>The World</u> & <u>The Methodist</u> come regularly.

Keep on writing.

Yours faithfully,

Andrew

My dear Jim,

As my friend Mr. Charles B. Stockwell leaves today for Havre to sail thence in the *Fulton* tomorrow for home, I thought I would send a letter and a little package by him. The package contains some stereoscopic views of Paris localities. Whether they will interest you or not I cannot tell. I got them because they were cheap. You can consider yourself in my debt for them, if you care to have them, at 18 cts. apiece. If you would like more at such a price (or possibly some maybe higher), I can get whole series of views of all sorts of places in Europe to any extent, besides interiors of churches and palaces and museums. I have been too much occupied to get a list of the card portraits of which I spoke yet, but will send it on some time soon. [p. 2] I don't want you to feel compelled to take these photographs for I shall be glad to have them myself when I come home.

If you can show any attention to Mr. Stockwell, I shall be glad. Of course, he has many friends in Phila[delphia], but it would gratify me to know that you were able to be polite to him. He has been at Bailey & Kitchens, but I think he intends going to Tiffany & Co.'s, New York, very soon. He is a very gentlemanly and kind fellow and his presence, especially when I first came to Paris, did a good deal to take off the utter loneliness of things here from me.

Until Friday, I had a sort of hope that I should start for the Rhine today. But I have no company, so I will not go. I do not care to go alone. I may leave about the first week in September.

The principal matter of interest to us now is that we are going to move our residence the fifth of next month to No. 10, rue Balzac, where Dr. McClintock [p. 3] has taken a small but comfortable "Hotel" for a year. We shall not have quite so much room as we have now, but on several accounts it will be more comfortable. The house is on the east side of the street between the Boulevard Beaujon and the rue Chateaubriand.

Dr. McClintock and Emory leave or have left this morning for Liége with Mr. & Mrs. John A. Wright, of whom Mr. Crowell spoke to you, to have a business interview of some sort with Gov. Wright,[1] minister of the U. S. at Berlin.

Downtown the other day, rummaging among the thousands of old engravings exposed on the quais and in the shops near at hand, I came across two terribly strong temptations. One, a beautiful impression of the St. John of Domenichino engraved by Müller, and the other an equally good impression of a Magdalen engraved by Raphael Morghen. The first was 25 & the second 20 francs. If you [p. 4] or Father or especially Sallie desire two really first rate engravings at a reasonable price, these would suit you. I don't know but I will buy them myself with the hope of disposing of them to some of the family if I should not be rich enough to keep them.

Sometime ago you asked me for an estimate of probable expenses of a journey to Italy. Whether I can go or not, of course, is yet uncertain, but I should not feel free to go pecuniarily without five or six hundred dollars more than I can command at present. For some part of this, say, two hundred dollars, I think I could undertake to become responsible after my arrival home; for the rest I see no way at present of providing, except by a long indebtedness, which I dread to incur. It is barely possible that something may turn up, some way may be opened for me to go without so much cost.

The Letters of Andrew Longacre * 41

Paris
August 20, 1860

[LETTER 9]

I have been hoping that some better [p. 5] provision might be made for me here, something like a salary. But the prospect is exceedingly dim. Dr. McC[lintock] is demanding now an additional thousand dollars for himself and, even then, his salary will fall about one thousand dollars below his expenses. He has a very expensive sort of way of getting along.[2]

Of course, with his claims so strong, there is little room for me to hope. I consider my engagement with him to hold me at present rates till November. What he will do then, or whether he will offer anything more than my board, remains to be seen.

Just living in Paris is pretty expensive even for me. Money goes in a great many ways. I have to live—in dress & habit—well or our good people would not like it. I mean the church people. Under these circumstances, if Dr. M[cClintock] does not think he can give me anything beside my board, I cannot afford to remain. This is all, of course, a good way off yet, all these [p. 6] arrangements &c. They float thro' my mind at times, and I should speak of them to you if I could see you, and so it comes very natural to write them. While I am unable to say what Dr. M[cClintock] will do, I think he will act kindly. He is certainly very kind to me, not in the least exacting, and apparently careful of my wants & my tastes. He is rather fussy, to be sure, acts and talks fussily, but he is kind with all.

Write me all about everything. I sympathise with you in the delay of your hopes, as to increase of salary, but am sure it is only a delay.

Love to all, especially to William Crowell.

Yours faithfully,

Andrew Longacre

My estimate for Italy is rather under than over what is probable.

Paris
August 23, 1860

[LETTER 10]

My dear Jim,

Your letter of the 1st & 3rd has arrived, after what seems to me like a long passage, with very welcome intelligence from home. If you know how much my heart had been travelling homeward the last few weeks, you would understand my pleasure in hearing regularly from you. However, you will have to cross the ocean to know it thoroughly.

The thought of the waste of waters between me and all I love gives a sort of hopelessness to my desires, a sort of faint sick-longing that could not well be were it otherwise. Tho' I am on the larger continent of the two, this eastern hemisphere, the old world, I feel as if it were a desolate island in the midst of a roaring ocean and I without a boat to carry me to the mainland.

One reason of my loneliness is I suppose the terrible weather we have had all summer—cold, cold, cold, cloudy, cloudy, cloudy, wet, wet, wet, with just little snatches [p. 2] of warmth and sunshine to make one feel the sadder by a glimpse of what it might be would the weather only change. It is now almost the last of August and still the same sad & dull season. You know me of old & you can understand then just how this dull weather takes all the heart and hope as well as health out of me. I feel most of the time unfit for anything, either for work or for play.

But I need not send my gloom across the sea to you.

I have written a letter to George West which I will enclose in this, as I do not remember his address, the No., I mean, and now for a while I shall leave you as I want, if possible, to see the gallery of the Luxembourg today. I have been going a long time but have not succeeded in getting there yet and if I leave it [until] later, I shall fail again today.

2 P.M. I have had a grand time at the Luxembourg and, having lunched and read letters from Irenee [Pepper][1] & Sallie, I [p. 3] [send] "a piece of penmanship" to you. Speaking of penmanship, I have wondered at your silence in respect to mine. Often I give a melancholy glance over a finished letter and wonder if you will be able to decipher it. But I must write fast if I write at all, and I certainly have lost the art, if I ever possessed it, of writing well and fast both.

If you care to follow my journey today on the map, you can trace a line from rue des Ecuries d'Artois, along rue de Berri, Avenue Champs Élysées to the Place de la Concorde, then across the bridge along the east side of the Palais des Deputies,[2] to rue de l'Université. Along that & the rue Jacob to rue de Seine, down to the Palais de Senat, as the Luxembourg is called. I was surprised to find it so large and handsome. The guide-book says the present edifice was built by Marie de Médicis after the plan of her paternal home, the Pitti palace at Florence. First I was shown thro' several very grand rooms full of pictures & emblems relating to the first and second Empire. The throne room is the grandest I have seen, surpassing, I think, both Fontainebleau and the Tuileries. [p. 4]

All the salons and passages are in what appears to be the French taste for palaces; that is, most overwhelmingly & elaborately & gorgeously ornamented. I confess it does not altogether please me tho' certainly when a room of fine proportions is thoroughly adorned in this style it is very imposing. I was shown the *Chambre a couches* of Marie de Medicis, a very elaborately ornamented room whose gilded & painted ceiling, where Rubens & Philippe de Champagne displayed their art, had looked down on the changes of more than two hundred and fifty years. It makes one feel strangely to go into such places and know they are the very same with scarce any change about them.

From this show part of the palace, I went to the portion I came particularly to see, the gallery. Here are hung up the pictures bought by Government which are the works of living painters. After the death of the painter, his works are removed to the Louvre. I cannot attempt an account of these. They are very fine, some, a few, of the kind which must be a "joy forever."[3] Not a few of them are [p. 5] very sad. The modern French painters[4] seem to delight in painting things that appeal to the feelings with the utmost intensity. One large picture represents the entrance to the arena at Rome, a view of the benches covered with spectators above and below, a party of Christians thrust in for some terrible exhibition. Two youths, one in priestly garments, are embracing in front & looking up with a lofty resignation, almost joy.

On the boulevard des Italiens the other day I saw a lithograph of a scene of the same sort, evidently modern. It represented a party of gladiators armed, in the arena, going to the part of the gallery where the emperor sat, & raising their swords. Under the picture were these words, "*Ave Caesar imperatore, morituri te salutant.*" "Hail, Caesar Emperor, those about to die salute thee."[5] In the same window was a terrible picture of the death of Julius Caesar. Very many of the pictures at the Luxembourg are of this kind, representations of terrible scenes, quite justifying the expression of a lady in regard [p. 6] "full of horrors." There are many landscapes and two or more fine cattle-pieces of Rosa Bonheur.

Of course, I am a little anxious to know always of the safe arrival of any packages I send. There are at least three which I have sent within some month or two past, of which as yet I have not heard. One, as I wrote you, by Mr. [Charles] Dunlap,[6] another of card-portraits by Dr. Beadle of New York, and the last by Mr. Geo. Stuart.

A good while ago I gave your shirt and socks, what I brought away in mistake, to Walter Palmer, who then expected to go home soon. He did not get off and what has become of the goods, I have not yet heard.

Another package of stereoscopic views, with letters, I sent this week by Mr. Charles B. Stockwell of whom you have heard me speak. He sailed in the *Fulton* but did not expect to be in Phila[delphia] till a week after his arrival. Of all these I hope to hear in time.

Yours faithfully,
Andrew

❧

Dear Jim,

Yours of the 7th, 9th, & 10th came to hand on Friday, and gave me a great deal of pleasure. You need have no fear of my finding any fault with your "matter" in letters. Anything from home would be valuable and yours are really too entertaining to be called under so general a name as that. You might tell me more of just little daily doings, whom you see, and what they say, what is projected and what is carried out. All items that pass thro' the minds of the folks at home become in a sort hallowed to me, off here, and are of real living interest.

You say I always have something new to write about, but after all, it is somewhat monotonous to tell what one sees all the time. I have a mortal dread of getting into a guide book style. Sometimes, I glide over things and make no note of them just on purpose to escape the catalogue character.

One thing, however, I really want to tell you of. Last week, after going thro' the show-rooms of the Tuileries, we went, the young ladies, Johnny and I,[1] into the Louvre and walked on till we reached the Museum of Sovereigns, as it is all called. It is full of the relics of different kings of France. There is the carved chair of King Dagobert, the sword, sceptre &c of Charlemagne and his crown, with suits of armor of many kings, royal robes decorated with gold and precious stones, a mirror [p. 2] candle-stand covered with jewels presented to Catherine de Médicis by the Republic of Venice, the prayer-books of kings, among them that of Louis the ninth called Saint Louis. In another room are the relics of Napoleon the first, his clothes, coronation robes, several highly ornamented saddles, his camp writing-desk & chairs, the cradle of the king of Rome, &c. Such things as these having a living interest, it requires no imagination to connect them with the persons and circumstances to which they belonged. One can almost see Francis first's[2] black eyes looking out from the suit of armor that stands head and shoulders higher than that of the preceding and succeeding kings.

The all absorbing topic with us now, to come from the dead to the living, is the state of affairs in Italy. Garibaldi has landed on the mainland of the Neapolitan territory and the *Telegraph* of Saturday reported a battle of some sort at Reggio. Today we hear he has been so far successful as to drive the Neapolitan troops into the fort. It is also reported that the huge sums of money in the treasury of that kingdom are being removed, so it looks as if the success of Garibaldi were hardly a matter of doubt. [3] What will the end be? People who ought to know predict a general war in which Russia and Austria will combine and fight against France and England. How Prussia will go no one [p. 3] as yet says. She has as strong ties with Russia as with England and it will be hard to choose. But the German hatred and dread of French preponderance may put her into the Russian scale. In which case the war will be terrible and right at one's door.[4] The troubles in Syria[5] have much of course to do with this.

Have you heard that it is said that the Druse have spared all the American Missionaries and also all who fled to them for protection? So it is reported here. These missionaries are said to have had under their care some thousands of Druse children before the war broke out.

Things keep quiet here. There are a few more carriages on the Avenue Champs Élysées than earlier in the summer, but there is no general return to town nor will there be for a month or more. Many stay out till after November, which is called the gloomiest month in the year here.

Strangers are arriving and departing continually. Every week we see new faces, and miss some we had seen before. One has the opportunity to scatter the seed widely, but it is not so satisfactorily, at least it does not feel so to the preacher. It is trying to lose those in whom one first begins to be interested. It does not do to waste much love upon them or life here would be a succession of heart-breakings. [p. 4] Just now I am anticipating a pleasant week at Versailles, whither I go today with Mrs. Curtis. I shall have a nice quiet time. I feel as if I needed the leisure and relaxation, and one could not find a more glorious place for it than the near neighborhood of those superb parks and all the great and little glories and beauties in and around them.[6]

Write to me always.

Love to all,

Yours faithfully,

Andrew

My dear Jim,

The *Adriatic's* mails are just received, bringing to me a joyous freight of half a dozen, counting from within the envelopes—no seven, in four envelopes. That is a very decent steamer, the *Adriatic*. If she often does as well as that, I shall think more highly of her than ever.

I am writing in my new home, of which I think I told you when it was in prospect. No. 10, rue Balzac. Occasionally, for a change, you can address your letters here—not newspapers or unpaid parcels. As for those, I have an account at Munroe's, and it is more convenient to have it all there. We are all agreeably disappointed in our "Hotel." When Dr. McC[lintock] came home and told us he had signed the agreement to rent it for a year, we were all taken by surprise. As soon as possible we came to look at it and began to be sorry at finding so little room. Dr. [McClintock] had really forgotten how large a family we were, and the new house seemed two rooms too small. However, the thing was done & not to be undone. [p. 2]

So we began at once to plan what was to be done with it. Having one servant's room more than was needed, it was with some change given to Johnny & makes him very comfortable, the servants' rooms being unusually good ones. Then we concluded a reception room was an expensive luxury and gave it as a bedroom to Emory. In this way we make our room correspond with our

Paris
September 6th, 1860
[LETTER 12]

wants and are really as pleasantly circumstanced as we could desire. It is a great satisfaction to have a whole house to ourselves—besides it saves expense. We are gainers too by the change in having much cleaner & quieter apartments. The furniture is very nearly if not quite new, and the whole has an air of elegant neatness which the old had not.

My room is a little gem, a sort of young Paradise with a window from ceiling to floor opening toward the south and looking over gardens of trees and flowers from which the much de-carbonized air floats into my room in the mornings like the fresh sweet air of Camp-meeting.[1] It is marvellously quiet here, too. Something is to be attributed to my deafness, but really, in the mornings I could imagine I were away off in the country. The house we occupied before was near one of the great thoroughfares [p. 3] by which the market people, &c, come into Paris. And as that street, the rue du Faubourg St. Honoré,[2] is not very wide and is very steep, a good part of the travel turned into ours [i.e., our street] which is next. As I am not a very sound sleeper, there was no rest for me from quite an early hour in the morning.

We are nearer the Avenue des Champs Élysées, although two streets are between it and us. We are a good deal higher, too, than we were. Indeed, we are very near the highest part of Paris, except such places as Montmartre and the heights of Trocadero. From our door to the Avenue des Champs Élysées is quite a steep down hill.

4 P.M. I have been interrupted and recommence after a long intermission. Dr. Maris called and took lunch with us. He has just been to Belgium and the Rhine, and will probably leave next week for Italy. He thinks I ought to like Paris having so pleasant a home, and especially so pleasant a room. It is pleasant. As I look round it now and notice the cleanliness and elegance of everything in it, and glance out the open window to the rays of the declining sun falling on the trees, it seems quite cheerful enough to make me contented with Paris.

After lunch I walked down town to the Hotel des Trois Empereurs where Mr. Walter S. Garner is staying. I do not know whether you remember [p. 4] his name. He was my room-mate on my passage in the *Vanderbilt*. He called and left his card the other day. I did not find him at home, so after a few purchases, I am home again in time to conclude your letter before dinner.

I walked up through the Champs Élysées which is quite a sight this bright afternoon. Have I described it to you in any of my letters? I do not remember it, so I will do it now to be sure. As "Champs" is plural, I suppose I should say "they," but we would call it park or square at home, so it seems more natural to say "it." It, then, is a long, unenclosed square extending, as you can see on the map, from the Place de la Concorde to the "Rond point," and from the Avenue Gabriel on one side to the Seine on the other. Thro' the middle from east to west runs the lower part of the Avenue des Champs Élysées but which does not take that name till above the "Rond point." I think there is only one street which crosses it from north to south and that only seems across the northern section, to the "Palais de l'Industrie."[3] This whole large space is covered with trees and this year has been laid out besides in flower beds, grass plots and fountains and walks with a great deal of taste. In it, you know, are a number of buildings—the great "Palais de [p. 5] l'Industrie," two circuses, cafes, &c. Along the main avenue are stalls; till now mere shells covered with canvas according to the taste or means of the owners. Now they are being replaced by neat carved oak (or oaked) summer-house-looking contrivances, quite pretty. In these all sort of cakes, candies, cigars, &c, &c, are sold. There are also quite a number of puppet shows, small stands representing a stage with curtains, &c, where puppets are made to enact sundry comical scenes. One that I saw this afternoon had a tall, fancifully dressed woman who came out and danced while, one by one came out from under her dress, a whole party of smaller figures, ending with four tiny little figures in white shirts, taking hold of hands. These all danced around her a while and then the scene changed. Sometimes these scenes are very funny. If I could understand the dialogue which is talked for them, I should enjoy it more. Right in front of each of these stands a rope is drawn around in a semicircle. Inside are low seats for the children & nurses and fond parents who mostly patronise these shows & [p. 6] outside a motley group of amused people, many just stopping as I did for a passing look & laugh. There are also circular machines composed of a canopy above & depending from it at intervals, wooden horses or sometimes boats. When a good many of the places are taken on these, the whole thing is made to revolve rapidly. The young folks enjoy this amazingly, and at night I have seen other than very young folks ride gaily around on them.[4] Besides these are two or three large enclosures where the "Cafés chantants"[5] are. All along the main avenue and here and there all thro' the place are thousands of neat iron chairs to be let for two or three cents apiece, if you wish to sit & enjoy what goes on. Of a warm summer night these are often all occupied. At least, so the folks tell me. This cool summer very few of them have been taken when I have been about. On the other side of the Champs Élysées, west of the Palais de l'Industrie, and rather toward the river, the "Concerts Musards"[6] [p. 7] are given, the orchestra occupying a gaily adorned and illuminated pavilion and the audience sitting out in the air all round.

You cannot conceive of the life and gaiety of this place of a pleasant summer afternoon and evening. Thousands of equipages crowd the main avenue and thousands of people—men, women, and especially children everywhere else. It is the great feature of the French that they know how to enjoy themselves. They do it admirably, with no grumbling or quarrelling, but in perfect good humor.[7]

There is one thing I may as well say now. I asked Eliza to tell you that Mr. Gerald F. Dale, a friend of William Crowell's, is coming to Paris in October. I met him here on my arrival, and I am sure he will bring anything to me you care to send. I have not yet been able to make up my mind as to money matters, but I think perhaps, if convenient to you to send me two hundred dollars on my own responsibility, I might use it. However, perhaps it would be as well to wait till I really need it. I [p. 8] suppose you would not have any difficulty about sending me a bill of exchange for that amount (I believe that is what you call it) whenever I should write for it. If you could send me some photographs of you folks at home, it would be a great consolation for I have no certain prospect of coming home soon. I have wished for them often. I only brought a picture of Sallie.

How much I long to see you all. Keep on writing.

Love to all,

Yours faithfully,

Andrew Longacre

Mr. & Mrs. Baker[8] of New York are expecting to come over to Paris this fall, about the last of October, I believe. Won't that be joyful for your uncle?[9] How I wish some of you would come too.

I enclose a letter to Orly.[10]

My dear Jim,

It is after ten o'clock and I have a head ache, and so, "by rights" ought to be going to bed, but I am not sure I shall be able to secure time to write to you tomorrow, and, as I feel like a small talk to you, I shall indulge myself.

Things look more cheerful and more pleasant now than at any time since I came to Paris. The weather is fair and fine, dry, and would be intolerably dusty were it not for all sorts of watering machines which keep our macadamised streets muddy notwithstanding the sun.[1] The early mornings (steel pens are too slow so I resume the gold) are special luxuries. I wish you could step into my compact little paradise of a room and share with me the delicious morning hour which I manage to be up in time to secure before breakfast. My room at all times is very cheery, but it seems especially so in the morning. I don't believe there is another such place [p. 2] in Paris—and if not here, where?

I had a great delight last Sunday[2] in seeing quite a number of our own people coming back after their summer travel, among them, first and chief, my special idolatry, Mr. Woodbury Langdon[3] who as a grandson of John Jacob Astor is very rich and is besides tall, remarkably handsome, and particularly kind to your uncle. He and wife and beautiful little son waited after church to speak to me in the afternoon. I called on them the next day and dined there, running the visit into the evening till ½ past 10 yesterday. Of course, by this time I am in a state of blissful excitement, difficult for you to imagine being quite peculiar to my unduly excitable disposition. But, alas, he leaves again on Monday and will not come back to stay in Paris till December. How I shall exist till then, I can't tell. Really and seriously, I cannot help liking Mr. Langdon very much indeed. He has treated me from the first as if he really liked me, has seemed to enjoy [p. 3] seeing me, and besides, from having been a very gay man of the world, he has during the last year or two settled down into a serious seeker of religion, is one of the most regular in his attendance at the chapel (he lives next door to it), and seems to desire to talk only on religious matters, specially his own spiritual state. His wife is not at all handsome, but intelligent and also kind to me. The boy is a fair miracle in the matter of religion. He is the means of influencing both parents for good, tho' only twelve years old, is never absent from church and listens to sermons as eagerly and interestedly as any one in the church. His eyes never wander. Altogether they form a family where I know I should love to be as much as was consistent with other duties.

To comfort myself in their going away, I expect to go to London next week. Mr. Francis Lycett, No. 2 Highbury Grove, who was in Paris, a Sunday some two months ago, has been asking me in sundry notes to come, and Dr. McC[lintock] says if [p. 4] he were I, he would go—so I think I shall leave next Monday or Tuesday. I wish I did not dislike travelling alone so much. It is worse here than in America you know—passports and custom-houses are annoying and there are a thousand inconveniences from having so slight a knowledge of the language as I have. I do not advance very rapidly in French.[4] One improvement I find, I am growing familiar with the sound of it and can distinguish words much better than at first, so that generally I can form some sort of an idea of what people say to me. If I fairly overcome my difficulty in this respect, increased somewhat of my deafness, I think I shall learn something. I have improved very much in my reading.

The last steamer brought me no letters from any body, so this whole week I have had not a word from America. Please don't do so any oftener than necessary. I know you are justly faithful so I will not complain, but only suggest that any word is a comfort.

Yours faithfully,

Andrew

On Monday, September 17, Andrew left Paris by the "Western Railway" bound for Rouen and Dieppe. He took a steamer across the channel to New Haven and then "the cars" to London. Thus began his first and eagerly anticipated visit in the home of the Francis Lycetts at Highbury Grove, where he found "an elegant house and fine gardens" and a warm and welcoming hospitality (cf. MS Diary, September 17-27, 1860).

My dear Jim,

I was compelled to send off my letter to Father this morning without enclosing, as I had intended, one to you. I snatch a few moments now and will jot down at odd times as I am able the thoughts that crowd my mind.

Mr. & Mrs. Lycett, my kind friends here, spare no effort to give me pleasure. They seem determined that I shall see as much as possible of London during my short stay. This has [been] my third day with them and, as the two others, it has been diligently occupied in sight-seeing. This morning a Mr. Enser who is staying here, an uncle, I think, of Mr. Lycett, went with me to Greenwich Hospital and the Park there. We got home just in time for lunch and before lunch was over the carriage was at the door to take us to the British Museum. Our party consisted of Mr. & Mrs. Enser and a nice little Mrs. Hughes, sister-in-law of Rev. Geo. Hughes, now presiding elder of Bur- [p. 2] lington District, New Jersey Conference.

With the British Museum I was not a whit disappointed. I question the wisdom of its arrangements, but the collections in it are very grand. Four museums might be made out of it— one for Art, another Natural History (Zoology & Mineralogy), a third Ethnology, articles illustrating the customs & habits of nations, and the Library.

The first of these was of course of much interest to me. Here are the Elgin Marbles, arranged with the most perfect art, having models of the Parthenon, &c, so that it requires only a moment's reflection to reconstruct to your mind the great whole. Nothing could be better than the care & taste displayed here, as well as in the sculptures from Egypt and Assyria.

The Natural History was like our Academy of Natural Sciences and not on a much more extended scale.

The collection illustrating the manners & habit of nations was very interesting. All sort of curious things gathered & put together. [p. 3] Enough Etruscan vases for instance to have filled half a dozen considerable cro[c]kery shops.

Egyptian mummies with all kinds of relics of old Egyptian life, [al]so of the Greek & Roman periods, of the middle ages, of barbarous nations, &c. Of course, a vast amount of all this could only be glanced at hurriedly.

The Letters of Andrew Longacre ∗ 49

London
September 21, 1860

[LETTER 14]

The library is superb, and in its <u>antique</u> department wonderfully interesting. The autographs, old & rare books, & ornamented manuscripts of all nations & eras.

One could easily spend weeks in going thro' the great wealth of curious and precious things here.

I was pretty tired when we came home, but had not much time to think about it as we had company to dinner—quite a nice little English company dinner, afterward a sociable evening. My very kind entertainers certainly seem to lay themselves out to please and gratify me in every possible way.

Sept. 22   Today we drove in Mr. L[ycett]'s fine [p. 4] barouche[1] to the new houses of Parliament. You know them thro' the prints. They are exceedingly rich in ornament and inside are very grand. So, also, I suppose, outside, many people think, but the *tout ensemble* is not Gothic. The ornaments &c undoubtedly are, but no real Gothic pile had ever that vast rectangular mass of buildings with its ponderous & clumsy towers. I think our chamber of representatives finer than the house of commons, and it is much larger. The house of Lords is very gaudily gilt and painted, but is not impressive. Some of the corridors, halls and passages are the best things in the whole.

Except the noble old Westminster Hall, where Strafford, Charles I & Warren Hastings[2] were tried. To me that, both outside and in, is much more satisfactory than the new effort at grandeur by the side of it.

Then, acting on the advice of a friend in Paris, I hunted out the old cloisters of Westminster Abbey. Here the deep, old, solemn feeling has full sway. No glaring and in- [p. 5] consistent newness shocks you.

In conclusion I should number the New Houses of Parliament among the tolerably long list of British failures, tho' unlike the *Great Eastern* & Thames tunnel,[3] the failure will not be so generally appreciated, and the good men of England may fondly fancy it no failure at all. It must have cost an incredible sum.

I fear that modern attempts to use the old Gothic architecture, except in strict copying of old specimens, are likely to [be] pure failures. Modern ideas of cost and utilitarianism stagger under the load, which the enthusiastic religious spirit of an earlier age bore flying. We have so many notions, flight and air and heat and over all cheapness that we cannot rise to that pitch of heroic art which feared none of these things because it knew nothing of them.

With Westminster Abbey, all & specially Henry VII's Chapel, I was entirely and only delighted, as also with Westminster Hall [p. 6]—and scarcely less with those quaint old cloisters once resonant to the song or head of cowled monks & abbots of the old, old times. But good bye again for a while. I must stop.

Sept. 25th   My "stop" has been much longer than I anticipated, but unavoidably so. As a visitor, I have but little control over my own time.

We had a <u>nice</u> (Anglicé) party to dinner on Saturday. Rev. Mr. [William] Arthur & lady, Revs. [Samuel] Coley & [Richard] Roberts, all first-class men here.[4] Mr. Lycett has had company almost every day to dine since I have been here. He seems determined to do me all possible honor.

There is much more of an American look about the English people than I had anticipated. Continually, I see people who look as if they were just from the streets of Phila[delphia] or New

My 29th Birth-day

June,　　TUESDAY, 12,　　1860.

Ro
5¼ — Da. D — Bkf. 1.35 —
Home. Wrote to Sallie — dressed
Went to lunch with Mrs Curtis
Rode out with her & Miss Bessie.
Home. finished letter to Sallie.
Dined with Mrs Curtis — Mr. C.
being out of town. Spent evg.
A long convs. on American Chapel
& its interests. Home 10½
Retired 11.
Rec'd in the morning a beautiful
bouquet & a fine Geranium
in a pot from Mrs. C—
From little George a blk.
silk case & carry sermons &c
bands on Sunday.

Heartsease
from bouquet
Mrs. Curtis sent me

Andrew Longacre,
Manuscript Diary,
June 12, 1860.
"My 29th Birth-Day."

Right:
"Mrs. J. D. B. Curtis,
Versailles, Aout [August] 30[, 1860]."
Longacre Portfolio.

Below:
Andrew Longacre,
floor plan of the second floor at
No. 42, rue des Ecuries d'Artois, Paris
Longacre Portfolio.

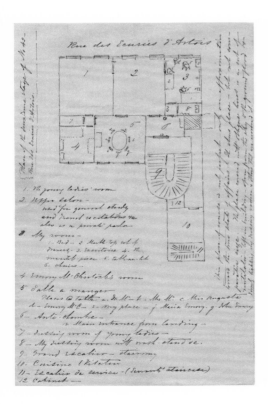

52

Left:
"Clock, rue des Ecuries d'Artois," July 1860.

Bottom Left:
"42 rue des Ecuries d'Artois, July 19 [, 1860]."

Bottom Right:
"Bed @ 42 rue des Ecuries d'Artois, July, [18]60."

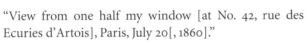

"View from one half my window [at No. 42, rue des Ecuries d'Artois], Paris, July 20[, 1860]."

"No. 41, rue des Ecuries d'Artois, Aout [August], 1860."

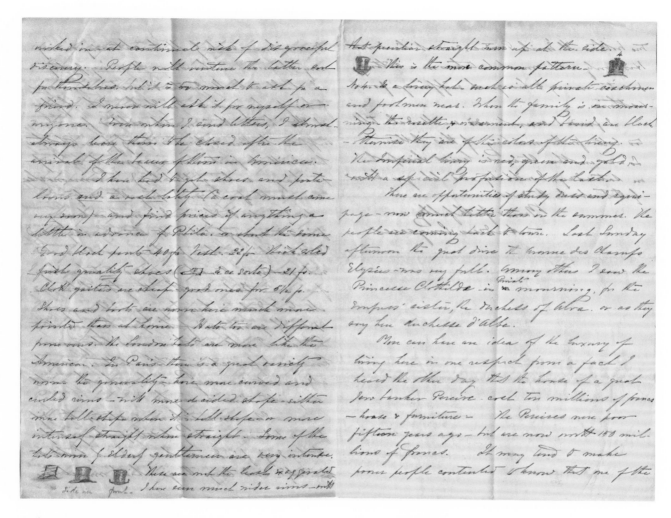

Andrew Longacre, to James Madison Longacre, Letter 15, October 8, 1860, with drawings of top hats.

Right:
Andrew Longacre's monogram.

Bottom:
"Bois de Boulogne," Paris, n.d. Longacre Portfolio.

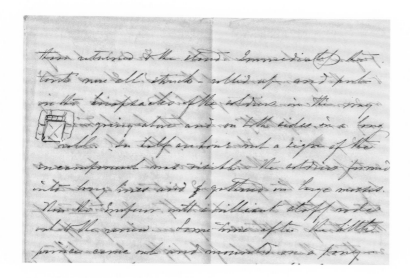

Left:
Andrew Longacre, to James Madison Longacre,
Letter 17, October 30, 1860,
with sketch of soldier's knapsack.

Bottom Left:
Andrew Longacre, *Manuscript Diary*,
May 1, 1861, captioned "Jour de la
morte de ma mère."

Bottom Right:
Andrew Longacre. Paris, April 16, 1861.

Right:
"From my window at 10 rue Balzac, June 27, 1861."
Longacre Portfolio.

Bottom:
"Biarritz, Villa Eugénie, Oct. 15, 1861."
Longacre Portfolio.

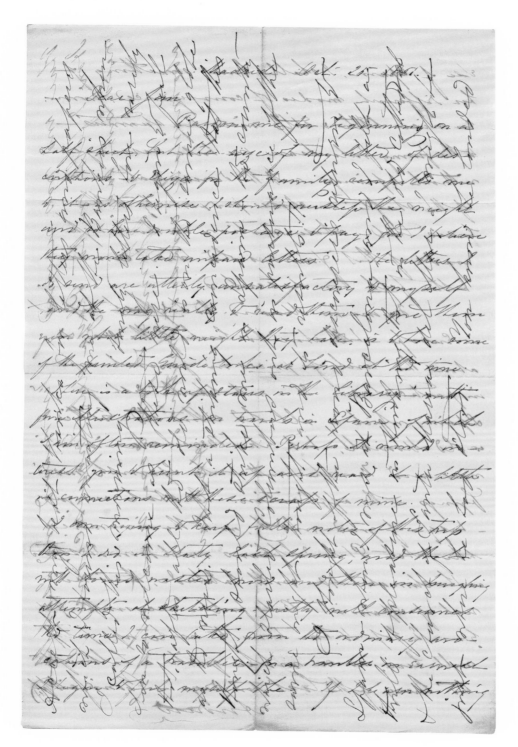

Andrew Longacre
to James Madison Longacre,
Letter 56, Madrid,
October 25, 1861.
An example of cross-writing.

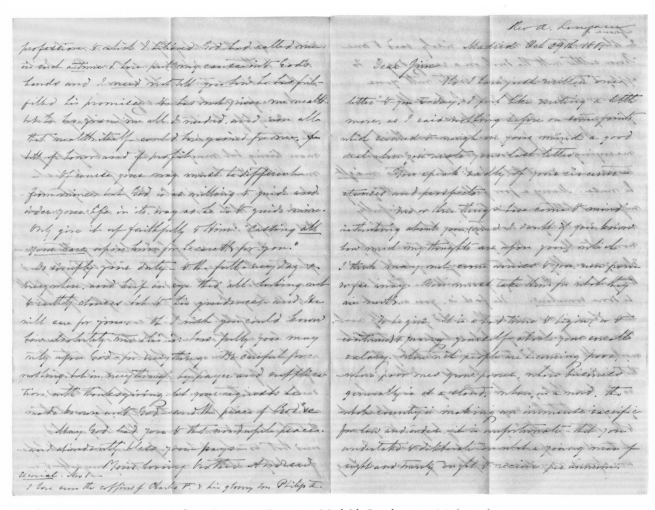

Andrew Longacre to James Madison Longacre, Letter 58, Madrid, October 29, 1861 (recto).
A letter of brotherly love and advice.

Andrew Longacre to James Madison Longacre, Letter 58, Madrid, October 29, 1861 (verso).
A letter of brotherly love and advice.

"Cart from Baelin to Cordova à Carpio[, Spain], Nov. 16, 1861." Longacre Portfolio.

"Cathedral at Cordova[, Spain], November 18[, 1861]." Longacre Portfolio.

York. The average of good looks is about as it is with us, [p. 7] tho' the women (not ladies) fall below ours. Yet the fine English complexion is a great improvement on the pallid delicacy of American faces. The grace of the women & men, too, is much below that of Americans & the politeness also. I speak, of course, <u>generally</u>. The children are lovely, large eyes, and bright, with a wonderful beauty of skin. When older this same skin grows to look a little coarse, but in childhood, it is lovely, the finest thing in the way of outside humanity I ever saw. I am surprised to see, but I need not have been in a city, the delicacy of the children's looks. Not that they seem ill, but I had fancied all English children must look like hearty country boys & girls. The fact is, they are as softly, delicately fair, as any with us & yet with much more a look of health.

Above, I said "not ladies," for I have not seen but one or two of that standing, so I cannot judge. As far as I have yet seen, either in France or here, [p. 8] I think the American ladies are most beautiful with an elegant dignity & grace of carriage rarely seen on this side the ocean. Of course, I mean in specimen cases, emphatically, & also in the average.

So, my young bachelor, if you would marry for beauty, you may as well stay at home.

I have had plenty of talk on <u>Slavery</u>—but I think people generally coincide with my own views.

Love to all,
Yours faithfully,
Andrew Longacre

Before leaving London on the morning of September 28, Andrew bid a sad farewell to the Lycetts and other friends who came to say goodbye. "Servants all weeping," he wrote. He was back in Paris by the next morning. The following week was filled with Chapel responsibilities, pastoral visits, reading, letter writing, etc. After his private devotions on October 6, he wrote, "Thought very seriously, as I have now better health, of a regular use and improvement of my time." On Sunday, October 7, he taught his "Sunday School class [at the Chapel] for the first time. 3 present" (MS diary, September 28-October 7, 1860).

My dear Jim,

Today, at last, the *Illinois* has brought me letters from home by the date of Sept. 21st, two weeks later than the last letters preceding. It may be all very well for you to suffer two weeks to pass without writing, but it goes rather hard with me. Do arrange matters so that <u>some one</u> shall write by every steamer. The Cunard steamers come every week. Every Tuesday morning I start off to Munroe's—and it is somewhat chilly to find nothing.

Hereafter, I should prefer to have your letters to come to the house. So let it be "noised abroad" that my address is ("<u>No. 10, rue Balzac—Champs Élysées, Paris</u>"). I find it will give me sometimes letters a day earlier than when sent to Munroe's.

As to what you say of the "affaire Italien"—my trip to Rome—I need at present make no remark. My last letter will set it to rest for some time. In one thing you are extravagant in your [p.

2] ideas of rapid travel. <u>Switzerland—Italy—& Rome—in a month!</u> You have not calculated the distances well—nor the character of the places to be seen. I was two weeks in London and did not half see it. I went pretty well through the town, streets and show-buildings, the standing lions, but pictures and sculptures, and the adjacent beauties, I scarcely attempted.

Merely to go to a place, to be able to say afterwards I have been there, is no ambition of mine. As far as that is concerned, I had quite as lief not go. I should consider two or three weeks for the city of Rome alone barely fair treatment. But, if it is to come, it will, somehow, & sometime. I am not at all impatient. I feel an occasional twinge of regret that I have to spend so much money in Paris, but I do the very best I can, use all the economy practicable, and for the waste of funds I must be resigned to my fate.

As I wrote to Eliza, in my last, Mrs. Alsop's [p. 3] dress is here, sent by Mrs. Leuschteming[?] during my absence in London. It is very pretty. I shall ask Mr. Curtis to enclose it in one of his packages to New York, to be left at the house there until called for. I suppose Mr. Keen (tho' it is hardly fair to bother him with it, for it is an ungainly sort of package—a long flat box) or some-one else can call for it and <u>pay the duty</u>.

As I wrote to Eliza, I cannot ask any friend to "smuggle" it into the country. And besides, it is such a package as I would not presume to ask a friend to take charge of.

But another thought strikes me. Mr. G. F. Dale is here, buying. It may possibly go in one of his packages to Phila[delphia]. I will see him and let you know before closing this letter, or at all events in my next, which will be quite time enough.

You can easily understand the difference between sending little packages by the hands of friends, such as are not liable to "duty," and large things which must be [p. 4] worked in at continual risk of disgraceful discovery. People will venture the latter sort for themselves, but it is too much to ask for a friend. I never will ask it for myself or any one. Even when I send letters, I almost always have them to be closed after the arrival of the bearer of them in America.

I have had to get shoes and pantaloons and a vest lately (a coat must come very soon), and find prices of anything a little in advance of Phila[delphia] or about the same. Good black pants—40 f[ranc]s, vest, 22 f[ranc]s, thick soled first quality shoes ([small drawing of a shoe] *de ce sorte*) 21 f[ranc]s. Cloth gaiters are cheap—good ones for 5 ½ f[ranc]s. Shoes and boots are worn here much more pointed than at home. Hats too are different from ours. The London hats are more like the American. In Paris there is a great variety worn—the generality have more curved and curled rims—with more decided shape, either more bell-shape when it is bell shape—or more intensely straight when straight. Some of the hats worn by elderly gentlemen are very intense. [Here, Longacre has sketched three versions of top hats; the first is marked through for deletion; the second is labeled "side view"; the third is labeled "front".] These [sketches] are not the least exaggerated; I have seen much wider rims with [p. 5] that peculiar straight turn up at the side [another drawing to illustrate the front view]. This is the more common pattern. [Again, another drawing, numbered "4" to illustrate the side view.] No. 4 is a livery hat, such as all private coachmen and footmen wear. When the family is in mourning, the rosette, & ornament, and band are black; otherwise, they are of the colors of the livery. The Imperial livery is red, green and gold, with a special profusion of the last.

There are opportunities to[1] study dress and equipage now much better than in the summer.

The people are coming back to town. Last Sunday afternoon the great drive to Avenue des Champs Élysées was very full. Among others I saw the Princesse Clothilde [sic] in private mourning for the Empress' sister, the duchess of Alva or, as they say here, duchesse d'Alba.[2]

You can have an idea of the luxury of living here in one respect from a fact I heard the other day that the house of a great Jew banker Péreire[3] cost ten millions of francs, house and furniture. The Péreires were poor fifteen years ago, but are now worth 150 millions of francs. It may tend to make poorer people contented to know that one of the [p. 6] two brothers, M. Émile Péreire, cannot lie down. His only rest must be when in a sitting position, owing to his great sufferings from asthma.

I find I cannot see Mr. Dale till too late for the mailing of this letter. So, as another steamer leaves Liverpool on Saturday, I will try and let you know by that about the dress.

Yours faithfully,
Andrew Longacre

My dear Jim,

Yours by the *Kangaroo* & the *Adriatic* have come to hand, and I was much obliged for them, altho' for three or four letters past you have been promising long letters and actually forwarding apologies. I was glad to hear from you at any rate and hope when you cannot send long letters you will continue to send some sort.

The other day, Monday, I think, we had the Rev. Dr. Deems,[1] a prominent man in the Church, South, to lunch with us, and with him a right good sort of young man from Lexington, Ky, named Shaw.[2] With the latter, Emory and I took something of a tramp in the afternoon thro' the mud and drizzling rain. We went first to the Dome des Invalides, to see the tomb of Napoleon,[3] but found it shut; then a slight turn brought us to the Champ de Mars whose immense stretch of unbroken plain looked like a desert in the gloomy light. Passing by the Artesian well of Grenelle, a beautiful iron [p. 2] observatory-looking affair,[4] we turned into the rue Rousillaye[5] and stopped to look at the exhibition of an engine upon a new principle intended to supersede steam. It looks very like an ordinary steam-engine. In the cylindrical chamber where ordinarily the steam is introduced are, instead of steam pipes & valves, apertures for the admission of street gas, and also electrical fluid from a battery. As the piston is driven to one end of the chamber, the gas is exploded by the electrical spark & the violence of the explosion forces the piston forward to the other end, where the same process is repeated. A waste pipe from the center of the cylinder carries off the exploded gas. The whole affair is as simple as possible and engines on the plan are coming into general use. There is no trouble of fires, and the rapidity of motion is easily regulated by the force of gas turned on.[6]

From there we visited the church of Ste. Clothilde [sic],[7] which I had seen before, and [p. 3] then the Pantheon,[8] which I had not seen. It is very splendid with an interior quite different from anything else in Paris & somewhat recalling St. Paul's, London.

On our way from there we stopped a moment at the Fontaine St. Michel on the Boulevard de Sebastopol[9] opposite the new bridge. It is much the finest fountain I have seen. The ornamental stone work reaches as high as the top of the houses. The main figures are St. Michel standing on Satan prostrate on some rocks. Under these the water falls in quite a fine cascade into a large bronze basin. Lower down, one on each side, are some sort of dragons spouting water into the basin, with boys all in bronze standing by them. Like many of the Paris fountains, this is up against the block of houses, exposing only the front to view, not standing out.[10]

After a short visit to Notre Dame, we turned towards home. Passing the "Morgue," we went in. I had never been there before and never expect to be there again. It is a lone [p. 4] one story square building on the bank of the Seine. Entering you find it has but one apartment, stone paved, at one end of which, behind an iron railing, are two rows of long narrow lying places, slightly inclined. Two male bodies were lying there, blue, bloated, with the dark purple marks of the discolored arteries distinctly prominent all over. They were naked, except a stiff wide leather apron over the loins. Bodies are kept there for three days for recognition, and they say it is <u>never</u> empty. Sometimes three, four & five & more even are lying there at a time. What a horrible view behind the gay scenes of Paris does such a place give.[11]

Beside that single day, I have kept pretty quiet, not feeling quite as bright as usual. Yesterday, I took a long walk in the Bois de Boulogne, turning into the quiet, out of the way paths, where I was quite alone—for squares, tho' the more public thoroughfares, were thronged with gay equipages & equestrians with many like myself jogging on on foot. [p. 5] A gentleman in an open carriage passed me near enough to allow me to see that his carriage-fur spread out over his knees and falling a little outside on both sides was of <u>ermine,</u> white with the black tails. Up by the Arc de Triomphe the Emperor passed me, driving himself in a sort of open carriage. Some gentleman occupied the seat next to him and two footmen sat in the dickey behind. He had no other attendants. Of all the men I saw he seemed the plainest and most unpretending—dressed in a drab overcoat which did not strike me as very well-fitting. His face I saw very plainly, for he was quite near. He looks well, hearty, but has nothing remarkable about him—a cool, easy expression, eyes not very wide open, with a tawny moustache and imperial. Dressed as he was then, he might have been any ordinary, plain, well-to-do gentleman taking his afternoon drive. One could hardly imagine that so active and subtile a mind lay under [p. 6] that steady and half-sleepy exterior. He looks fully fifty years old. [12]

How I wish you could see the vast variety of equipages on the fashionable drive here. Very few are at all like those we have at home. The most striking feature, generally, of difference is the high seat occupied by the coachman. It is almost as high as an omnibus driver's place. You will see sometimes a half a dozen or more near together of large barouches with this high seat in front and either another man on the box or else sitting in a dickey behind & all in livery. There are many elegant little one-horse carriages like the ladies have in Phila[delphia], then stately coaches, with & without dickeys. By & by comes along a nondescript with four horses, a high omnibus seat in front & another behind & two down in the middle between all facing one way & all open & square looking, a mingling of carriage & omnibus-sleigh. But I must close. *Tempus fugit.*

Your faithfully,
Andrew

My dear Jim,

I'm glad to get your letters, such as they are, <u>altho</u>' I sometimes long for a little more particular and intimate sort of talk. But I suppose pleasure must yield to the great matters of business. Yet, once in a while, if you could spare me an evening when you are at home, it would not be thrown away, at least so far as the conferring of pleasure is concerned.

You are very kind to compliment my letters. They are not meant to elicit things of the sort. Having not a few to write, I have only to dash them off as fast as I can without regard to Grammar, Composition, or Penmanship. If they fall into any tolerable order, it is more than I calculate upon. If I were to attempt to make good letters, I should many a time miss the mails for it is no infrequent thing for me, even here, to have many days to pass when I feel altogether incapable of any sort of mental exertion.

Today, Emory, a Mr. Shaw[1] of Lexington, Ky. [p. 2] and I started off to see as much as we could of a review of the "Garde Impériale"—or some fifteen or twenty thousand of them.[2] It was held on the race ground at Longchamp, a great level green sward exactly fitted for the best display of anything of the kind. Before we arrived, a sort of camp had been formed exactly as the camps are made during the marching time of an army. The tents were little low things hardly more than three, certainly not over four, feet high, very loosely put up on a few sticks. When we arrived, the soldiers were walking in and out among them with a very free and easy air, awaiting the arrival of the Emperor. After some time of expectation, he came. We were in good places and saw him very well. First he walked out from the stand, leading the little prince by the hand who was dressed in full military uniform, cocked hat and all. They went right in among the soldiers who crowded around them with cries of *"Vive l'Empereur"* and quite hid them from our sight, who were of course some distance off. They remained in the camp some time and [p. 3] then returned to the stand. Immediately the tents were all struck, rolled up and put in the knapsacks of the soldiers in this way [here, Longacre drew a small picture of the knapsack surrounded by the rolled tent], going above and on both sides in a long roll. In half an hour not a sign of the encampment was visible. The soldiers formed into long lines and gathered in large masses. Then the Emperor with a brilliant staff rode out to the review. Some time after, the little prince came out and, mounted on a pony, rode after the Emperor's staff, led by an officer also mounted who held the pony by a strap wrapped round his arm. The little fellow rode, very erect, and occasionally put up his hand to his hat with the military salute. Both the Emperor and prince seemed well received by the troops and the spectators. It was comical to hear the commoner class of women cry out at the appearance of the prince, "Oh, ah, ah," in quite an extasy [sic] of delight. The Emperor does not show to much advantage walking. He stoops and seems to shrug one shoulder a good deal, nearly amounting to a deformity. On horseback you do not see it, tho' even there, his [p. 4] figure is not remarkable. We did not stay to see the grand review at the end. It was cold and we became thoroughly chilled, besides growing very uncomfortably aware that lunch time had passed. There is not, after all, much satisfaction in these reviews. The numbers are so large, and the spaces and distances so great that but little is seen distinctly. In pictures of these things, battles, &c, you are always apparently in the midst of the fight. In reality, a spectator and not an actor is at a considerable distance and all particularity is lost. I have seen now three large reviews under quite favorable circumstances, and I don't think I would go for or pay much to see another.

I was glad to see that the (London) "Times" correspondent gives a very kind & even enthusiastic account of the Prince of Wales' reception in New York.[3] I hear nothing, however, of his stay, if stay it may be called, in Phila[delphia]. I am writing early this week as I must get as much time for study as I can. I suffered last week from having to "crowd" Friday and Saturday.

Yours faithfully,
Andrew Longacre

Paris
November 5, 1860[1]

[LETTER 18]

My dear Jim,

How in the world could you misunderstand me so? When I wrote to you setting the consideration of Italy aside for the present, I meant only and simply what I said. There was not a shadow of feeling about it which I did not express. I am a thousand times obliged for your kind offer, and advise you not to forget it as I shall not. But for the present I can decide on nothing and, as I wrote, it may be that I shall need nothing but what I can get here. This, however, is the unlikely alternative.

You ask me to keep the account of pictures I send. I have not done it hitherto, and I am such a poor hand at such things that I think I never had any sort of account with any church or society or individual in my own hands but some [p. 2] how I seemed a loser by it. So I will send over the packages, and the prices, and you will have to keep the account.

I believe I told you that if you did not want all those Swiss pictures you could let Sallie have the others. I think she will like to have some.

From your estimate as to how much you wish to expend in such things I imagine I have sent over quite enough stereoscopic views. Tho' they are in such incalculable abundance and variety that one hardly knows where to stop in buying them. I will keep on the lookout for other things in my rambles.

There are many things I should like to get here; but Paris is not a cheap place; and they seem to estimate elegant and pretty and rare things at their full value. People say that in Germany, at Dresden, &c, many very nice things can be had at very much less cost than here. But I see no way of getting there to buy them.

You speak of your half envy of my [p. 3] London visit. Let me just say one thing. Things of the sort, wonders of travel, seem much more strange and grand from our side of the ocean than when you get right in among them. "They are no such great shakes after all." Of course, it is a great satisfaction to see them with your own eyes, and there are thousands of new and odd circumstances about them of which one never dreamed: but after all one might have a more pitiable fate than to die in blessed ignorance of the whole of them. There are such revelations of misery and immorality and of people governed to death, guarded and watched and kept down, that makes one sigh long and often for the pure free air of dear America. Then there are very many <u>old</u> things that to our vision with its prejudices of younger growth seem rather <u>silly</u>. For instance, the soldiers at the "Tower" (one of your cherished wishes) are decked off in funny coats of red and green cloth, and black velvet odd-shaped hats [here Longacre draws an illustration] with bunches of bright colored ribbons around where the band [p. 4] goes. They look to me like fancy men got up for a show. Then, too, the idea of judges in ugly little crisped and powdered wigs and all sorts of officials in all sorts of outlandish robes. I declare, it makes the whole affair, government and all, look like child's-play—a thing of dressings and deckings. I dare say it is all very imposing to people accustomed to it, and I don't know but I rather like it myself <u>in pictures</u>, but when it comes to real actual live men, it seems carrying it <u>too far</u>. Of course, I know this sort of feeling is only the result of a different education. But I am sure it would seem as funny and ridiculous to you, especially as you could not help being reminded, at every new scene, of "Mr. Pip's his diary." You would laugh over poor old "Gog and Magog" in the Guildhall. They are two ugly misshapen, painted images that would be a disgrace to any tobacconist's shop in Phila[delphia]. Yet there they stand, aged and time-honored, and you are bound to respect them in spite of their ugliness & fresh paint. [p. 5]

You need not come to Europe yet. Things are growing, especially in Paris, and the longer you wait the more will there be to see when you come. But when you get rich and middle-aged, and after your comfortable dinners, your patriotism sometimes falls asleep: that's the time. Just pack up a small trunk (leaving out books on account of weight, and cigars on account of duty) and come over for "a year abroad." If it don't wake up your sleepy patriotism, I think I may venture to promise to foot the bill of travelling expenses. My "year" is not "up" yet to be sure, but I fear sometimes, unless something stops the downward progress of my sentiments in regard to life in Europe, I may even quit the scene in disgust before it is up. Dr. Maris is going home, "home-sick," the day after tomorrow; and yet he has been in Belgium, Germany, along the Rhine, several weeks in Switzerland and several more in Italy. I have a great many movings within to follow his example. But I'm a fixture for [p. 6] another six months, I suppose.

Of course, living as I do, with my regular pastoral life and work, I cannot be supposed to <u>enjoy</u> foreign life as much as those who come for mere recreation. My work is similar to work at home, but I am without the aids and sympathies and kindnesses which are almost always connected with such work at home—at least so it has been with me. People are kind, it is true, as kind I really believe, as they know how to be. But I fancy, I am too much a Methodist. I grow hungry for real warm-hearted Methodist communion.[2] Perhaps I am a little out of sorts today and things may look more gloomy than usual, but certainly I feel quite blue in seeing other folks going home and <u>me</u> left behind.

Yours faithfully,
Andrew Longacre

Dear Jim,

Since I wrote to Father and Eliza an hour or two ago, John has brought me your letter with one from Eliza of Oct. 26th. They must have had a long passage as two days ago we had news to the 30th. But they are none the less welcome, though I have been feeling all degrees of indignation at the silence of two weeks which has rested over home correspondence. After the disappointment and delay of the last two weeks, I would say more emphatically than I have ever said it before that it would be much more agreeable to me to have a letter from someone at home by each steamer, say, you and Eliza write one day, and Father the next time. If Bets[1] chooses to take the time, she might write both times (as I do almost always), as Father always could enclose another sheet without making his too heavy.

I was interested and amused with your account of your visit to Mrs. Golder [p. 2] and think you must feel very badly in prospect of Miss Koon's marriage. My dear old boy, you will be an old bachelor if you don't take care. You can't be so "onreasonable" [sic] as to expect the girls to keep waiting so long while you are making up your mind. The first thing you know, Mary Ludwig will be going off with somebody and you will be narrowed down to quite a small party, unless you increase the number in some way. I am sorry I have never seen Miss Veazy. From past appearances, she seems to stand as fair a chance as any of them. Well, I suppose it will all come out some day. Don't you pity them that are waiting for either of us? I'm thinking "Patience" will have full exercise in their tender minds.

There are some few young ladies here; enough to make quite an agreeable circle—if one choose to go in to it. Next door to us a family named Edgerton, from New York, have one right pretty young lady, who shows her sense by being particularly afraid of coming in contact with [p. 3] Emory McClintock and me. She is quite a friend or companion rather of Miss Augusta's. They sing together, go to the choir and to prayer-meeting together, &c, &c. I might go though the list but it would not be very interesting, as they are all unknown to you. Come over and you shall see them for yourself.

Every morning in my early walks I see a comical sight: a troop of cavalry with cloaks on. They have long light cloth cloaks, almost white, which often stretch out quite to the horse's tail. You can hardly imagine how odd it looks to see a quantity of them together. I see that all the soldiers and policemen, &c, have very comfortable cloaks for the cold weather. They are of different shapes and colors, but all look ample and warm. Some have capes, as the cavalry I spoke of, and others have pointed hoods hanging down the back which they often pull up over their heads. Every where it is apparent what good care the government takes of the soldiers. And well it ought. The army, and I was about to say, the army [p. 4] only sustains the present régime. Certainly, it was so at the first. Now the people generally seem, so they say, to look up to the Emperor and feel interested in his rule.

The Empress has just gone to Scotland on a visit to the Emperor's cousin, the Duchess Marie Hamilton, a princess of Baden, I believe she is, and daughter of one of Napoleon Ist's nieces, Stephanie of Baden.[2]

Things are quiet here for those like myself who are quite outside of the gay world and indeed for those in it. I believe the regular round of frivolity has hardly begun. I am hoping for a good pile of letters tomorrow. Remember me if you please to the Ludwigs. Emily used to go to school with Augusta McClintock at Mr. Cleveland's. Also, return my compliments to Miss Lucy Hill.

Excuse the manifest hurry of this letter, but I am just at this moment pressed for time.

Yours faithfully,

Andrew Longacre

Jim

Don't forget to address 10, rue Balzac.

My dear Jim,

Your letter of the 14th *ult*[1] came with the others yesterday. I was looking for later advices by the Liverpool steamer, but there is no tidings of her yet, altho' she is several days behind time. The ships of that line are so regular that one cannot avoid a little anxiety, even at a little delay. But I suppose we cannot expect very quick trips at this season.

Your faint intimations, for they are scarcely more than that, of a better prospect at home politically is somewhat cheering. You can hardly imagine the interest felt here of all Americans in affairs at home. The distance seems to add a sort of intensity to the expectation. We wait to know, not so much what will take place, as what has taken place, and all sorts of opinions are held on all sides.[2] The family here, Dr. McC[lintock] is quite a decided Republican and almost in favor of a quiet secession of as much of the South [p. 2] as chooses to go. We had two or three warm talks, but as he is vastly more a politician than I, infinitely better read on all points, having lived on newspapers for a number of years past, may be all the way back to the beginning of them, it is hardly a fair fight. I fix on general principles, of which the chief is that religion & politics ought to be left apart, that political confederations ought to be made and conducted solely on political principals, the parties waiving all questions of conscience except its freedom. Two or three times we tried it and in a short time landed at the same place, so I thought we had better give it up. The last time he offered battle I rather gruffly declined to enter the lists. Since then, we have gone on, each in his own course of private opinion.[3] The President's message is universally condemned.[4] People only hope the South will hold still long enough to cool a little—altho' we all fear it. South Carolina, at all events, had gone too far to secede with decency. [p. 3] You will oblige me if whenever you write you let me know something of public affairs. Everybody's opinion is of some value over here now.

There is some probability that Mr. & Mrs. Baker will not go to Italy at all this winter. He thinks he must return to America to take care of business and she is hardly willing to stay without him, and if she does, will prefer to remain in Paris where we are & other friends. I mention this as affecting possibly my own Italian prospect. Tho' at present no matter what were the offer, I could not leave Paris. Dr. McC[lintock] after two months of lameness is hardly any better,[5] and I could not think of leaving him, even if he should suggest it. You need not be surprised, however, if sometime in the course of the next four months, I should ask for the fulfillment of your offer made some time ago.

My work here becomes more interesting to me than ever. The people are more kind and I hope more profited [p. 4] than ever before. In very many respects no field of labor could be more delightful. It is rather a melancholy view of the case, however, to reflect that, with me, it is a serious question: how long I can afford to stay. Money steals away all the time, and tho' my board & lodging is given me, there is no perennial spring to refresh my wasting funds. However, I am far from melancholy about it. It hardly ever enters my head & then rather amusingly than otherwise. I have no fear but all will be right and the best for me, whichever way matters turn. One thing I should like, to be able to stay here long enough to accept Mr. Langdon's kind invitation to spend a week or two next summer with him in Switzerland at his home there. But I dare hardly hope for it. It seems almost too bright a prospect to be realized.

Since I wrote this, just now, Dr. McClintock has been in my room. I spoke to him of my inability to stay as being what I could not afford. He then [p. 5] told me what, it is funny, I never had a

Paris
January 2, 1861
[LETTER 20]

distinct idea of before, exactly what he understood as the terms of my engagement with him. He expects to pay my passage both ways, besides the $360 I receive of salary for the time I was here alone. This gives me something more than two hundred dollars more than I had calculated upon. He says if I stay longer than my year, after next May, some arrangement for a salary must be made. At the same time, he is not at all certain that he will remain longer than that time. As matters look now, there is very little prospect of an increase of salary and he says he cannot afford to stay without it: besides, if matters grow worse at home, his own affairs may compel him to return. In such an event, I may stay here, for at least some time after his departure, until the place is duly filled by the Society[6] at New York. Indeed, one gentleman here has suggested that I take the chapel, really as pastor, if Dr. McC[lintock] should go. All this is purely confidential.[7] [p. 6]

You must use your well-known discretion and keep it in your own heart. One thing is certain. I am in the hands of a wise and kind Protector who is fully able to take care of all my interests. It is a great comfort to me to know that I do not have to guide myself, that as I came here, not by my own seeking, I may look to be kept here or released by the same divine power.

I am hoping to have an opportunity of sending some things home next week. Quite a number of gentlemen are going to America, called thither by business perplexities. This time, I shall have nothing for you. Were I rich, I should dearly love to make up a box of presents, but I can afford exceedingly little in that line. I am practising all the economy I can.

In speaking of the letter or some part of it as confidential, I do not mean to exclude the family from participators in it, but only to <u>confine it to them.</u>

Yours faithfully,
Andrew

∞

Paris
January 7th, 1861

[LETTER 21]

Dear Jim,

Yours of Dec. 18th I rec'd last week after I had closed my last to you. It was late coming, as you remember I spoke of the delay of the steamer which carried it.

I am much obliged for the little portrait, which is so far better than the large one in that there is less of it. The figure of the other is stiff, and that is lost in this. I shall expect the other one of you with some desire. Cannot you folks have "*carte de visite*" pictures taken, like those little ones I sent. Every body here has them, and it is the custom to exchange them among friends so that each person has an album full of the pictures of their friends. People often keep two albums, one for celebrities & the other for friends.

[p. 2] As to the commission business—since they have the pictures now for sale in America, and I hear—on this side—quite a trade is springing up of it, I would just as lief be excused, except for any special thing you may desire.

As to what has been done, I leave it altogether to your judgment.

As yet I have seen no photographic copies of Vernet's pictures. I believe copies can be had of Delaroche and others. There are very many copies of paintings exposed in the shops, for sale, and some of these days I will inquire as to price, &c.

There are also large photographic views of places, churches, rural scenes, &c, many of them very fine, but I fear held at high prices. You can let me know how high you are willing to go for such things—views, copies of pictures, &c.

We are having an agreeable [p. 3] change in the weather—now & for some days, a clear bright sun, like our own winter sun, making the whole world cheerful.

The river Seine is very high. Yesterday we heard from the Ambassador's family that they had four feet of water in their basement, from the river, nearly on the level of which they live.[1]

On Saturday, riding out with Mr. Langdon on the bank of the river we saw the road on the other side in many place[s] three feet under water. All the islands were covered and in some place[s] on the banks the houses were standing in enclosed lakes, as the water had come within the walls & flooded the grounds. You can have an idea of the size of the stream when I tell you that even now it is hardly as large as the Schuykill is ordinarily. [p. 4]

I shall try to send off a few things by some gentleman going in the *Arago* day after tomorrow. Mr. Baker would take care of anything, but he has sent his trunk on to London & I would not bother him even if he would consent to take anything in his packet.

My own health is very good. I wish I could say so of Dr. McClintock. His knees keep about the same & he is now seriously thinking of going fairly to bed and leaving all things here in my hands for a week or two.[2] I don't know but it would be the best thing for him—and I would cheerfully bear it to have him well again.

Yours faithfully,
Andrew Longacre

Enclosed with this letter was a list of more than seventy prominent persons of the time whose photographs were available for purchase.

My dear Jim,

On Sunday morning your favor, with others of [the] 4th, by the *Fulton,* came safely to hand, and yesterday the regular Liverpool steamer brought me yours of the 7th.

For your promptness in the matter of the photographs, I am very much obliged. The pictures might have been a little lighter, but they are not too dark for use. The likeness to my little friend is more striking in them than in the card-portrait I sent you.

I was glad to hear at last of the safe arrival of the photographic album and that you were pleased with it. I thought of sending it as a gift, but I knew I could not afford it. I am tempted all the time to do such things. There are so many little things I could get here that I know would give pleasure to some of you dear folks at home that I have to maintain a spirit of perpetual economy. Even with all that, "the money goes." One item—I have just bought my third pair of shoes since [p. 2] I came to Paris. For a pair of low shoes, light, for summer, I paid 16 f[ranc]s; for a heavier pair, ditto; for winter 22 f[ranc]s; and now for a pair of heavy walking gaiters 32 f[ranc]s. These are pretty good prices, yet I avoid going to the most expensive places. Gloves cost me a great deal. I pay for Jouvin's[1] 4½ f[ranc]s a pair and I have to get a pair every month, I am not sure but oftener. I could go on thro' these items but I hardly suppose it would interest you.

At last, after three weeks of ice, we are in a state of un-freezing. Whether to say it is an improvement in the weather or not, I don't know, for the air is raw and moist and both days and nights are foggy. But cold or warm, dry or not, the weeks fly so fast that one has not much time to think how they are. Sometimes I sigh for home, so as to find more time. It seems to me I accomplish nothing here, except a little painting, which I have serious thought I should [p. 3] abandon.[2] Yesterday and today, I have been working on the large picture of Bets which Mr. Baker brought over. I think it improves and in the end will make a good picture, one of my best, if I am a judge.

Friday evening, the court had a novel entertainment, a skating party on some one of the ponds in the Bois de Boulogne. The Emperor & Empress were there. He skates well, and she tried it but could not go alone. They had many chairs on runners for the ladies, which are made very prettily of light iron work and cushioned with velvet. I had a pretty full account of it from young Evans[3] who was there.

The Americans here are all on the "*qui vivre*" ["on the alert"] in expectation of Mr. Faulkner's ball, to come off on Friday. Dr. McC[lintock] and I had cards of invitation. Many here think it quite in bad taste for our Ambassador to be giving a ball while things at home are so sad. The ladies, however, seem to regard it with great satisfaction, such of them as will go. Some will not, I am happy to say. [p. 4] The Faulkners are funny people. A lady told me that on Sunday, after morning service, Mrs. F. turned to her in her pew or just by it in the aisle and said, "Did you receive your card for Friday night?" "Are you coming?" Upon the lady's saying she had not intended to do so, Mrs. F. asked for her husband &c, &c, and rattled on until they were out of the church. She has done the same thing before and, of course, as a minister, I can't admire it very much. It may be all very well for a Virginian, but we should call it bad breeding and bad taste in Pennsylvania to speak of it at all—and especially at such a time. Excuse the gossip, but the thing was so characteristic of the Honorable lady that I could not help mentioning it. She is very kind tho', heartily so, and to everybody. At the same time, Sunday morning she sent word to Dr. McC[lintock] that he must not hire a carriage to take him home from church if his lameness prevent his walking but he should always use hers. If she were not out, the children would see him home.

For fear of making Eliza's letter too heavy, I'll put some last words in Father's.

Yours

A.L——

My dear Jim,

Altho' I have nothing from you by either of the last two arrivals, the *Kangaroo* or the *Australasia,* still as I am sure you write when you can, I'll do the same.

I told you in my last of Mrs. Faulkner's ball, which at that time was to be. It has been and was a success. I ought to say in this connection that she spoke to some one of the current objections to it at such a time, &c, and added by way of apology that she felt it due to the many who had given her invitations, to make some return, and that this was only one, and she had intended to give four: the reduction in number being on account of the times at home. I say this by way of doing justice to the fair and honourable lady.

The famous Bonaparte trial has been attracting considerable attention here.[1] It came off, that is as far as it went, [p. 2] last week. I suppose you will see full reports. The counsellor for Madame Bonaparte (or Patterson) made an able speech and gave a strong & effective representation of her side of the case. The common people, I hear, think she has the right side, but how it will be decided no one can tell. Some delay has occurred in the affair now, but what it is or means, I do not know. The old lady herself must be a pretty hard specimen. She told some one at some time that "her husband was the worst man she knew except her father." Her grandson, you know, is a captain in the French army. Some time ago, a year or two I think, a decoration was offered him in the name of "Patterson" which he declined to accept. Since then, he has had no promotion, the Prince Napoleon, his <u>step</u>-Uncle, treats him with contempt, calling him, "the little Patterson," but the Princess Mathilde is quite fond of him.

An odd speech of the Emperor's is reported. [p. 3] On some occasion Prince Napoleon taunted him with what is pretty generally understood, not having any Bonaparte blood in his veins (the son of Hortense but not of her husband). "It is true," said the Emperor, "I have no Bonaparte blood in my veins, but I have the whole Bonaparte family on my shoulders."[2]

But enough of Parisian gossip. I don't hear much of it and what I do, taking this as a sample, is hardly worth writing.

We have had tolerably good weather lately overhead but the streets are intolerably muddy, covered with a perpetual moist slime which splashes up on one's pantaloons and penetrates the very soles of one's boots, making it extremely disagreeable to walk.[3] The sun seems to have no evaporating power at all, and every night a dense fog bathes everything afresh. My reminiscences of Paris climate will be far from favorable. Sometimes, I grow quite impatient, wishing for our fine [p. 4] walking weather. The only two seasons of the kind we have had here were six weeks in the fall and two or three weeks of freezing after Christmas. The name of Paris should be written in <u>mud</u> on the pages of the world's history.

I have been trying to paint one of those heads of little Langdon (the second series not yet having arrived). He was here for a couple of hours yesterday and I worked from life, but I find it almost useless to try to overcome the heavy black of the shadows. What do you say to sending me a lighter impression of his head (as well as the others)? If it would not trouble you, I should like to have it. When am I to have another of you? How would Gutekunst[4] succeed in a *carte-de-visite* picture of you? All of you folks might have those little pictures taken.

Yours faithfully,
Andrew Longacre

My dear Jim,

Your good, long and really comfortable letter came yesterday—the one dated Jan. 29th. Just two weeks after the writing came the reading of it. I calculated the days and found it exactly which little operation gave a sort of reality to the letter, quite unusual.

As to your project for Niagara & Pittsburgh next summer, I am more than willing if I shall be at home. Present appearances, however, are against my arrival before sometime in September, if so soon.

While on the subject of my movements, I may as well say that a day or two ago, I offered to give Dr. McC[lintock] a month more of my time in the summer (till June 15th) if he would allow me to make a holiday of next month: March. I did this for the reason that if I am to go to Italy,

June will be too late to go with safety. He accepted the proposition quite readily as he thinks of going with Mrs. M[cClintock] [p. 2] to a water-cure establishment at Homberg in June and will have to have some one in his place in Paris. I am now on the lookout for a travelling companion. There are quite a number of people I know now in Rome, and the matter is only to find one to keep me alive on the road.

I should not like to go alone, tho' if it comes to that or nothing, I think I will try it. How I wish you were over here to join me. I hope to get thro' the trip on less than two hundred dollars, which Dr. McC[lintock] will have forthcoming. After that he will still be in my debt for as much more, but if I travel at all in the summer, besides living expenses till that time, I shall need the sum you very kindly offer to send over. There is no hurry for it as I hope to be able to do without it till June or July, and who knows what may turn up by that time?

I really need some change, my sleeplessness seems on the increase, and [p. 3] otherwise I feel as if I were suffering from "Spring fever" or some other anomalous disorder not set down in the books. We are having fine weather like our best days in March, rather than February, but like March, it does not seem to improve my state of health very perceptibly.

The carnaval [sic] is over. Today is Ash-Wednesday and Lent is begun. Yesterday was *Mardi-gras,* a great day here, the last of the three on which the *Boeuf-gras*[1] parades the streets. The procession (pictures of which you have seen) I did not see. They say it is a very small affair. On the streets yesterday, I saw several masked figures, generally men in women's cloth[e]s, which afforded amusement to some of the people, but by the most part were passed with indifference. The day is a general holiday, and seemed to have something of the stir of Hallow Eve or Christmas Eve with us. Funny pranks were allowed by the police, and the people seemed in an [p. 4] easy good humor.

Calling in the afternoon on Mrs. Edward Pepper, I met a Mrs. Sims (Philadelphia but resident here for seven or eight years) who was giving an account of the doctor's appointment of her daughter (Miss Ellen Sims, about 18, rather pretty, whom I saw one evening at Peppers'). She was to have her "presented" at court on Sunday, was dressed & *coiffér,* all ready to start, but no card of admission came. It turned out that no Americans were presented, altho' sundry English & other Europeans were. Some six other ladies & twenty gentlemen in that way missed the last ball of the season. After Lent, I believe, the court keeps a quiet time. The court season has not been very gay on account of the Empress's mourning for her sister, the duchess of Alva, or as they say here, "La Duchesse d'Albe."[2]

For my part, I was ashamed to hear that any Americans were expecting presentation on a Sunday, after so many oppor- [p. 5] tunities on week-days as I hear there have been this winter. Our Ambassadress never goes out on Sundays, neither she nor her daughters. In this I think she has set an excellent example; tho' I am sorry to say there are many Americans not disposed to follow it.

By the latest news things at home seem in a state almost of crisis.[3] Secession inevitable—and with war. I can't altogether agree with you in laying all the blame, or so much of it, at the door of the Republicans. Tho' I am not at all in sympathy with many of them, I think their most eminent, Mr. Seward, the President-elect, &c, have shown great magnanimity and prudence. The South— or So. Carolina at all events—seems determined to secede no matter what may be done to prevent it; and this, they say, has been their intention for ten, fifteen and even twenty years. Reason is lost and argument or compromise is mere chaff in such a state of affairs. [p. 6]

What is to be done by Government now is a very difficult question. I am convinced that prompt action at the first, not allowing any violations of Federal law—in forts or revenue or Post offices—would have averted the danger. <u>Now</u> the case is a thousand times more intricate and I fear a war more or less extensive must come, and a secession, more or less extensive, will be the <u>permanent</u> result. The question for the sincere lovers of their country is rather how to make the war as brief a one, and the secession as small a one, as possible, thus how to avoid either. At least so it looks from off here.

As to European politics, the most important item I have seen for a long while is in today's paper, to the intent that Victor Emmanuel assures Austria he will not attempt any military demonstration against Venice in the Spring.[4] If he adheres to this, the general war looked for may not come off [p. 7] but be indefinitely postponed. Still if Hungary is fairly roused as she seems and gives Austria trouble on that side, I fear Victor Emmanuel's virtue will hardly be able to resist the temptation to tease her on the other. Both at home [and] abroad, "rumors of wars"! We can only wait and pray that out of all such strife, the true and right may come forth victorious. Yet I have little confidence in the victories of <u>right</u> gained by mere <u>might.</u> Blood has always proved a poor preparation for the gospel except when shed by its enemies. The blood of martyrs has been the fertiliser [sic] of the vineyard of God[5]:—the blood of the wicked have made it barren. The apostles of truth & right, like their great Lord, are made perfect thro' suffering. "Shall conquer tho' they die." Conquer most gloriously in the dying. [p. 8]

But no more of this. I don't care to make my <u>letters</u> rhetorical, however necessary I find it in my sermons.

I suppose Eliza is at home again by this time. I hope she enjoyed herself, and wait with a good deal of eagerness to hear of her visit.

You must excuse all corrections, erasures, &c, as well as my terribly degenerate chirography (anglicé <u>hand-writing</u>). I have had to write so much that I have fallen into all sorts of bad habits in the desire to lose no time in it. I hope you succeed in deciphering my scrawls without too great difficulty. I should not be surprised, besides, if my increased nervousness had its deteriorating effect on my writing.

Yours affectionately,
Andrew Longacre
10 rue Balzac

Dear Jim,

I am sorry not to get a letter from you today, but I suppose you were too late for the Cunard mail. However, having a little time on my hands, and not sure that during this busy week the same thing will happen again, I shall my regret at not hearing from you exhale in the next pleasant thing—writing myself. As recent letters, especially one written yesterday to Father, have informed you, I am looking towards Rome. The whole thing seems <u>just right</u>; all matters arranging themselves almost without an effort on my part. Mr. Dale,[1] whose son is to be my *compagnon du voy-*

age, is kindly attending to everything, will inquire as to routes, hotels, &c, obtain letters, make out one letter of credit for both of us ample enough to cover everything, &c. Besides all this, Nelson is a very nice sort of a [p. 2] boy to travel with. As to his peculiar qualifications, he is good for all the French and German we shall need, and has a smattering of Italian (they keep an Italian servant), he has travelled a good deal, enjoys the fun of it and does not get tired easily. He is intelligent, very well read for a boy of 15 ½ years. Altogether I am delighted to have him, and since I have known he would be with me, have looked forward to the journey with much more satisfaction and pleasure than before.

You see that, altho' you are not here, Providence takes care of me. Sometimes our old proverb comes into my head, "The lame and the lazy are always provided for." I must be one or the other for certainly things do <u>turn up</u> in the most unexpected manner for my especial delight and consolation.

Among other things, I feel like mentioning particularly the comfort I have had in Mrs. Baker's² society here. [p. 3] I go over to her room which is only a very few steps from our house, in No. 7, of this same street, every day, and sometimes twice a day. We talk together an hour or half an hour and mutually cheer and encourage one another. It seems more home-like than anywhere else. I can talk just as I please, and the world at large would be greatly enlightened could it know all that transpires in such seasons of free conversation.

You will see in the papers how the Bonaparte case is decided.³ The court take ground that the decision of the Imperial family council, some time ago, concluded the matter according to the Code Napoleon. So Mr. Bonaparte, as they call him in Baltimore, is henceforth in France Mr. Bonaparte-Patterson. I heard that in calling somewhere immediately after the legal decision was pronounced instead of giving his name as he has always done heretofore in the American form, he gave it with the "<u>Patterson</u>"! For myself, I did not [p. 4] imagine any tribunal in France during the Empire could annul two family decisions, one of the old Emperor and one of the present one. Of course, no one doubts, here or elsewhere, that the simple right, the <u>equity</u> of the case, lies with the American family.

You must not be surprised if after this you do not hear from me for a month, as in travelling in Italy where the post-rates are enormous (I hear), and must be <u>pre-paid,</u> I shall not be able to afford much epistologizing. And as I shall not receive your letters till I return to Paris, you need not write, unless you feel like it, for a couple of weeks after you receive the — No, that won't do either. For <u>one</u> week you can rest, but as I shall be here again by the last day or two of March, you will have to resume writing about the middle of the month. I shall run greatly in your debt I know, but I will try & make up in interest [p. 5] what is lacking in number. My trip to places, of which I have dreamed and thought so long, cannot fail to furnish agreeable material. Your "own correspondent in Italy" will do his best to gratify and enlighten the rather limited "public" who have access to his periodical sheets.

11 P.M. I have just returned from a pleasant dinner at Dr. Evans', the dentist's.⁴ Dr. McClintock and the high-church English preacher here, Rev. Archie Gurney, were there. Mr. Gurney is a very pleasant man with an unusually good English face. Dr. Evans gave us, as he has a weakness for doing, plenty of stories connected with royal personages. He was very emphatic in proclaiming the virtue and innocence of the Countess Castiglione who has the unenviable reputation of being

one of the Emperor's chief favorites. He told us that once when he dined with his majesty in company with sundry other gentlemen, the Emperor declared upon his honor as a [p. 6] gentleman and as Emperor of the French, that he had never visited Madame la Comtesse. Even after that, it is pretty hard to believe there is nothing in the reports.[5] Dr. Evans has any quantity of incidents and anecdotes of royal doings which can all be collected under one head, that crowned men and women are wonderfully like all other men and women. Yet it is one of the funny things in human nature, that even the simplest things, of people in high place, have an air, a something in them, that awakens curiosity and interest.

I dare say nothing in the English papers is read with more interest, or by a greater number of persons, than the little bulletins of the court, telling who dined with her majesty, and at what time of the day she took a drive, or by what route she walked over to see her mother, and which of her royal children accompanied her.

How odd it would seem in America to find a column or part of a column regularly devoted to retailing the minutiae of Mr. [p. 7] Buchanan's ordinary life; for instance, "the Pres. rose this morning at nine in his usual health. At eleven he rode out accompanied by his private secretary, Mr. —— and Mr. —— of ——, &c," *ad infinitum.*

I have been making a few visits P.P.C.[6] before going off. People all seem interested and wish me a good time. Sometimes I wish it were all over and I safely back and at work again. Pleasures of the kind are always more to me in recollection than in anticipation. Visions of noisy hotels, rude waiters, troublesome custom-houses, and cheatings and losings innumerable rise before me to take off the too keen edge of expected enjoyment. But I mean to be as free from care as possible and get all the real, genuine enjoyment possible out of the trip.

Half a dozen times a day I find myself wishing for you. I dislike responsibility and care and bother about trunks and hotel bills and finding out where and how to go to places. But I must get broken in to it sometimes. It might as well be now [p. 8] as ever. If I mean to be a man, it is high time I was thinking about it. I don't believe preaching is good for the development of the business part of man's nature.

Feb. 20. 8 P.M.

You see I have to write when I can. I have been busy all day, not seriously busy either, that is, not occupied with serious things, yet so as effectually to put writing out of the question. This morning, Mr. Proeschel,[7] Dr. McC[lintock]'s secretary, brought up with him a wonderfully compact and perfect machine for taking photographs, and all the morning was spent in efforts to get pictures, in some of which we were quite successful. All the afternoon was given to Mrs. Munroe, first accompanying her to a superb private collection of pictures[8] and then making sundry visits. Now it is night again and much left undone that I had hoped to accomplish today.

At last I must say, "Good-bye" for a good while.

Yours faithfully,

Andrew Longacre

My dear Jim,

As I shall be even more hurried on Monday than I am today, I will snatch a few moments now to acknowledge the rec't of your favor of the 4th & 8th, with the draft for fifty francs and the little pictures, for all of which accept my sincere thanks. Altho' as a rule, it will never be worthwhile to make a draft for less than a hundred francs and, indeed, I could quite afford to have you in my debt more than that, yet your remittance just now is opportune, as I shall feel free to invest it in any little things I see in Italy which I think likely to please you; nor will I be very strict in confining myself within that small sum, which I think you will decide is "all right."

My arrangements are now pretty well completed. Mr. [T. N.] Dale got a letter of credit from Munroe's for Nelson and myself in my name and to leave us sufficient margin—had it drawn for 5,000 francs—fully [p. 2] 3,000 more than we shall spend as we each carry 500 with us. I left my passport at our consul's this morning to have the visas of the Sardinian & Papal legations. Besides these necessaries, I am taking some letters, for Florence & Rome, in both of which cities I have some acquaintances. A lady who has a house in Florence gave me quite a strong invitation before she left Paris last fall to stay with her if I came there.[1] I don't intend to do that, but I shall certainly call. In Rome I have quite a number of good friends, people who have attended the Chapel here.

Today, passing Mr. May's[2] studio, I went in *pour prendre congé*[3] and he offered me letters to some of the artists both in Rome & Florence which was exactly what I wished. They will take me among them in the best way coming from an artist. Mr. Dale has, I believe, got letters to two members of the Italian Parliament now sitting at Turin. Thro' them, I hope [p. 3] to be admitted to their session, so as at least to <u>see</u> the first Parliament of United Italy.[4]

One very good thing Mr. May did. Besides giving me some letters, he gave me a list of good and cheap hotels in Florence, Naples & Rome, which will be of great use to me, who have not a long purse. Most of my friends here recommend hotels without considering the expense at all, as it is a point they rarely consider themselves.

I intend keeping a very strict account of everything, places, names, people, prices, &c, as well as I can. I know I am not very good at such things but the consideration that it may be useful some day to others makes me wish to do it as well as I can.[5]

You ask about papers. I have rec'd one or two lately from you—all in fact which you mention in your letters. As to Phila[delphia] papers, there are none at Munroe's. I see only those you send [p. 4] me. They interest me even in their columns of "Local Items." Everything from <u>Home</u> is invaluable here.

I shall enclose with this the <u>notes</u> to my air "We would see Jesus." Could you get it <u>arranged</u>? I mean with an accompaniment. Miss Warner, whose sister wrote the words, asked me for the air and I promised to let her have it. If you can get it done, I will trouble you to enclose a copy with a note to Mrs. Julia M. Olin (Rhinebeck, N.Y.),[6] stating that it is from me for Miss Warner. Mrs. Olin will forward it. The score I send was made by a Mr. Fairlamb[7]—a composer of some songs, &c, who put it on paper for me one evening not long ago.

And now, my dear fellow, I must say "Good bye." How often you will hear from me in the coming month is altogether uncertain. God bless you.

Your affectionate bro[ther],

Andrew

For their sightseeing tour of Italy, Andrew and Nelson Dale left on Monday, February 25, 1861. Traveling by train by way of Sens, Dijon, Mâcon, and Lanslebourg (at the foot of Mont Cenis), they reached Turin on February 28. During the next month, by land and by sea, they went to Genoa, Leghorn, Pisa, and Florence, Naples (where they visited Pompei and ascended Vesuvius), Civita Vecchia, and Rome. In his MS Diary *Andrew kept a detailed account of their various modes of transportation, of towns, villages, historic sites, museums visited, of purchases made, and of people he met. Some of his acquaintances from Paris were also touring Italy, and these friendships were renewed in new settings: Edward Harrison May, Dr. and Mrs. Gould, Alexander Van Rensselaer and his young fiancée, Miss DuPuy, et al. Andrew traveled with his sketchbook and made a number of drawings on this trip. He also kept a meticulous account of his expenses (including receipts of hotel bills) which were evenly divided between himself and Nelson Dale. For their return, they went from Rome to Civita Vecchia, where Andrew penned the following letter (cf.* MS Diary, *February 25-March 27, 1861).*

My dear Jim,

It is long since I have written to you, but you know why. While in Rome, Mr. Baker himself sent on your letters & the rest from home, as they arrived, so I have yours of the 4th, but hope to have in a few days more and later which must be awaiting me in Paris.

First, a little matter of business. While on my tour, I picked up one or two things especially for you, having rec'd your draft a little while before I left Paris. As the Dales kindly offer to take all I care to send, I shall send them on, now, that is, if I get to Paris in time to do so.

In Pisa, I bought for 11 francs a little alabaster model of the celebrated Campanile.² It seemed to me cheap and I thought it would please you for, if you do not care to retain it, it will do for a present to some one. In Rome, I was much struck with variety & beauty of the antique marbles and after picking up some stray pieces, I came across a [p. 2] cheap chess-board containing some twenty-five kinds in it. I remembered that you used to wish for a chess-board, so I got it. It cost 2 ½ scudi, which with the <u>exchange,</u> will be somewhere near three dollars.³

There are some other things of less account which I got in different places, of which I may send you some, but I cannot settle about it now. Another time will do for them, or indeed, if I have time in Paris before the sailing of the *Fulton,* I may send them with the others.

The Dales will take over for me also two bronze columns, which were Nelson's⁴ Christmas present to me and which I thought would give more pleasure at No. 1206 Spring Garden Street[, Philadelphia,] than at No. 10, rue Balzac, Paris.

What else I shall send I cannot say now. There are at most only a few little matters, and I will make out a list of them when I make up my parcel.

Well, I have been to Rome. Of course, my whole trip has been hurried, almost provokingly so, if one had [p. 3] not sense to be satisfied with what was possible rather than what was desirable. Almost all things have conspired to make my journey pleasant and satisfactory. In Rome, particularly, I was very happy. Surrounded by friends, in the midst of things of beauty, and of associations most deeply interesting, the time went on golden wheels. It was hard work, day after day, going and seeing, going & seeing, but the result will remain when all thought of the fatigue has passed away—the treasured store in my memory written out in indelible letters on these faithful tablets to be looked over with pleasure thro' the years yet to come.

5 ½ P.M. To pass pleasantly some hours of this afternoon, when it cleared off, Nelson and I set out for a walk about the harbor and along the shore. If we were not in a state of compulsory attendance upon the irregularities of the Neapolitan steamer, we might find enough in the shore of the Mediterranean to while away [p. 4] whole days. A few odd needs and little shells we gathered as mementos.

I cannot tell you how much nearer home I feel by the seaside than elsewhere in Europe. The same water & the same sky reaching from me to you makes a sort of <u>conductor</u> for feeling and fancy.

Another thing I cannot tell you how many times and how heartily I have wished for you during the last four weeks. You know what a poor traveller I am, how I hate bills and accounts and bargaining and counting change, all of which whether you like them or not seem to come natural to you. Somehow, it seems as if you are the other part of me, having <u>plus</u> where I am <u>minus</u>. Yet it is odd that we have never had a real journey together. Why won't you come over here and take a tour in Switzerland next summer? I suppose you think our family too poor to keep two gentlemen of leisure abroad at a time. Isn't it funny that I, the poorest of the lot, should have the expensive luxury?

Love again, you shall hear from me more at length.

Yours lovingly,

Andrew

[Postscript written at the top of page 1:] "I have written the names of the different marbles in the chess-board on <u>corresponding places</u> on the under side."

When Andrew and Nelson Dale arrived at Civita Vecchia on Wednesday, March 27, they learned that the boat for Marseille would not leave until the next day. Checking into a hotel, they then called on the British Consul, took a walk about the town and on the beach. The next morning, however, they were disappointed once again when "there were no signs of the steamer." To pass the time on this day they called on the American Consul, walked about the town, along the quai, and looked into several churches. Late in the day, Andrew "walked out alone and tried to find my way to God more perfectly and fully than I have of late." Finally, on the morning of March 29, they were able to go on board the Vesuvio. *"Got along pleasantly through the afternoon, passing Elba, etc. Plenty of room on board having only a few passengers." At Marseille on Saturday, March 30, they took the night train for Paris, having been away from the city a little more than a month (cf. MS Diary, March 27-31, 1861).*

Dear Jim,

In sending off my letters and bundles, I want to add a few more words to you.

You were mistaken in thinking my travelling companion was a son of Mr. Gerald F. Dale. He is no relation, but a son of Mr. T. N. Dale, one of our most prominent Am[erican] Chapel people in Paris, with houses of business both in Phila[delphia] and New York. Please let Miss Mary Ludwig know of your mistake and, at the same time, give her my kindest love, and my regards to her Father, Mother & Miss Emily, with all the handsome speeches befitting the occasion.

It is very possible that you will see some of Mr. T. N. Dale's family in Phila[delphia]. I need only say, that they are among my kindest friends & that Nelson has proved a pretty fair [p. 2] substitute for yourself in my recent journey, to insure all the attention you can give them. I have asked Nelson to stay at our house if he can. I know his particulars of our journey given *viva voce* will be of interest to all of you. He is shy & timid but in many things mature and manly for a boy of only fifteen.

You mention an offer of Will Maddock's[1] to you. I ought not to advise, and yet I should say, if I were to do so, that you ought by all means to accept it. Whatever favor you might expect elsewhere, you would certainly have a surer prospect with him than with others. The field is a fine one for the development of an energetic business character.

At the same time, it is no easy life and unless you are willing to put yourself down to three or four years of hard work & no play, it [p. 3] would hardly be worth while to accept it. May God guide you aright in the matter.

I have thought about Will a great deal lately—in his anxiety for his father, his new position in business, and his danger of too great attachment to this world. I shall write to him very soon, altho' I think he manages to keep in my debt almost all the time.

This letter has no complimentary close or signature.

❦

My dear Jim,

Yours of the 18th March has just come in, the *Niagara*[1] having had, for some reason, an unusually long passage. I have to acknowledge besides it several newspapers, two Bulletins & a *Pennsylvanian* which I found awaiting me when I reached home a few days ago.

You speak of my scoldings for your delays in writing, &c—tho' not by way of any present reproach. Let me say, once for all, that I think you are perfectly splendid as a correspondent. Only on odd occasions, when the steamer is delayed, I feel sorry, and perhaps I don't express myself well, so you think I'm blaming you when it's only the lazy old boat; or, at other times, when only a small piece of a sheet comes (and it's sure to happen, just when I am voraciously hungry for two or three sheets) and then if I express disappointment you go & [p. 2] and [sic] take it all to yourself when I mean it for the mean old Insurance Office that will not let you have more time.

Rest assured if I was in the habit of addressing epistles to the steamers or the Ins. Office, you would not hear a word of complaint, but as I do not, why, what can I do to relieve my mind but just "blow out" on the first sheet of paper I come across.

Please understand in future how the thing is.

I have just been adding up and arranging my expenses of travel while in Italy. Perhaps a very rough and inaccurate (I am incapable of accuracy in such things, you know) may be agreeable to you. I will put it under several heads.

R.R. & Steamboat	F[ranc]s	569.25
Living, Hotels, &c		290.45
Porters, stewards, &c		25.17
Cab hire		36.00
Fees – at galleries, &c		31.35

[p. 3] This last item has no regular charges in it, but it is as necessary and ten times more inconvenient than if it had. It is the same with Porters fees, &c.

Purchases (some necessary) 106.20 [francs]. I put separate also our trip to Vesuvius & Pompei which came to 21.03 [francs].

In all cases I count only my share in all the expenses. Of course, in very many cases I should have had to pay much more had I been alone; that is, the fare which was really divided, I should have paid alone.

These foot up [i.e., add up to] 1079.45 francs. There are some other items which swell the amount to 1103.30 and to this some 50 more can be added for loss on exchange and money not accounted for. I may reckon my expenses as between $225 and $230. This, you see, is considerably higher than the estimate you made some time ago and is something more than I hoped it might be. Had you been with me [p. 4] or some one who understood & who could manage affairs, I know it might have been much less. As it is, I am glad it is not more. It runs me quite ashore in money matters. I shall barely make out to live for the next three months on the few francs I have remaining, so that if I am to go to Switzerland & the Rhine, not to mention England, a kind Providence must find some way of filling my exhausted funds. To be able to accomplish even this has required prolonged economy. I am very thankful that so far I have not run in debt. How much of your money I have in hand I do not exactly know. Please let me know when you write.

I have some misgivings as to whether you will like the little <u>tower</u> & the <u>chess-board.</u> If you do not, do not take them. I shall be very glad to give the <u>tower</u> to Sallie & the chess-board to Orly as presents. So don't feel bound in the least to keep them. [p. 5]

It is a great pity we are not rich, but since we are not, it is wisest to be as resigned as possible. I say this because just now there are images floating before my mind of sundry beautiful & interesting things I saw at Rome & elsewhere that I should delight to send over to Father & Sallie & you and Eliza & Orly & Cline. I thought of you all often, and the children, the dear little souls, besides, and half-murmured that God had not given me as large a purse as my heart.

But "*J'ai fait ce que j'ai pu*" ["I did what I could"], and one must be satisfied after that.

I was interrupted by remembering suddenly that I had an engagement to breakfast with Mrs. Baker at 12—and when I took out my watch I found it ten minutes after one. Hurrying over, I found I was not too late, for as no one was expected beside myself, Mrs. B. delayed ordering it till I arrived. Since [p. 6] then I have had a very nice ride with her and Willie in the Bois du Boulogne, which looks beautifully now. The early spring is opening all the leaf buds on the trees, and the bushes are covered with thin veils of small green leaves, the grass is green and little meadow flowers are scattered everywhere.

I wait with some eagerness for conference news. Will it trouble you to send a copy of the minutes to Geo. W. Brindle, Lyons, Iowa?[2] I am afraid no one will do it now I am away. Of course, you will send me a copy.

I hope Providence will choose the right man for Union.[3] Some day I may be very happy to have "a call" as you call it from there, but the time is not yet. I feel as if I would rather have for some time after I come home some small & not well known place, where I could take some lessons in plain & simple doing of good to common people. God bless you.

Yours faithfully,

Andrew

[P.S.] Please use better—i.e., blacker ink.

Dear Jim,

Your half-sheet of March 26th, in company with epistles from Orly and Eliza, came by due course of mail. Several of your late letters, this last among them, have been written with very pale ink. Perhaps when you write you indulge the hope that it will grow dark, but it does not; and I can hardly decipher the writing on the semi-transparent paper. As I make it a point to have first rate ink myself, I find it not easy to be satisfied with a poor article. It has been really a serious drawback on the pleasure of your letters.

It seems almost as odd to me to be absent at Conference-time as it can do to you. To know that business is going, friends are together and, especially, at home preachers are coming and going, Cline and Eliza are off to Conference, & speculations of all kinds are rife as to appointments &c— all without me—[p. 2] seems odd indeed. I can only comfort myself with the thought that I shall be with you by the next Conference—in all human probability.

It seems singular to me that you have no light upon the subject of the new pastor of Union. Such entire ignorance as you all plead is really funny. I suppose good old Union must be sliding gently back into good old fashioned Methodist usage and be giving up the delightful privilege of "<u>calling</u>" her desired shepherd.

I rather fear the truth is that some of the old officials have managed things with unusual secrecy and discretion, so that nothing of their sage planning has got wind abroad. Among Methodist stewards and leaders of the present day, not to mention Trustees, there is great fault in the old adage that "Providence helps them that help themselves," so they keep an open eye toward all [p. 3] providential indications and are always ready to do their part should things seem to them to need urging a little. Some of these days when you are called to "come up higher" into some official dignity, you will learn all about it, and who knows but you may keep things as quiet as Bro. Whiteman[1] and the rest have done this time.

I have no doubt that Union will get the right man, tho' I fear nothing can save her from going down hill—except setting out and pitching her tent further west. I only hope she won't delay such a step until her members are so scattered as to make it beyond the power of anyone to reunite them.[2]

I wonder how [J. F.] Chaplain[3] will suit them at Trinity. I hope you will go to hear him sometimes and let me know about the size and attention of the congregations as well as what you think of his sermons. If you [p. 4] can make it convenient to meet him occasionally, I shall be glad. I am sure you would like him if you knew him well. He is solid gold—no sham about him: one of the most genuinely pious men in the Phila[delphia] Conference.

Of course, I shall want to hear how everybody is pleased with all their preachers, so you have ample field for your powers of composition.

As to myself, I am quite over my bilious attack, having had recourse to my old friend, Extract of Taraxacum,[4] only that I took it in the fluid form which is much easier to swallow than the solid. I mean to keep on taking it till the weather becomes more settled and the danger of biliousness is passed.

Mr. Baker is coming out again about the middle of May. If you could get a box of tooth powder to him for me in time, I should be obliged.

Yours faithfully,
Andrew Longacre

Paris
April 17, 1861
[LETTER 31]

Dear Jim,

Yours of April 1st I have just rec'd. Somehow I have been intensely anxious for a few days to hear from you and now I am gratified. I wanted to hear all about Conference, the appointments, &c, and shall feel in a more settled state now I have your letter and shall soon have the papers you speak of. Papers are always delayed some time.

I am quite surprised to hear that [J. Talbot] Gracey[1] goes to India. As our mission there is in a very healthy part of the peninsula I don't know but he may find the movement a pleasant one in its results. I fear a little for his wife who is not strong. How changes come out of our class. Gracey to India, [J. F.] Chaplain[2] to Trinity, and your uncle in Paris. One hardly knows what to look for next.

The crowding of married men—or the haste of the boys to marry—in my opinion, ought to be peremptorily stopped. Few of [p. 2] them would dream of marrying so young if they were in any other business, and I think it is a shame to show such haste when its inconveniences are so manifest.

April 18th

This letter was begun yesterday but could not be finished. However, it will be no worse for the delay of a day. I shall enclose with it a little photograph—a view of our house. On account of an embankment which [is] in front of it, the view is not complete. You only see the upper part of the gate & posts & hardly any of the railing running between the posts. Neither do you see the steps up to the door which run from the pavement on each side of the door, two flights of six or eight steps. Under the landing at the front door is another door by which the servants go in and out.

The door opens into a small hall, chiefly to the left & extending only a little way back. The rest of the space to the left, behind the left-hand windows all the way up, is occupied by a stairway. On the right of [p. 3] the door is a room which was Emory's bedroom till he went to Germany (he went to Göttingen while I was in Italy); now it is Mademoiselle's atelier (we call Miss Augusta Mlle.).[3]

The two right-hand windows of the second story are those of Dr. McC[lintock]'s bedroom & the two above them are of the young ladies' room.

The parlor is on the first floor back to the right, and the dining room to the left. My bedroom is on the second story back of the stairway and, therefore, back of the left-hand window of that floor in the picture.

I went out the other day and bought a new light overcoat for the spring & summer, a "Macfarlane"—cost 55 francs.

With Mrs. Baker & Willie I went yesterday to Ken's[4] photographic establishment and pictures were taken of us all. It is as good a place as there is in Paris. Of course, we have no idea whether the things are good, bad, or indifferent, and we shall not be able to make up our minds on that point in a hurry as the [p. 4] pictures will not be sent home for two weeks. Of course, a specimen or two of my phisz [physiognomy—i.e, face] will find its way across the Atlantic.

The weather now is quite warm enough for summer and perfectly delightful, the finest decidedly that Paris has exhibited since my coming. There is no further light on the proposal made sometime since for me to remain another year.

The two papers came last evening and you will please accept my best thanks for them.

When you are in receipt of letters from me, please indicate them by the date, & if they come by private hand, say so. I wait with some anxiety to hear of the safe arrival of sundry letters and packages I sent by the Dales. Mr. Baker does not leave for Paris till about the middle of May. So I hope for my tooth powder. You had better send two boxes of it.

Yours affectionately,

Andrew

❧

Dear Jim,

Do you often feel as if you were a particularly good boy? Now, don't get excited. I am only about to say that your recent epistolary regularity has especially charmed me. When I thought of the long cessation of letters from me which would follow my going south, I began to fear like little children do sometimes when they have been left for a while that their parents will forget to come for them—that not receiving anything from me you might forget the "steamer-days." Of course, I might have known better. I might have remembered what a capital good brother you are. But at any rate, the evidence of the fact comes very refreshingly to me now in the long and uninterrupted letters written with the <u>faith</u> that I would be in Paris sometime to answer them. That with the date of April 9th containing the music of my poor little air (for which receive a thousand [p. 2] thanks) arrived today. I was in some suspense as to whether my letters from Rome would get safely to America and your assurance that Father had received his was very satisfactory. I am now getting up a small anxiety about the safe arrival of sundry goods and epistles by the Dales. Your next may tell me something about them or at all events the next but one.

Yesterday Dr. McC[lintock], Mrs., baby, and nurse set off for London, so at this present writing I am Lord paramount, doing the paternal to the two young ladies and a sort of nondescript article called John[1] of whom to say that he is at "<u>the uncomfortable age</u>" (for himself and others) is to say all. I ought not to say a word against him, however, for in spite of my apprehensions, he quite surpassed himself yesterday at dinner, was "as good as pie," and went to a meeting with us at Chapel afterward as beautifully as could be. His [p. 3] nearest approach to a breach of etiquette was a somewhat malicious inquiry as to who was "regent" in his father's absence. When his sister intimated that I held that distinguished position, he glanced toward me, but seeing nothing but an intense meekness depicted on my averted face, he concluded to prosecute his investigations no further. He is a youth of delicate sensibilities, which in his particular case, take the form of a strong desire to be let alone. His chief misery seems to be a haunting apprehension that somebody wishes to interfere with him. I suppose the secret of all is he's "a growing boy."

Besides my role of *pater-familias* I have to sustain the more onerous dignity of sole Pastor of the American Chapel. In that capacity I presided at a very singular meeting we had last night. At the request of some of the English clergymen here we opened our church to Mr. Reginald Radcliffe (quite a name for a novel, is it not?), [p. 4] one of the laymen of the Church of England who have helped on the recent revival by their exhortations and meetings. There was quite a good congregation, mostly of English people. After I had given out a hymn, Mr. R. read a portion of Scripture on which he commented and then went to prayer, asking people to pray as they might feel drawn to for a minute or two each. After this came more singing, one of our old familiar Methodist tunes, some more prayer, an address by a "young convert" who had come over with him from England, then his address. Toward the close of his remarks, when he was about to address himself to the unconverted, he sent quite a small crowd of us into the vestry to pray for him. After his address, he directed the senior men of the congregation to go into the vestry to be talked to & prayed with and sent in some people to attend to them. He remained with the serious female part of the audience only such being supposed to remain, as the larger part of the congregation had gone home. He went about the church [p. 5] talking here and there a few minutes at a time and calling to his aid all young converts and many women. All the people who joined in these exercises were unknown to me. I have no doubt some good was done, but the whole affair had too irreverent an air for my taste. It was too busy & fussy and without much evidence of feeling. On the whole I am glad it is over, and is not likely to be repeated in our chapel at all events. They did not break up till after 10 o'clock and then I had to speak to him on the subject and I fear he thought it rather cool.

These people don't understand using the Methodist fire-arms. They do not make any noise, as we are apt to do, but they lay themselves open to many objections which we avoid.

I hardly know whether all this talk about the affair will interest you much. It comes up as the last event.

Some time ago you said you intended going to see Cousin Huldah.[2] Have you [p. 6] done so? You know I shall be glad to hear from you anything you know about her. I am anxious, too, to hear something more as to Will Maddock's proposition to you. If Will does not mention it again, there can be no harm in your recalling it to his mind, that is, if you care to accept it. Of course you can judge much better than I as to what you had better do.

I feel for Will very much. My heart almost aches to see him. I have tried to urge upon him to connect himself with the church. I dread lest he should put it off, as an indifferent thing, until he loses all interest in the matter. Yet I cannot do much. Will must have his own time and way for action. Prayer at least shall not be wanting.[3]

I shall take the liberty of enclosing a letter to Rev. J. T. Gracey[4] which you will do me the favor to enclose in an envelope and forward to him. You can learn his address from the Thompsons or at Heggins & Perkinpine's.

Yours faithfully,

Andrew Longacre

My dear good brother Jim,

Your long and most welcome letter of April 15 I received yesterday. At the close of it you express a hope that by another mail my letters will begin to come in again. By this time you have had quite a series of them. Once and twice a week for a month past I have been sending you letters so that when this reaches you, you will surely feel that our correspondence is fully resumed, not to be broken off again, I trust, until we meet face to face, for in all future travel I shall try to move more at my leisure and so have time for such pleasures as letters.

In the music to "We would see Jesus" which I rec'd sometime ago, there is a little fault toward the close. The last two bars should be [Longacre draws a staff with notes]. This is quite decidedly an improvement on the writing you sent me, as you will see in making the change. You have had this done so nicely for me, I may trouble [p. 2] you with some other things of the sort. I should particularly like to have "Rabboni" and "Couldest thou not watch one hour?" written out. Some sort of transcription of the first exists somewhere at home, tho' I have not the least idea where.

You ask what I think about Orly's entering the navy. I hardly know what to say about it. If he keeps his old desire for it, and really prefers it to anything else, it may be as well. He is old enough now, and I hope settled enough in character not to be led away by the terrible examples he will find around him in such a life. Entering now, he may find his way open to good advancement; altho' that is not so certain, as a great deal is done both in the army and navy by patronage. As to there being nothing else for him to do, of course, just now there must be stagnation in all sorts of business. Such a state of affairs cannot last always [p. 3] even in a time of war.

I am very glad to hear so favorably from Cousin Huldah. I am not sure it would be best for her to go home. A visit of some months to the country, especially among the mountains, which she always loved, I think would be far better. She would in this way become familiar with active life again, gradually, and there would be far less of pain in it than in attempting at once to go back to the old places and ways of living.

I was much interested, of course, in your suggestions as to a change of your business relations. My own preferences would be for you to take some mercantile position. The field is wider and while it has more risk it gives a man more and I don't know but a better development. I am still inclined to think favorably of Will Maddock's[1] proposition, even after the news of Mr. Stitt's failure. Your connection with Will could not be merely a common one no matter what terms were agreed upon. [p. 4] Perhaps, indeed, the least said about terms in such a connection the better. Entered as a friend rather than as a servant and you would confer an obligation rather than receive one. However, as I said before, I am sure your own judgment will guide you. As to Bro. Aldridge, I am not very sure it would be the best thing you could do. He is one of the men that cannot be relied on very confidently, simply because neither he nor anyone else can venture to say what he will take it into his head to do.

For myself, I do not feel at all in a settled place here. I mean, as to the length of my stay. I may come home early in the fall, which I most heartily desire to do; on the other hand, I may remain for an indefinite period. Now and then Dr. McClintock talks as if he would go home himself in the fall. In that case I should stay indefinitely. But there is little prospect of that, I think. He will stay if it is at all possible for him to do so. He has no wish to go home, [p. 5] nor have any of the family. However, I don't allow myself any uneasy thought about my course. I am trying to do all the good I can, and I think there are more hopeful signs now than I have seen before. It is not like working at home, with a sympathetic people around one assured of their prayers, and with almost daily evidences of good done. Here, one must work patiently and learn to be thankful for the smallest indications. Yet I suppose it is good discipline.

4 P.M.   The papers you sent me came to hand and were very welcome. Once in awhile to have a familiar Phila[delphian] sheet does me good. Almost always too there is some item of interest in them of a local character which is not of course given in the New York papers which come to the house. The last papers you sent contained the announcement of the death of my old teacher, Joseph C. Engles, the only one of all my teachers I really loved [p. 6] if I except one young man who was assistant at Mr. James' school.[2]

Just this moment, while I am writing, John comes in with the intelligence that Virginia has seceded from the Union[3] and that Gov. Hicks of Maryland refuses to allow Northern troops on U. S. service to pass thro' the state. This is a complication I had not anticipated. It will bring the war right to our own borders. It seems to me I never saw before how weak our central government really is. My heart bleeds for my country, and I know not what to fear nor what to expect. It is hard to believe that the things we hear are really true. It seems more like a fearful vision or a wild tale. I still hope the contest may not be protracted nor bloody. But it is terrible in any aspect. We wait now for every mail with intense interest.

God save our unhappy country.

Your affectionate brother,

Andrew

Phila. [i.e., Paris] May 8, 1861

[LETTER 34]

My dear Jim,

After a long experience of gratified expectations, I have had a dismal disappointment. The *Persia* brought me no letters; not a line from you nor any one. The disappointment is the more keen at such a time when we look with intense interest for every scrap from home. Besides this interest I have been a little restless to hear of the safe arrival of the goods I sent over by the Dales. However, you have been so good that I will not scold you. I shall quite forget my disappointment when my next letters come, which may be this week.

Tho' I shall say little about home affairs, you will well understand that I am not the less interested. My heart bleeds, but there is little to say. All that can be done is to wait and pray.

Mrs. Baker has very sad news from Mr. B. Their family in Baltimore is entirely [p. 2]

Southernin sentiment, and it seems as if there would be a breach between the two brothers, both my dear friends Charles and Henry.[1] Another thing, Mrs. Jones (their sister) and her daughters are all strongly for the South, while Matt Jones who has been several years in New York is in Washington with a N. Y. regiment.

But no more of these sad things in my letter.

Dr. McC[lintock] is home again from London. He seems to have talked pretty plain English to them on American affairs.[2] I am afraid, however, nothing will stop them from a policy of at least partial recognition of the South. After goading on the Abolition excitement & feeling in America for years, they will probably now take advantage of our troubles resulting therefrom.

Ah well! Our trust must be in God and not in earthly governments.

The great art exhibition is now open in Paris at the Palais de l'Industrie, some 4,000 pictures, statues, &c, being on [p. 3] exhibition—as many more having been refused. I spent Monday afternoon there but shall have to go often to see the great affair well.[3] Last evening I attended the *Séance Musicale* of an Amateur orchestra to which one of my friends here belongs. It was of course <u>free</u>. The place was a very elegant tho' not large hall at the establishment of the piano-makers Pleyel, Wolff & Co. The company performing must have numbered between thirty and forty if not fifty. About 25 violins, 3 bass-viols, hautbois, clarionets [sic], flutes, french horns, &c. The playing was very good. A solo on the violin by one of the members would have charmed you. At several points in it the audience, who listened well, cried Bravo (sounding exactly like bow-bow as if they were imitating dogs barking).

Quite a boy, <u>Tissot</u>[4] played remarkably well on the piano. There was some singing, tho' not extraordinary, except two or three things for their <u>funniness</u>. Imagine two [p. 4] songs, one called "What is it to have eyes," and the other "What is it to have a nose." ("*Ce que c'est que d'avoir des yeux,*" &c).

Another piece represented an auction of poultry with prose comicalities interspersed. And a fourth, the trials of a cheap lawyer (*"L'Advocat [Avocat] à deux francs l'heure"*). In this last he gave a conversation between the advocat [avocat] and an Englishman who could talk but little French, which was exceedingly funny.

I observed, and I report it for your benefit on such occasions, that the performers all wore white cravats (except in playing) and gloves (kid of course) and also the young gentlemen engaged in finding seats for the audience. One fellow was very like Charley Adams & seeing him flitting (?) about made the affair seem quite home like. Instead of saying, on the programme, "M— will <u>preside</u> at the piano," they write *"Le piano sera tenu par M.—"* <u>will be held</u>.

The whole affair was quite an agreeable break in the general monotony of my life in Paris. Hoping for a letter soon.

Yours faithfully,
Andrew

My dear Jim,

The first delivery of the Cunard mails has taken place this morning and no letter has come from you. One from Mr. Baker poorly supplies the lack of your accustomed letter. With some anxiety I wait to see if by some neglect your letter has been overlooked in the morning delivery and will reach me this afternoon. If none comes at all, I shall begin to feel a little hurt, as last week's steamer, the *Persia*, failed to bring me a line from home and just now we are all intensely anxious to hear all we can. It would be more gratifying to have your letters increased than diminished in these "troublous times." I don't know, of course, how closely you are engaged, but it would be a great comfort to me to hear from you as fully on all matters of interest as you could find time to write.

In one of my late letters to Eliza, I [p. 2] sent a very brief message to you, which I will now give to you more at large.

Mr. Proeschel,[1] Dr. McC[lintock]'s secretary, has invented a very small and compact camera for taking small photographs. You could carry it, stand and all, in one hand, without serious inconvenience. It is perfectly complete, containing the glasses, collodion, baths, &c—all; and it will be accompanied by a book of instructions which will be full & complete as to the manipulation & the chemical preparations. There will be nothing to be done but to prepare paper for printing; which you know does not keep. The whole affair can be bought for a hundred francs. If you care to invest so much in a thing of the kind, which I have seen used, for it has been here at work on all of us often, you have only to let me know your wishes.

Now, I have a word to say on a long neglected topic: money matters. I am not sure that I shall need any [p. 3] more than I shall get here, but I may do so. If I conclude to leave here this summer instead of remaining till the winter, I shall need about a hundred dollars to enable me to visit Switzerland and the Rhine—for England I hope to be provided at least in part in some other way.

I have thought that I might as well borrow that money from Mrs. Baker, and request you to return it to Mr. B[aker] by Mr. Keen in New York. That would be simpler and safer than doing it by the mails. If you will agree to this, I shall be obliged; and I think it necessary I may even act upon it before hearing from you as Mrs. Baker will leave Paris in a few weeks. She wishes to go home from Liverpool and has asked me to go with her that far on her way home. In that way I may get to England without expense.

I have been the more anxious to hear from you as I have no word from you since the Dales arrived in America. [p. 4] Whether you have rec'd the things I sent or whether you liked them, I am yet ignorant. Of course I shall not feel altogether satisfied till I hear from you. Eliza's last letter speaks of the arrival of some of the things, but not of others. I suppose they [will] come on as Mr. Dale finds it convenient to send them.

I shall not finish this letter until I either have your letter, which I hope for today, or am forced to give up the hope of it.

May 15th. Your letter came after all, with Eliza's enclosed. It has happened several times that my letters here come later than the others; the reason, I think, must be that you address them in a delicate hand, and in the first rapid sorting at the office they are thrown on one side. If you were to write the address in a bolder hand, I think this delay would be avoided. But it is a little thing— too trifling to speak of. Mrs. Baker will leave Paris either about the 10th or 22nd of [p. 5 (half-sheet)] June. She has not yet decided which—to sail from Liverpool either the 22nd of June or the 7th July. If she goes at the earlier of these dates, I shall hardly have time to hear from you in response to this letter. I may not need the money and, if I do, I feel confident you will let me have it in the way I have mentioned.

I should not be surprised to find myself packing up and starting for America some time in August, and it may be even in July. As yet, there is no formal application for my stay here, and I have strong doubts whether it will come [p. 6 (verso of half sheet)] at all, owing to the poverty-stricken condition of all American purses. It will be a great relief to me, if it does not, as then my way home will be open and plain.

I don't give myself much thought about the matter, as I believe it will be all "ordered" rightly. I shall do what God pleases; and I pray for grace to be ready for that in patience & meekness.

Write good long letters.

Your loving brother,

Andrew

⤬

My dear Jim,

Please consider "the present writing" a birthday epistle to your excellency commemorative of your twenty-eighth.

My thoughts were with you a great deal on Saturday. In the evening, particularly, I took a long lonely quiet stroll in the Bois de Boulogne to pray and to think of you. I wonder if my celestial telegraph carried over to you some shadow, some wave, some spark of tender influence to remind you of the loving heart across the wide sea.

I forgot to say in my last, how much obliged I was for the picture of Steve Darlington. He must have improved in looks since I saw him. Some of these days I shall send you a letter to forward to him.

Eliza tells me that your chess-board has come and that other things are on the way. As I sent so many and such inconvenient things, I did not expect [p. 2] a very speedy delivery of them. It was very kind in Mr. Dale to consent to be bothered with so much. I hope you will have some opportunity of showing him your appreciation of the favor.

Mrs. Baker leaves in the *Persia* June 22nd. I shall go with her from Paris on the 10th. She means to go to Ireland for a day or two visiting the lakes of Killarney. As I never expected to see the Emerald Isle, the trip there will be clear gain. Returning to Paris, I shall try to secure some two weeks in London with my dear, warmhearted friends.[1]

Even yet, I cannot say positively whether I shall need to ask her to lend me anything or not. If I do, it may be $150.00—which I hope you will be able to forward to Mr. Baker as soon as convenient after I notify you of the loan. You may think me rather confident and free in this matter, but it is on the [p. 3] strength of an old offer of yours, as you will remember. How much obliged I shall be for the favor, I hardly need stop to say.

So much for such items. Inside the hidden world which people do not see there is just now the movement of two feelings: a great hunger for home, and a strong desire to be "a better boy."[2] It takes a much greater amount of effort to be good here than at home. There you are reminded of

Paris
May 20th, 1861
[LETTER 36]

The Letters of Andrew Longacre ⋆ 93

duty, recalled to God, by a thousand things. It is almost a fight <u>not to be good</u>. Here the good desire comes from God & finds very little countenance from external things. A very small allowance of goodness will take one through his daily life without awaking the faintest suspicion of inconsistency. People will think him perfect if he only keeps from open offences. They will not expect him to try to do good.[3] I thank God that the monitor within [p. 4] is more exacting than friends without. I am tortured half the time with the thought of the littleness, the variableness, the inconsistency of my efforts to do good. It is painful, but I am thankful, oh how thankful, that it is so. Lately these feelings have arisen upon me with renewed force. I must do more for God. My life must be a more faithful witness and testimony for him. The world has a right to demand it of me, and I know God expects it of me.

After all, when we think how near eternity is, and how the fires of the judgment will test all human things, it seems as if the only real things a man does are what he does for souls.[4] Money, learning, &c, of earth will be of no account when we once cross "the narrow stream of death."[5]

God bless you my dear, kind brother Jim, and give you many more years and each, better & happier than the predecessor.

Yours very affectionately,

Andrew Longacre

[P.S.] No new letter of yours since my last—expect one tomorrow.

Paris
May 22nd, 1861

[LETTER 37]

Dear Jim,

Yours of the 7th acknowledging recp't of the chess-board, &c, has come to hand. I am glad it pleases you and hope the little alabaster tower will suit you as well. I have still some four or five dollars of yours on hand to get rid of, but I dare say it will not be very troublesome. They say that Switzerland is a famous place to pick up things pretty, little and cheap, so if I go there this summer I may have another budget to send or bring home.

My heart trembles a little as I write "bring." Last evening, Dr. McClintock told me that things [are] taking a definite shape as to my remaining in Paris, that arrangements were almost complete for putting the thing into such form as would bring it up for my assent or dissent.

As yet I wait. <u>I want to go home</u>. Just as if I were not almost thirty years old, I feel the year of absence as [p. 2] a very long time. Often the feelings of home love wash over me tumultuously, the wonder how you look, the desire once more to have part in home pleasures, to talk with you of affairs, to hear you and Eliza play, to go to the Schuylkill, out to Woodlands,[1] or visit Sallie and see how the children have grown. The spring is beautiful here, much more beautiful than I ever saw it at home, but it is not home. And even the beauty is new and I look at it as if it were a picture, something lovely to look at but in which I could not have part. I am surprised at myself to find how the keenness of my desire to have some of you here with me does not diminish. Really I did not know I loved you all so much.

Mr. [T. N.] Dale writes to Dr. McC[lintock] today and sends word to me that he meant to take some other things to Phila[delphia] himself the week after writing and that Nelson would go with him. Of course, [p. 3] it will be all over when this comes, and I am sure you will do what you can to make Nelson's trip a pleasant one. I hope he will stay at our house while he is in the city.

You ask about the ink. It is all I can desire and I assure you, however you may be inclined to think, it is a vastly better kind than what you used before, which I always had great difficulty in seeing.

I shall be glad to have Dr. DuBouchet's recipe for tooth-powder, especially as Mr. Baker is not coming over and I suppose you will have no friends coming.

Do you know that Charley Stockwell is married? You remember him as my fellow passenger in the *Vanderbilt* when I came out and who with Dr. Maris made my circle here till Dr. McC[lintock] came. I had a very nice letter from him and a photographic picture of himself & his lady. She was a Miss Grossholz. He is now at Tiffany, Reed & Co.'s, New York, where I [p. 4] should like you to call with my compliments any time you go to that city.

Our chief political question over here is still the perverse blindness of England in reference to the real nature of the struggle in America. They regard it as simply a contest between the South & North for dominion and evidently consider the South as the aggrieved party which is simply contending for its independence. They put the slavery question altogether out of the business, and esteem themselves very honorable when they put the two parties on a sort of equality between whom England is to preserve a strict neutrality. Treason, robbery, lawlessness and persecution, instead of making rebels, raise their perpetrators to the rank of recognized belligerents waging a just war. Of course we are annoyed at all this, but we begin to feel, I speak for many Americans here in this, that England has not yet forgiven her revolted colonies & is more fond of monarchy & of cotton than of human freedom.[2]

Yours faithfully,
Andrew Longacre

❧

My dear Jim,

Mrs. Baker has had a note from Mr. B[aker] which came by telegraph as far as Nova Scotia and so is very brief, which has put a stop to her arrangements for leaving Paris when she expected. In a day or two more, she will have letters which will tell her exactly what to expect. At present, we are hoping that he means to come out for her himself. If this should prove correct, my anticipated Irish and English excursion will not come off. Still, I hope to get to England some time this summer. I really long to be once more near such warm hearts and such simple Christianity.

Yesterday, the Americans in Paris, or a good part of them, had a grand demonstrative breakfast at the Hotel du Louvre.[1] As they sent me a ticket, I went. About 170 people were there of whom I should think 60 were ladies. The notabilities present were Hon. Wm. L. Dayton,[2] our [p. 2] new minister here, Anson Burlingame[3] (Min[ister] to Austria), Haldeman[4] of P[ennsylvani]a (to Sweden), Cassius M. Clay[5] (to Russia), & Col. John C. Frémont.[6] It was an interesting thing to see Frémont & Dayton sitting side by side at the table. All those I have mentioned made speeches, which seemed to be carefully prepared. Mr. Dayton's in particular was a noble one, and he has risen fifty per cent in my opinion of him since I heard it. Mr. Frémont spoke but little, a few earnest, simple sentences. Mr. C. M. Clay spoke more strongly than any one with regard to England. He was a little stimulated by the rather contemptuous treatment of a letter of his by the London *Times*. Mr. Burlingame had more feeling, I mean pathos, than any of them, and his speech was full of beauty. Dr. McClintock spoke well, and did a good deal, I think, to soften the tone of the meeting toward England.

The meeting was very enthusiastic, and but one sentiment seemed to prevail. [p. 3] I was glad to have so pleasant an opportunity of hearing some of our rather illustrious fellow-citizens.

Mr. Frémont, I believe, is *en route* for home, in obedience to a call from Gen[eral Winfield] Scott[7] summoning him to military duty. He was enthusiastically cheered when reference was made to that by one of the speakers.

The sentiment seems now to be a general one here that the government is to be sustained in putting down the whole southern rebellion. Whatever may come afterwards, whether states or sections, that may by a majority, in a <u>free</u> expression of opinion, desire to withdraw from the Union, are to be permitted to do so or not. All are agreed that rebellion and treason are to be put down at all cost, even tho', according to one of the speakers yesterday, that cost should be 500,000 lives and $1,000,000,000.

Many of us hope still that before actual bloodshed shall proceed very far, the [p. 4] South will become so divided in its counsels as to compel them to abandon all idea of a prolonged war. Their want of money, if nothing else, will drive them to desperation. Everybody here is thankful that Gen[eral] Scott is still living and able to take charge of the U. S. Army. Mrs. Scott was at the breakfast yesterday, and she must have been pleased to hear how warm a response was made when her husband's name was mentioned.

I have written you quite a political letter; however, it will do to have one once in a while for a change. I shall not promise another very soon as I try not to mingle my feelings of home too much with the thoughts of sorrow that rise from all political views of American affairs.

I received the papers you sent by the last mail. I believe they never fail to come when you send them. What are your plans for the summer?

Your affectionate brother,

Andrew Longacre

[P.S.] I enclose letters to Eliza & Harry Rex.

[Written at top of letter:] Tell me if this <u>steel</u>-penmanship is more easy to read than the ordinary <u>gold</u>-penmanship of my letters.

Paris
June 7, 1861

[LETTER 39]

Dear Jim,

I had not intended writing to you by this mail, as you will see by Eliza's letter, but so great a change has come over may [i.e., my] European programme—or to speak more definitely, so great a point has been decided which directly affects all my arrangements that I cannot forbear telling you of it.

The point, long in suspense, has been decided. Dr. McClintock told me yesterday that the few persons who had been spoken to on the subject were feeling just now too embarrassed in money matters to undertake any greater charge in church expenses than they now had to bear. A number he said were willing and would be glad to do their part, but they were so few. So my way is open to go; for which I am very thankful.

This will make it necessary to do what I suggested a week or two ago [p. 2] to borrow some hundred dollars from Mrs. Baker. I shall spend as little as I can and will let you know all about it when I see you, as it will not be necessary for you to do anything in the matter until I come home. My reason for borrowing at all is that I am quite drained of money now—and I borrow so much because I should be sorry to return home without seeing the Rhine and a little of Switzerland. When I shall be able to repay you, in these hard times, it is hard to say, but I imagine you will not be very much troubled on that score.

My idea now is, to remain in Paris a week or two longer, then to take a short trip, about a week, to the Rhine & Switzerland, again a short interval in Paris, and leave for England about the 6th or 7th of July, to leave for America the 20th from Liverpool. On the way I hope to spend a few days in London. [p. 3]

This will bring me home about the 1st of August.

I hope I shall be in time for some of the Camp-meetings,[1] if in the excitement of the war they find time for such things. Please let me know what there is to be known on the subject.

Mrs. Baker will remain until I can go so that we will go over home together.

Don't write to me after the 1st of July as letters written after that will not be at all certain to reach me. I must be content to have a short time of silence before comes the joy of meeting you all once more face to face.

I have not time today to write more.

Yours faithfully,

Andrew Longacre

[p. 4] June 8th. My letter did not get off yesterday owning to a forgetfulness really excusable under the busy circumstances of yesterday, so they will have to wait till Monday when the Londonderry steamer will take them. Before closing them up, I shall add a few more words at the latest date possible.

June 10th. I resume my letter again this morning. Since Friday I have thought over my affairs pretty thoroughly and have come to the conclusion that as I have not much time and don't want to spend much money, and have no one to go with me, I had better give up my trip to the Rhine. I should not like to feel hurried—I should want to stop here and there a little, and on the whole I shall feel better to give it up altogether. Perhaps I may come over here again sometime and if I don't, well, it won't matter much. I have seen a great deal already. Still, matters are not quite decided. I expect to leave Liverpool on the 20th of July in the *Africa*.

Yours faithfully,

Andrew Longacre

[Postscript written at top of page 1, above the inside address:] "I enclose a few lines to Sallie."

My dear Jim,

I am without anything from you for a good while, and that too when I want to hear answers to some of my recent propositions. However, I suppose I shall not have to wait much longer.

Some time ago, a week and more, I borrowed a hundred dollars from Mrs. Baker on the strength of your offers made a good while ago. Had I known what has since transpired, I might not have made the loan. When I asked for the money, I had no expectation of receiving any more from Dr. McC[lintock] as my year had expired and there was no arrangement for my longer stay in Paris. I was expecting and preparing to go home, as you have already found from my last letters. Now, things are changed. Dr. McClintock had had a matter put into his hands which at once makes him able to give me an adequate salary and calls him, [p. 2] at intervals, away from Paris. So it seems to be necessary for me to stay at least three and perhaps six months longer. I thought it best to consent for, several reasons—among them, the simple one, that I am here, with work and a salary, whereas if I were to go home I should have neither one nor the other. Besides, it would be rather difficult for Dr. McC[lintock] to make any other arrangement, and the people seem very much to desire me to remain.[1]

A few words more as to my loan. I shall be able to return to Mrs. Baker from $25 to $50 of the amount and shall only have to ask you to forward the balance to Mr. Baker, after you hear again & definitely from me on the subject. I shall soon be able to have the amount for you either to be spent at your order here or kept for you till I have some easy way of transmitting it.

I have bought for you several fine [p. 3] photographic copies of good pictures besides one or two more card portraits & three glass stereoscopic views, which last I thought good & cheap, only 2 f[rancs] apiece. Some of these things I want to send on by Mrs. Baker, but I am not sure whether I will venture to ask her to take charge of the pictures as they are on large sheets & would be troublesome. I paid for them six & eight francs apiece. They are as fine as can be.

The change in my plans is very sudden, and as it only happ[en]ed yesterday morning, I am hardly used to it yet. Until then, I had been getting ready as fast as possible to leave Paris, seeing a few of the remaining lions and making sundry purchases of knick-knacks. This change makes quite a lull—and I am again thrown back into the dim distance of an uncertain prospect of home.

I am fixed for three months longer [p. 4] and how much will be added to that before I get away, it is impossible to say.

I expect to go with Mrs. Baker to England & Ireland, *en route* to Liverpool, as was first arranged. We start (D.V.[2]) about the 8th of July. On my way home, I shall stop a little while in London.[3]

It is now probable that I shall get to the Rhine & Switzerland sometime in August or September.

I wait to hear from you with some degree of impatience. Your single letter from Washington interested me very much. I regret it has had no successors. I shall be glad when you are home again and able to write to me regularly. Why can't you come over on a business visit to Paris & run down to Switzerland next August? We should have a jolly time.

Yours lovingly,

Andrew

[p. 5]

Dear Jim,

I take another slip of paper to say that I shall only keep fifty dollars of the loan I made from Mrs. Baker; the rest I shall return to her. It will take some economy to get along with so little, but I don't like the feeling of a heavy debt. I hope to be able to live on so little as to have enough left to go to the Rhine in September.

Some time ago, I saw what I think you would like to have—a set of things for "Parlor Gymnastics," consisting of two lines of steel springs, long and closely curled, which you fasten on the wood-work, one on each side of a door or window, merely hung on hooks. The exercise consists in various pullings of these so as to call into play almost every muscle in the body. There is another shorter line of springs with a handle at each end to take the place of dumbbells & I [p. 6] should think much better. The set, with a book of directions, costs $16—80 francs. If you want it, let me know, and I can get it to bring on with me when I come.

As I am fifty dollars in your debt, I shall be ready to get whatever you wish, or to use any part of that money for you as you may desire. In a few months, if I stay so long, I shall have no difficulty in returning it in this way.

I must beg you to excuse my writing, but my arm aches & my hand is unsteady from flogging my donkey yesterday in the forest of Montmorency.[4] If I hurt the noble beast as much as I have wearied my arm, it will not soon forget the jolly ride, for a full account of which see Eliza's letter.

Yours lovingly,

Andrew

[Postscript written at the top of page 1, above the inside address:] "Please think about a P.S. I put in Eliza's letter on the subject of Orly's taking another letter to his name. I have thought of it a good deal."

Dear Jim,

Your little but very welcome favor of the 10th has just come to me. I am glad your trip has been so satisfactory to yourself and to the gentlemen of the company. I hope to hear more about it in your next.

My object in writing this morning is as much to relieve my own mind as to give you any information; as for the latter purpose, a day or two later would do just as well. A few minutes ago Dr. McClintock came into my room with a rather startling proposition. After the many shocks I have had lately, I ought to be proof against surprises.

He said that it was doubtful whether the congregation here and the society[1] at home together could make up his salary, that if they could not, he could not afford to remain, and even if they could, it was doubtful. He then [p. 2] asked if I would consent to remain here upon a salary of $1500. He thought there would be no difficulty about raising that amount. He asked, he said, because he was writing home and must have something definite to say to them. I told him that I would consent to stay till next spring but could not speak for any longer time. So the matter stands.[2] What will be the result I cannot say. The prospect of a continued residence here is rather

Paris
June 25, 1861

[LETTER 41]

dark. Were it really to come to pass that I should remain, I would insist upon a holiday in which I might make a visit home.

However, I cannot think of it. It feels like breaking my heart to remain so long away, to think even of making Paris a sort of home.

Yet I suppose it is not well to consult only one's feelings. It might be wise for me to consent to it. The [p. 3] position is an honorable one, and the salary sufficient so long as I am unmarried. You see I am just looking at it. I can do no more now—and, who knows, perhaps I may not have the offer.

You have not yet sent me Dr. Du Bouchet's recipe for the tooth-powder. I should just as lief have it written in French as not. The English druggists are much dearer [i.e., more expensive] than the French ones.

June 28th

This letter has lingered on but must be closed today. Eliza's letter of the 14th has just reached me telling me that you are off again to Washington. The long letter you promised me in your last little one, I suppose, is postponed. Perhaps, however, it will only be the better and longer for the delay when it does come.

For the last few days I have not been very well, something of my old dysentery—& home-sickness has come [p. 4] in with a rush. I don't think I can persuade myself to stay here much longer. Were the proposition of last Tuesday to be made to me now, I should not give so kind an answer. What a blessed thing we do not know the future. We travel on into it with all our hopes and keep hoping always in spite of myriad disappointments.

I have your reply about the photographic machine. I shall see more about it before making the investment. The probability is that I shall not get it.

I greatly miss your letters. My correspondents generally seem disposed to fall off. To Father I am more obliged than I know how to say, for his steady punctuality. I had hardly dared to hope for it on time.

You see I have not much to say. The fact is I am still in a sort of prolonged collapse from the effects of my disappointment about going home.

Yours lovingly,
Andrew

⚬

Paris
July 4, 1861
[LETTER 42]

Dear Jim,

Tho' it's the fourth of July, I don't feel a bit jolly. For some days I have been crawling out of a fit of dysentery I had last week and tho' the weather is superb, wonderfully fresh and bright, I haven't yet got up to my ordinary condition, either in body or spirits. Besides there are to be no doings of any sort this fourth except a private pic-nic this afternoon and evening, which I can't join on account of our prayer-meeting. I should like to go very much as I believe they want me; Mr. Munroe asked me as if he did, and I am quite sure I should enjoy it. They go to St. Germain[-en-Laye], a lovely place, where I spent a day with the Curtises about a year ago.[1]

Almost every mail from home brings Dr. McC[lintock] some fresh tidings of a character to draw him thither. [p. 2] It begins to be highly probable that he will leave Paris this fall, say, about

October. If he should do so, I suppose I am in for some months more here, with no definite prospect of the end. It remains to be seen whether the Society[2] at home will request me to stay, on what terms, and for how long. Of course, until something comes from them, it is idle for me to speculate as to what I shall do. A thousand schemes and dreams fly through my brain, all mere shadows.

I suppose by this time you are home again from Washington. That long letter, too, containing full accounts of all things, visits to Mrs. Robinson, &c, is doubtless either on the way or under way. Remember I am just as anxious to know all that you have seen, heard, said and done, as if I were at home. Home news of all kinds is, I think, even more interesting [p. 3] away here than at home itself.

Nothing seems to be going on here of more than mere daily interest. People are leaving town as fast as possible. When I start off next Monday, I shall be in the height of the fashion. The only draw-back will be that I don't intend to remain away so long as the world generally. But still four or five weeks will make a good summer holiday in England, Ireland & the Isle of Wight. How I wish you were to be with me. It is really <u>too bad</u> that I have to go all over these scenes of which we all have read and talked and thought with no one of my own kith and kin to bear me company. It seems such a half and half sort of enjoyment not exactly selfish, because it is not from my choice, but somewhat melancholy.

Ah well! We shall have a good joyful reunion some of these [p. 4] days, all the better and sweeter perhaps from the long pain of this enforced absence.

I have been getting you a few things to send home by Mrs. Baker. I don't know exactly how our account stands, but I have spent for you somewhere about 25 francs. Hereafter, you know, I shall hold myself ready to get anything you want without remittances, as I shall be in your debt fifty-dollars. You must let me know, however, what part of that you are willing to expend over here. If at any time Sallie should want me to get something for her, you can receive the money and credit me with it, while I will buy what she wishes.

Won't you ask George West some day whether he knows what has become of an old friend of his, Charley Tompkins, who went to West Point? Is he the Lieut. or Capt. Tompkins in the army now?

Your affectionate Bro[ther],
Andrew

In addition to Andrew as a compagnon de voyage *on this trip to England and Ireland, it is not clear from the* MS Diary *how many were traveling with Mrs. Baker. One would assume that her son, Willie, and other members of the household were in the party, but only her Irish maid, Margaret, is mentioned by name. They left Paris on July 8, making a stop at Rouen to visit the cathedrals of St. Ouen, St. Maclou, and Notre Dame before crossing the channel and continuing to London.*

*The next day they traveled by train to Holyhead where they boarded a steamer for Kingstown (Dun Laoghaire). The approach from the Irish Sea, "the hills and sweep of the coast," reminded Andrew of "a reduced copy of the Bay of Naples" (*MS Diary, *July 9, 1861). From the port, they took* *the train into Dublin. Although their accommodations at the* Gresham *were the best the city had to offer, they "would be called third class in America." The next morning a walk along the quay, "the walled river, small boats and bridges," were reminiscent of Florence, although "the buildings [were] far less interesting."*

The party left Dublin by train for the cross-country trip to Killarney, "at first [through] pleasant English-looking scenery, changing to a vast stretch of wild and unpopulated country." Rain the next day kept them inside, but on Friday, July 12, they began their sightseeing in earnest with a trip to Muckross Abbey, Torc Mountain, and Torc Waterfall. On Saturday, they took a car through the Gap of Dunloe by Purple Mountain, then ponies to ascend the pass by Serpent Lake. They descended in view of Black Valley, took a boat to the head of Upper Lake and went through the three lakes stopping at Eagle's Nest and on the island of Inishfallen. On the 15th, they returned to Dublin and crossed the Irish Sea to Liverpool. See MS Diary, July 8-August 2, 1861; and below, Letter 44, July 25, 1861; Letter 45, July 27, 1861; and Letter 46, August 1, 1861.

Liverpool July 19, 1861

[LETTER 43]

Dear Jim,

My head is aching too much to attempt much of a letter today. Some things I need to say about the package of pictures which Mrs. Baker takes for me. I think you will find with them a list with prices on it, tho' I am not sure I put it in. The large photographs were 6 f[ranc]s apiece, except one, which I sent to Sallie (which cost more), "*Les Girondins*." One other I send to Father, "*Rembrandt dans son atelier*." If you like either of those pictures well enough to have them added to your collection, [p. 2] I will send them on to you at some opportunity, or perhaps bring them. The glass-views (stereoscopic) I got because they were good & cheap—2 f[ranc]s each; the card-portraits I thought you would value. If you care to have likenesses of other musicians I can get Schulhoff, Berlioz, Musard and others.

I spoke in Eliza's letter about a book of popular French songs—children's airs & ditties. It would not go well in the bundle, so I have kept it for another time.

As to your cards,[1] and Orly's, I can and desire very much to get you others, if the style of these does not suit you, if you will only send me out a pattern. I suppose Orly would wish U.S.N., or perhaps Asst. Engineer U.S.N. on his card now. If any change of [p. 3] the kind is desirable for him or for you, I particularly request to be informed of it and to be allowed to make my trifling present complete by having it done here—of course, you and he retaining the plates which will now be in your hands.

How my account stands with you I don't know. I leave all that in your hands, as I feel very keenly that I have no head for accounts. With regard to Sallie, for instance, I am hopelessly involved, and can't for my life say whether I am in her debt or she in mine, but I incline to the belief that I yet have some dollar or two of hers unexpended.

I go to London tomorrow after seeing Mrs. Baker fairly off on the voyage which I was to have had the happiness of sharing. [p. 4] I like Liverpool more than I expected. It is decidedly provincial with less attempt at <u>city</u> character and resident completeness than Baltimore or Philadelphia. A few fine buildings give it a fair look in places, but most of it is second rate. The suburbs remind me of Germantown and Chestnut Hill, as much as anything in England can remind one of America. The scenery is English, which means broad, level or any gently rolling plains and long low hills, all rich in fields, trees, both scattered & in groves, and houses—cottages & mansions alike neat and well-to-do. These seen thro' the perpetually beautifying <u>haze</u> of English air meet you everywhere. Our own scenery is more varied, more romantic, but generally much less <u>rich</u>, less suggestive of luxuriance & abundance. And where equally <u>rich</u>, decidedly less beautiful.

Yours always,

Andrew

⚘

After two days of sightseeing in the Liverpool area, on Saturday, July 20, Mrs. Baker boarded the steamer Africa *bound for New York, and Andrew returned to London and his friends, the Francis Lycetts. On Sunday evening, he preached once again in the chapel at Highbury Grove and spent the following week sightseeing in London and its environs.*

Dear Jim,

I shall put a few lines only in this letter, reserving the rest for another time. But since I have rather the advantage of as to the number of letters written lately, I am sure you will not complain.

After several fine days in London, yesterday and today have been dull and rainy. The dullness forces itself into my spirit. I feel sad and homesick. "Oh, that I had wings like a dove," etc.[1]

I am glad you are once more at home again so that I may hope to hear from you regularly. Even in your holidays, you need not fail to write, as there are many odd hours at the sea-side.

Here with my kind friends, Mr. & Mrs. Lycett, I am enjoying myself, as much as I can so far from home. I cannot account for nor describe their kindness and that of the friends who make up the little circle here.

You will see from my letter to Eliza how my time has been occupied—I need not repeat it. I am very much obliged for the [p. 2] picture of Orly but sorry to see his is so thin in face. However, he has become a man since I saw him. Before either of us see him again there may be much greater changes.

I believe I wrote some time ago, definitely in regard to your sending $50 to Mr. Baker. If you did not so understand it, let this inform you. You can forward it, in any form that seems proper to you and to him, at No. 182 Water St., simply referring him to Mrs. Baker for information in regard to it. She, of course, knows all about it. I think I shall be able to have that amount ready for you almost at any time, to be kept or spent, as you think proper, or forwarded to you if you desire it.

July 27th. Even this trifle, you see, I could not finish for want of time or disposition. I leave you to guess which. Bishop Janes[2] is now here. I went yesterday to the Botanical Gardens at Kew and thought over that interesting rhyme,

"I'm her highness' dog at Kew

And pray (I forgot just here) whose dog are you?"[3]

Your affectionate brother,

Andrew

**London
July 27, 1861**

[LETTER 45]

Dear Jim,

If I can secure time to fill this sheet this morning I shall put it in Father's letter. If not, well, you will not be the wiser.

I had a very pleasant day yesterday in company with my dear friend, I can't consider him anything less, Mr. John Edward Hughes. We went to Kew as I said in the half sheet in Eliza's envelope.

A few steps from here is a station on a sort of city rail-road running right thro' dense parts of the town in a deep cut, and crossed by bridges at all the streets. We changed cars at one point and were in half and hour or little more at Kew on the Thames some dozen miles or more from London. I was there with Mr. Hughes, when in London before, on our way to Richmond and Hampton Court. It was the recollection of that day that made [p. 2] us both wish for another one that would come somewhat into the same associations. He considers that some remarks of mine then brought him to the decision to be a Christian, a decision which he put into execution some month or more afterward. His thankfulness and gratitude for the little part I had in that matter are very touching to me tho' I feel them undeserved. He is a noble fellow in looks and in character—a thorough and rising man of business and a most active Christian, working energetically in every way in his power. He is superintendent of the Sunday School and on Saturday evenings with one or two more young converts meets a class of poor working men, called here navvies.

With him I should have enjoyed a trip anywhere. But the place itself at Kew, the river, with its islands and wooded banks, and the meadows here and there, all bright and beautiful in the sunshine after the rain, all was [p. 3] beauty and enjoyment.

The Botanical gardens, as the name implies, are full of specimens of trees and flowers of all sorts. Such as will not grow in the open air have houses built for their accommodation. There is a house of Ferns, and some of them are large enough to help one to understand the tree-forms of the early Geologic periods. There is a house of tropical water-lilies, and a perfect palace of glass appropriated to Palms.

There is a museum on the grounds which, however, I had not time to enter. Towers of different kinds, a pond and fountain, &c, adorn the grounds which are of very considerable extent.

We got into London in full time to keep an engagement I had to meet Bishop Janes at the R.R. station on his arrival from Paris. The English rail roads, and stations, deserve a chapter in somebody's book of travels. They are wonderful in completeness, decidedly the most perfect of any I have seen, and [p. 4] evidently perfected at immense expense. At this London-bridge station, for example, there is a great area, right in the heart of London, where the trains have ample room to run in, each line having its own place, and running in on one side of a long & sufficiently broad foot-way, right on the other side of which the cabs are standing, as one has but to get out of the car, finds plenty of porters ready to attend to his baggage (that is, to go with him to get it, for there are no checks), or if he has no baggage, he takes three steps into a cab just opposite the door of the car. But it must be seen to be appreciated.

Bishop Janes, at Mr. Lycett's invitation, came home with us and has gone off this morning on a tour thro' the city, I remaining at home with the agreeable company of a diarrhoea for a change.

I don't regret it, as it will probably relieve the biliousness from which I have been suffering lately.
Yours affectionately,
Andrew

Later in the day, Andrew toured the West End, Hyde Park, and Regent's Park. The next day, Sunday, he preached in Highbury Chapel at the eleven o'clock service; on Monday he went shopping for books, music, and "stereoscopic views." He went to the South Kensington Museum and then called on a friend at the reading room of the British Museum, a "superb circular room." On Wednesday, he left London for Ryde, Isle of Wight, where the William S. Moores were his hosts. Together they toured Carisbrooke Castle and other points of interest on the island. His friends from Paris, the Munroes and the Danas, were also at Ryde. The drive back to the Moores' was "of great enjoyment, the setting sun, soft summer air, and beautiful scenery" (MS Diary, July 27-August 1, 1861).

Ryde, Isle of Wight
August 1, 1861
[LETTER 46]

My dear Jim,

Yours of July, accompanying one from Eliza, & another from Reese Alsop,[1] gave me much pleasure, altho' so short. Just such glimpses of summer travel and plans of different kinds abridge the distance from me to you. And particularly, I must thank you for that faint gleam of a visit from you and Father to this side of the ocean next spring. Your figures I think are quite too low, as they scarcely cover the item of steamship expense, but for the benefit accruing, or certain to follow, I think you might set your mark somewhat higher. To Father, if he could obtain leave of absence, and taking in view the benefit to be obtained by a visit to the mints of France and England, I should think he could easily manage that. The expense would hardly be a consideration, as of course he would not care for the house at home to be kept open during his [p. 2] absence, and Eliza's board (unless she came with him, which I think ought to be the case) would be a trifle compared with the regular home expenses. Indeed, I think Father might even come himself and bring Eliza, and yet lay up money the same year, as he is now free from all expense except for himself and her, with his salary remaining the same. But I suppose these are matters more in his province than ours. I will only say this, that if Dr. McC[lintock] should leave Paris and I remain, I will cheerfully and only <u>too</u> gladly make Eliza's visit of no expense to Father, beyond the passage money or travelling expenses. Her <u>living</u> here shall be my affair. I only regret that I am not rich enough to make the same offer to you and to him.

From some things that have recently come to my knowledge, I fear the affairs of our Chapel are not likely to improve much for some time to come. The depressing influences that affect people at home must be felt very keenly by our people here. Whether any serious result is to be apprehended or not, I [p. 3] cannot say.

Aug. 2nd. Providence has certainly smiled most approvingly on my visit to the Isle of Wight. The weather has been delightful beyond description. The long, golden, glorious yesterday I can never forget. Sea air never was so soft, and a northern sea never looked so blue. The country itself is beautiful, and our ride thro' it of 13 miles, going along the cliffs on the coast of Brading, Sandown, Shanklin and Shanklin Chine, Bonchurch to Ventnor seem[ed] to combine more varied beauties than in any ride I ever took before.

We stopped to go into the quaint old church at Brading with its ancient tombs, and in the grave-yard the gravestone of "Little Jane" whom Legh Richmond[2] has immortalised. Brading too is the neighborhood of the Dairyman's daughter. We climbed up the romantic glen of Shanklin Chine, stopping here and there in delight at its wildness and enjoying at other points the look-out over the sea.

After a very merry time with Mrs. Munroe & family & Mrs. Dana, dinner, and a delightful ramble, Mr. & Mrs. Moore and I drove quietly back [p. 4] to Ryde as the sun was setting and the long luxurious twilight came on. The twilight here you know is much longer than at home, and last evening it was wonderfully soft and beautiful. The Isle of Wight combines so much, the sea, and right upon it, down to the edges of the white cliffs, the most luxuriant cultivation, with trees & gems of gardens where fuschias live out all winter and grow to be quite large trees.

To-day, I must leave this Fairy-land, after a visit so short yet of so much enjoyment.

I have been away long enough to look forward to the quiet and regularity of my Paris life with a good deal of pleasure, much more than I had dreamed of. It is well to find pleasure at both ends of one's travels, the going & the returning—mine has had pleasure all along besides. I can only wish your sea-shore experiences may be as pleasant as my glimpses of England, Ireland & Wales.[3] God bless you, my dear boy,

Yours affectionately,

Andrew

On Friday, August 2, 1861, in a heavy rain, Andrew left the Isle of Wight for Southampton, where he found the Munroes waiting. They walked about the town and dined before Andrew took the boat for Le Havre. "A very rough night—many sick. I escaped" were Andrew's diary comments. He arrived at Le Havre the next morning, had breakfast at the Hotel de l'Europe, walked about the town and the quai before boarding the train for Paris, "A fine day, beautiful ride."

Sunday, August 4, was filled with church duties. In the evening, "Sad news from home; the shameful defeat at Manassas Junction." Monday, August 5, was devoted to writing letters. On Tuesday, August 6, Emory McClintock returned from Göttingen, Germany, where he had been studying chemistry. Andrew made another visit to the Louvre "thro' galleries of the French painters." His correspondence with James resumes the next day (MS Diary, August 2-6, 1861).

Paris
August 7, 1861

[LETTER 47]

My dear Jim,

Your letter with notice of the defeat at Bull's Run[1] I rec'd on Tuesday. We had news of the defeat on Sunday evening—a telegram to Mr. Munroe.

There is no use of making any remarks on it. All we can do is to hope for better tidings soon. In the meanwhile, if some body would burn, buy or shut up the New York *Tribune*, it would be a national blessing. Any man who takes such an occasion as this to lower confidence in the executive, merely to gratify his own personal malice, ought to be—well, I won't say what, but something awful. The English papers, on the whole, are more moderate than I had ventured to hope for.

You have doubtless heard from Father that there is again a prospect of my coming home. This time, it comes more gradually and I think more surely. The facts are simply these. Dr. McC[lintock] is going to stay and he can't afford to keep me with him. There is a talk of my being asked to preach next winter [p. 2] in Rome. But the prospect is very slight for a support there. It would be very pleasant, especially if I could, in the meanwhile, run over home for a few weeks. On the whole, the present prospect is that I shall set my face homeward sometime next month. If the *Fulton* sails in September, I shall try to arrange to come by her.

Since I got back, we have had, or rather are having, real summer weather, such as I have not seen since I left America. The days are clear and bright and still, just like some of our midsummer days. The evenings were quite warm, but last night it was quite refreshingly cool. I find myself a little oppressed by the heat, more however because of some internal disarrangement than from the mere "outside pressure."

The streets are full of imposing preparations for the fête of the 15th.[2] Great frameworks are rising around the Arc de Triomphe, as if permanent structures were to be erected & not the mere [p. 3] staging for the illumination of a single night.

Emory McClintock, who has been at Göttingen since last March, came home yesterday morning with his health very much improved. He has been studying chemistry and at the same time has been careful to keep up the physical part of his education.

This morning, we have another arrival, a Miss Lamb from Chicago, a friend of the family, who crossed in a sailing vessel in thirty days. So we are pretty full.

Our crowd comes at an odd time. Dr. McC[lintock] gives up his house at the end of this month and we must seek other quarters. Please remember this and address hereafter (care of Jno. Munroe, 5 rue de la Paix). However, you won't have to mind this very long. In a few weeks I hope to send you word to discontinue writing in view of my speedy return.

Of course, the Dr.'s conclusion to remain here another year knocks in [p. 4] the head my suggestions about Eliza's coming. For her sake, and yours, and Father's, I almost wish I was to stay. But on many accounts I shall feel better to be at home, in the regular work once more. This half-work don't suit me, now that I feel well enough to do full service. When a man gets to be <u>thirty</u>, he hardly can feel at ease in a <u>junior</u> position. Of course, if it were my duty, if I felt it so, I should stay. But as it appears that the way will be open for other service, I am not sorry to go.

As soon as I can find a friend who knows anything of Meerschaums,[3] I will get one for Thad. I wish tho' that he had made some suggestions as to style of casing, &c. I shall have to consult my own taste & run the risk of not pleasing him. I hear that they are to be had here for all prices from one franc to thousands.

Love to all,

Your affectionate bro[ther],

Andrew

[P.S.] Enclosed find letters to Eliza and Orly.

Dear Jim,

We are having real American August weather. I do not remember to have felt the heat more at home than I have done here for the last week. Today, I have been out in it for several hours so I can speak understandingly. Dr. McClintock and I have been out to secure my berth on the voyage home. For some days I had thought of sailing on the *Great Eastern* on the 10th of next month, but when I found it would go from Liverpool, and that they had no arrangement for carrying my heavy baggage thither, I gave up the idea. It is much more simple and direct to go to Havre, which will avoid all the trouble and expense of hotels and changes, as I can leave here in time to take the steamer the same day by taking the night line from Paris.

On Tuesday last, I got your letter of the 22nd *ult* with tidings of our defeat,[1] and on Friday later news from Father.

We have full files of papers, and I am [p. 2] as much as ever indebted for Phila[delphia] ones. I feel tho' as if I did not wish to see or hear anything more from America until the rebels have been thoroughly defeated. The work of organizing, and especially of getting decent officers, must be a slow one, I suppose. We can hope for nothing from the men when those who command them are so utterly worthless as too many proved to be at Manassas. We can only live in hope of "better luck next time."[2]

Sometimes, when I think of coming home and finding things so changed, the figure and color of the whole people altered from a nation at peace to a nation at war, there are misgivings and regrets that crowd into my mind which I cannot express. A strange reluctance seizes me. Will it seem like home to me? Is it really the dear country I left smiling and happy but little more than a year ago? How will the change seem to me? The uniforms in [p. 3] the streets, the papers teeming with war news, the people everywhere all excited, absorbed, occupied with one topic. Will it not seem strange?

My mind generally, however, dwells on another picture. I think of home, not as a country but as one city, one or two houses, and the people in them, with all the familiar amusements and pleasures of old times, old walks and drives. Your violin and Eliza at the piano. True, Orly has gone, but then there is not so much to dread for him on the sea as there would be on the land. I am very very thankful that as yet this fearful strife has not cast over us the dark shadow of personal loss, as well as public calamity. We can be happy together in spite of the war.

It seems almost as if any happiness were wrong when our land is the scene of so fearful a strife. But I rather think we may and ought to take what blessings are vouchsafed to us [p. 4] thankfully.

Nothing is going on here but the gigantic preparation for the fête next Thursday.[3] The illuminations will be something far beyond anything yet attempted here.

Unless the weather should become cooler, I fear there may be many fatal cases of sunstroke, as multitudes will expose themselves on that day to share in the general festivities.

I am happy to say that notwithstanding the increasing heat I am getting better. After a week of dysenteric pains, I am now free from them, and feel better than I have done all summer. Perhaps the use of some Mercurius in Homeopathic doses has something to do with my improvement.

You dear old fellow, how glad I shall be to get a sight of your face once more. I think I have learned to appreciate home-folks as I never did before.

Yours affectionately,

Andrew

Dear Jim,

This afternoon I went out on a long shopping tour, and among other things I bought the Meerschaum [pipe] for Thad Webb. I am half afraid he will not like my selection, but after thinking what I should choose and wondering what his taste would be, I concluded to buy what accorded best with my own. So I got a plain pipe, with no carving, but of an elegant shape; the simple white bowl and a curved amber mouth-piece cost 31 francs. For 40 f[ranc]s I could have got a nicely carved Zouave's head, but they are very common, lining the windows of almost all the tobacco shops. Were I a smoker myself, the one I have bought would have been my choice. I hope it will please Thad. I am sorry he did not make some suggestions as to the shape or style. It is too late now to wait for advices.

Aug. 19th. I have been thinking over the matter of Thad's pipe, and have almost concluded to go change this one for another, a carved Zouave's head at 40 f[ranc]s. I will let you know more about it. [p. 2] I am in doubt about getting for you the photographic machine. I see that it takes a great deal of experimenting to get acquainted with the business. The instrument itself is good, but I doubt if you would have time to use it. Emory McClintock has just got one. If he succeeds in making a good picture before I leave, I will get an instrument. If he does not, I will take it as evidence that it would not be worth while getting it.

After two weeks of oppressively hot weather, it has been somewhat cooler yesterday and today, for which everybody who has anything to do cannot but feel thankful.

This is a mean specimen of a letter to send in return for your last long one. But somehow I have nothing to say today. There is nothing going on in Paris, except that people are still going out of it. The last clearances for the summer take place this week. Two or three families will go to-morrow. You shall hear from me soon again. You know you need not write after the lst of September—<u>unless by the *Persia*</u>.

Your loving brother, Andrew

[P.S.] I enclose letters to Eliza & Reese Alsop.[1]

Dear Jim,

It hardly seems worth while to write when I am hoping so soon to see you. However, it is well to keep up the line of communication. I shall have a break of some ten or eleven days at least, but you need have none. My letters will reach you to within a day or two of my own arrival.

After several considerings of the point, I have concluded to return the <u>plain pipe</u> which I bought for Thad. It strikes me as decidedly more elegant than any but the most expensive carved ones that run up to 100, 200 or 300 francs and even more. Fine work commands fine prices in Paris.

As to your pictures, I will do the best I can. Unfortunately, I have less money than I thought I should have and so cannot go very largely into purchasing. I have not seen the "Battle of the Malakhoff"[1] of which you [p. 2] speak, but there are some good battle pictures to be had, and I may get you one.

Paris
August 17, 1861

[LETTER 49]

Paris
August 29, 1861

[LETTER 50]

So far, this week, that is Monday, Tuesday & Wednesday, I have been too much an invalid to do anything of any account. To-day, tho' better, I am feeling quite unlike going out and exerting myself. But I have only three days more here, and I must use them. How I wish I had your cheering voice and vigorous arm to support and encourage me. It is so desolate, going out to look at things alone, or to buy things alone. I am altogether a baby about it, I know, but I can't help it for all that.

I hope I shall be fatter and stronger before I reach home. Just at present, I am as thin and weak as I was a year and a half ago.

Excuse this short epistle. I am too weak & have too much to do to write a longer or better one.
Yours faithfully,
Andrew

The McClintocks had been looking toward finding another place to live, and on August 22 Andrew went "with the young ladies" to look at an "appartment" at 3, rue de la Plaine, which McClintock subsequently leased. In the meantime, he moved the family to a "summer resting-place" at 3, Boulevart du Roi, Versailles, "a grand old apartment on the third floor containing ten rooms thoroughly furnished with old style French furniture—everything comfortable and nice. No carpets: some of the floors are waxed, others are tiled, but all as clean as a pin. Clocks in almost every room—and very elegant ones, too—writing desks, and, in fact, every convenience" (Crooks, p. 305).

They lived in Versailles through the week; on Sundays, Andrew and McClintock took the train into the city to perform their official duties at the Chapel. By the middle of September, however, Andrew was beginning to go into town earlier and spending Saturday nights in Paris at the Edgertons', former next-door neighbors, as his arrangement with McClintock for living accommodations had drawn to a close.

Versailles
September 4, 1861

[LETTER 51]

My dear Jim,

Yours of the 17th I got yesterday. It came out to me from Paris. You have already heard of my disappointment, if it may be called so, in not getting off in the *Great Eastern*. Eliza or Father has told you of the proposition Mr. Alexander Van Rensselaer[1] made in his letter from Geneva, which I rec'd last Sunday. I answered it yesterday. I told him how gladly I would accept it, that there was no duty in the way—only, I had no money and could not undertake anything that needed any. I said this plainly tho' delicately. What he meant by his invitation, whether it will be possible for me to accept it, remains to be seen. I shall stay here until I hear further from him. I try not to think much about it preferring to have no more disappointments if I can help it.

I am not sorry to be out here. The change of air is very great, and I fancy I am better already for it. Decent drinking water [p. 2] would be a wonderful addition to the comforts of Paris[2] and of all the "region round about."[3] Except this one drop of bitter in the cup of Versailles existence, one could be happy and comfortable here if anywhere. The palace, a vast museum of paintings and sculpture, the park and gardens, and the palaces of the "Grand" and "Petit Trianon," afford study and pleasure for much longer than the short month Dr. McClintock expects to spend here.

Whether I shall stay as long as he does is, of course, not settled and cannot be till I hear what Mr. Van Rensselaer expects.

Have I ever spoke of him in my letters to you? I must have done so for his friendship has been one of the cheering things in my life on this side of the ocean. He was kind from the first, used to call upon me in the rue de l'Arcade and, until he left Paris, never failed to do all that was kind to me that came in his way. Before Dr. McC[lintock] came out, he asked me to go to Russia with him. At Rome, he was exceedingly kind, and gave me a pretty little souvenir when I left of a set of studs & sleeve buttons in [p. 3] Roman gold. He is, I should judge, somewhere near forty years old, rather over than under that, very pious, gentle, quiet and affectionate with, as far as I can judge, a remarkably even temper. Of course, he is a cultivated and refined gentleman as he was born and brought up so. He has never had any profession, I believe. Sometime last fall or in the winter, he was engaged to be married (he is a widower without children[4]) to a Miss DuPuy, with whom he travelled, her aunt, Mrs. Wurtz, being of the party. She is very handsome, and young, not twenty. He writes me that the engagement is broken, and report says, by her, which I can readily believe. They are hardly fitted to be happy together. She is too gay, but she is a great dunce not to love a man who is one among thousands.

When I was in Rome last winter, he told me that if he could control matters he would be married by me then and there. It is better, I guess, as it is. It would have been miserable to find out afterwards that he was not loved, and that, as I suspect was the case, [p. 4] Miss DuPuy had married him because he was "a good match" and to please her aunt, on whom she is quite dependent.

Here I am giving you a whole account of my friend's affairs in true gossip style. I hope you are edified.

You speak of the possible loss of your check sent to Mr. Baker. I don't think you need be alarmed. His numbers are (for he has <u>two fronts</u>) 142 Water – 183 Pearl Sts.—that is, if I am not mistaken. You can easily settle it by looking at a New York directory if you have not heard from him by this time.

As to the funds of yours in my hands, I have spent, since I wrote to you, 31 f[ranc]s for Thad Webb's Meerschaum, & 44 [francs] for photographic pictures, large size—among [them] the "Taking of the Malakhoff" which you mentioned. Whether I shall be able to devote to you the remainder from the very small allowance I am likely to have, I can't say, but I will buy nothing more for you at present. If I go on that Eastern tour, I have no doubt there will be little occasional odds & ends in which it [p. 5] might be agreeably, if not profitably, invested.

When I wrote about my readiness to use that amount for you over here, I had in prospect a stated salary of ten dollars a week (beside my board) from Dr. McClintock.[5] That is all over now, and I should be utterly without funds, had it not been for a very handsome gift I received the other day after baptising a little girl—twenty-five dollars in sovereigns.[6] This will at least keep me till I hear from Mr. Van Rensselaer, as my tailor's bill can wait for several months. As Dr. McClintock will pay for my passage home, when I go, I am not anxious, tho' the sum I named is rather a paltry one to have to live on. However, Dr. McC[lintock] thinks that my services are quite worth my board, at which rate, indeed, he would be willing to keep me as long as I chose to say— so I shall try to live according to the commandment, taking "no thought for the morrow."[7] My way has been opened marvellously up to this present time, and I shall not now begin to fear that I shall be forsaken. [p. 6]

I sent by Mrs. Baker two pictures to Balto [Baltimore] ordered before I came to Paris, which will bring me fifty-five or sixty-dollars sometime, at least I hope so. So if I should not be able to spend anything on your account over here, more than I have done already, I think you will be safe in trusting me. However, I hardly think you need assurances of that sort. I said it rather to finish the "exposé" of my financial affairs that I was giving than for anything else.

You must save all you can this winter as if <u>I stay</u>. I shall want you and Father to come over next spring as you talked of doing some time ago. I know it would be good for you and it would add a dozen years to Father's life. It would make him young again. If you two come, Betsy ought to. However, we cannot tell what may occur by that time. It is too far ahead to look at in these times of commotion.

Yours faithfully & affectionately,
Andrew Longacre

Versailles
September 19, 1861

[LETTER 52]

Dear Jim,

My hand is so tired that I take up a half-sheet so as not to be tempted to write too much. Don't think it, however, a mark of special weakness. It only comes from writing a good deal. As to my health generally, I am "getting better fast." For the last week I have felt like a new being, better a great deal than for months before. I sincerely hope it will last. The pure air of Versailles is enough to make anyone feel well.

I am very glad, as you may suppose, that you sent off those last letters from Eliza and Orly. They are the last, I suppose, that I shall have for a week or two, owing to the unfortunate alteration of my plans at such short notice. As it was quite unavoidable, however, it is folly to grieve over it. Another time, I think, I shall not send word to stop writing. Who can tell, however, when that <u>other time</u> will come? The probability is too far away to speak of.

Altho', of course, I am glad of the opportunity to go to the East, I feel keenly the disappointment of not going home. The *Fulton* sailed from Havre yesterday; [p. 2] in a few days, less than two weeks, she will be at New York, and I think I might have been on board of her! Ah well! I must be resigned; and it ought not to be [or] require extraordinary virtue to be resigned with such a prospect as there is before me. Yet – yet – one glimpse of home, and of dear home faces would be marvellously comforting. Living in other people's homes, and with other people's families, is a very different thing from one's <u>own</u>.

I was thinking the other day of the music I asked you to send to Miss Warner, thro' Mrs. Olin, was it not?—"We would see Jesus"—and I wondered if you ever had received any acknowledgement of it? If you have, you never told me of it.

I enclose with this letters to Eliza and Orly. I suppose you send to Orly regularly. Do you know where he is now? Dr. McC[lintock] says his vessel has left its place at the mouth of the Savannah.

From late news the navy is looking up. After a long repose, it is stirring itself to take part in this war. I hope it may always be as successful as in this first blow.[1]

Your affectionate brother,
Andrew Longacre

Dear Jim,

Whether I wrote to you or to Father last, I cannot remember, but as I have some special things to say to you, I think I will address you this time at any rate.

Yesterday, I saw Mr. Van Rensselaer. He had written to me saying that he expected to be in Paris on the 25th. I went into town as it was the National fast-day, and we were to have service in the Chapel. I called upon him as soon as I could and he went with me to church. Afterwards, I took lunch with him, and then he took me first to the Tailor's, then to the shoe-maker's and finally to the hatter's, ordering all the things I should want on our tour. He was exceedingly kind in everything, and seemed to take this, which I had not expected, as a matter of course.

His kindness and thoughtfulness will save me from an outlay which would have involved me a good deal in my present shortness of funds. I have but a hundred francs to take with me on my journey. What I shall [p. 2] have occasion for more than this, I must borrow from Mr. V[an] R[ensselaer]. There will doubtless be times when I shall want to get little things, mementos, &c. It is probable, therefore, that I shall want to borrow about a hundred dollars from you. Already, I shall need fifty to discharge some debts I have had to incur. I shall not need it for some time, however, and shall give you full warning. It will probably be in April or May next. When I can repay you is, of course, uncertain, but I don't think that will trouble you as much as it will me.

Want of money is a bad thing, but it seems marvellous to me how Providence opens my way without it. I have had a salary for only about three months of the time I have been in Europe, and yet, I have been well cared for for five times three months and am likely to be for some time longer.

"The young lions do lack and suffer hunger, but they that wait upon the Lord shall not want any good thing"[1]—Something like that the Bible says and certainly my life is a striking sermon [p. 3] on that text.

There was a meeting last evening in one of the French Protestant Churches, the Chapelle Taitbout,[2] in behalf of America, that is, to pray for our deliverance from our present troubles. It was well attended, quite a crowd, almost all French, a few English, and a very few Americans. Dr. Baird was there. Pasteur Fisch, one of the French ministers who has lately been in the United States, spoke to me after the service, of his having preached several times for my cousin, Dr. Willetts. I didn't recognize the title, but I was very glad to own up to the cousinship, and I let the "Doctor" pass. I think I'll write to Alphonso some of these days tho' I had not thought of it before.

Mr. Van Rensselaer is anxious to get out of Paris as speedily as possible, and it is possible we may start a week from to-day. I am beginning to fear I shall have to go letter-less as I can hardly hope to hear from you until that day. Possibly the mail of next Tuesday may bring me something. This disarranging of my [p. 4] plans has had at least one inconvenience, that of putting me out of reach of you completely for a while. I want very much to hear something from you about what you think of my Oriental tendencies. To have the expectation confined to myself alone is not at all satisfactory. It feels lonesome and contracted. I do want to hear some of you folks say how glad you are for me, and how the thought of such an opportunity makes you willing to do without seeing me for some months longer.

One thing that I heard yesterday makes the whole matter seem more providential than ever. Mr. Van Rensselaer told me that he had not heard that I meant to go home soon, at the time he wrote his letter, but only generally and that he thought he would write then as it came into his mind. Had he left it one day later, it would have been too late, and I should have been with the frightened crowd on the *Great Eastern*. Does it not seem as if God took care of me? I hope to be more faithful to him than I have ever been.

Your affectionate brother,
Andrew Longacre

Paris
October 8, 1861

[LETTER 54]

My dear Jim,

Your kind letter of the 24th *ult* has just reached me, and tho' it is too late for my reply to go by this mail, yet as I have time now, and may not have it again, I will write something in reply at once. Coming home, a few moments ago, I found a note from Mr. Van Rensselaer saying we would not go to-morrow but the next day. Altho' this is the third little postponement, in all not quite covering a week, it suits me very well, as I have not packed up yet and, besides, have two or three visits to pay so that I should have had hard work to get ready by to-morrow, and in my rather reduced state, hard work does not agree with me.

I don't know whether you have noticed in my recent letters home how many things that have occurred to me lately seem to indicate peculiarly the care of my Heavenly Father. To-day, another thing of the kind has occurred, from the surprise of which I have not yet recovered. As I wrote you in my last to you, [p. 2] I found myself pretty destitute of money. Mr. Van Rensselaer's kindness & Dr. McClintock's had relieved me of some care in the matter, but still I had many little expenses which I found it hard to meet & in fact I have borrowed $30 from Dr. McClintock so as not to be entirely without funds in travelling. I went today to obtain the cash for Dr. McC[lintock]'s check and after doing so spoke a few words to Mr. Munroe. He asked me to sit a few moments and presently a clerk brought him a letter of credit for a thousand francs, drawn in my name, and which he signed & asked me to sign & then gave to me, saying that I would no doubt want to get little things here and there in my travels, and he hoped this sum would help me to do so. You may imagine how I felt. I hardly knew what to say. It was the largest sum I ever received as a gift, and was quite beyond what I would think it right to spend on the little things he spoke of. See how God takes care of me! Mr. Munroe has always been very <u>very</u> kind. Within a month he has presented [p. 3] me with two dozen bottles of a wine he thought would be good for me, and more than that, his manner has always been kinder than I can tell you altho' he is a quiet man and talks but little.

I heard a little thing today which gave me pleasure. You will pardon the repeating a compliment for it is not a common one. A Mr. Richard Hunt, lately come to Paris, whom I like amazingly, has taken a reciprocal fancy for me, so his wife says (they are both young, only been married six months). He said he was very sorry that I was going away from Paris, and that if I were settled over a church in the Latin quarter (where the students reside) he was sure they would cut off their hands before they would let me go. You know I have always had a yearning toward that same Latin quarter, and as Mr. Hunt has been a student here for several years of his life, his verdict, given so earnestly, has pleased me a good deal.

You must not think I am getting vain [p. 4] because I say this. It may lead me, or help to lead me, into some path of duty in the future.

I suppose I need hardly say that with Mr. Munroe's princely gift, I shall not need to ask you to send over the hundred dollars I threatened to borrow of you. It seems as if God had brought me here and that he means to provide for me while I stay. I dare not be anxious. With so many instances of his love around me, coming so wonderfully without effort, & even often without prayer (tho' I did pray about my poor little exhausted purse the other day), I can only dismiss every anxiety and submit to be led by my Heavenly Father from one blessing to another. Pray that he will add to all his blessings yet one more & give me grace to live & serve him more faithfully than I have ever done.

> "Perpetual blessings from his hand
> Demand perpetual songs of praise."[1]

My last day in Paris, the last for some time, that is, is coming to a close. I [p. 5] have been pretty busy getting a few last things and making a few final calls. Among other things I went to Ken's[2] and got some additional photographs, feeling able to lay out five dollars on the strength of Mr. Munroe's timely and liberal gift of yesterday. I will enclose two of them in this to you, and a third, for Cousin Cordelia Miles, who asked Father to get her one. If you will hand it to Father for her, I shall be obliged to you. The cost of the letter will be somewhat augmented, but I suppose you can submit to that.

A word about letters. In writing to me after your receipt of this, and during the rest of this month on to the middle of November, you may address: care of <u>Tod Rathbone & Co., Cairo, Egypt.</u> After that, unless you hear from me, send to Munroe & Co., Paris. You can enquire if there is any peculiar precaution necessary in sending to Egypt, but I don't suppose there is. Please let the folks at home know of this, for it is just as easy for you to send my letters there as for Mr. Munroe. [p. 6]

We start tomorrow morning and sleep at Bordeaux, going on the next day to Biarritz, where we will stay till Monday, on which day or the day following, we shall make our <u>entrée</u> into Spain.[3] I shall take such occasions as I can find to write of our progress, but I hardly think you would like the expensive luxury of very frequent letters. I want to keep a pretty full journal of the whole tour, & you must wait till I come home for the full particulars.

I have already written to Eliza about not sending letters oftener than once in two weeks for I shall get them in bundles even at that rate, as in travelling it is quite impossible to have letters coming just when you want them, and we shall only have two or three depots where they will accumulate & await our arrival. Cairo will be the chief one.

May God bless & keep us both.

Your affectionate brother,

Andrew Longacre

The travelers left Paris on October 10, bound for Bordeaux. From Orleans onward, Andrew found "beautiful country, well wooded and watered." Tennyson's Idylls of the King *occupied him on the long train ride. The next day they went on to Bayonne and then by omnibus to Biarritz, where they arrived in time to take a walk on the shore, "a smooth beach with high broken rocks full of minute fossils. . . . Good bathing houses in gaudy Moorish style." Over the next four days Andrew went swimming, painted several seascapes, and he and Van Rensselaer attended Sunday servic-es in the English church, "a good congregation, perhaps 100, the church plain, neat and evidently new" (MS Diary, October 10-16, 1861).*

Biarritz
October 16, 1861

[LETTER 55]

Dear Jim,

I have just come from the bath and feel a little too luxuriously languid to dress right away, so I spend a few moments in writing. It seems funny to speak of sea-bathing the middle of October, but so it is. From my open window I see now a merry group of bathers, and tho' I went in early myself for the time of year, about 8 o'clock, yet the water was no cooler than in the early bath at Cape May.[1] Later in the day, I have no doubt from the intense heat of the sun, it is as warm as it is with us in July and August. They say indeed that the warm weather here lasts till Christmas.

I have enjoyed the four or five days here exceedingly and think they have been of solid benefit to my health. With a good deal of journeying before me, I am really thankful for a little recruit-ing of nature's languid forces before I fairly begin it. During the past summer I had become pret-ty well run down in Paris, successive attacks of diarrhoea had left me hardly any strength, so that my duties at the American [p. 2] [Chapel] tho' not at all arduous were often a heavy burden. I got a little better at Versailles, but was[2] ill again as soon as I got back to Paris. I am not yet quite sure of myself. Thanks to Doctor Beylord's[3] prescriptions, I steer clear of actual breaking down, but I am not yet independent of the remedy. However, I hope for wonders from my travel this winter. With no care, nothing to do, and going no faster than is agreeable, with good mingling of rail-road, steamer, and diligence,[4] if not on <u>mules</u> also, I shall have variety enough to keep from fatigue. Today we are to start from Bayonne in the diligence and travel all night across the lower Pyrennes to Pampeluna[5] in Spain. It will be bright moonlight most of the time which is a great comfort. We shall not stay at Pampeluna at all, but go on to-morrow to Saragossa, and it may be the next day to Barcelona, where we shall remain two or three days, as there is a good deal to be seen.

Excuse my short letter this time, and keep me informed of things at home, especially of army matters, as papers <u>had better not be sent</u>.

Yours affectionately,

Andrew

They left Biarritz on Wednesday, October 16, traveling back to Bayonne by omnibus and then taking a diligence for "Pampeluna." They "rode through a beautiful country à Espellete," where they "changed [their] style of equipage for the Spanish, 8 mules and a horse, the latter ridden by a light postillion—15 years [old]." At Sandibar, they found the customhouse "rigid to a ridiculous

extent in its search." Arriving at Pamploma, they visited the cathedral, the cloisters of which Andrew thought "very beautiful, more so than any I have ever seen." Later, while sailing up the Nile, Andrew began "a little drawing of the cloisters at Pampeluna," which he finished on New Year's day (MS Diary, December 26, 1861; January 1, 1862).

From Pamplona they traveled to Saragossa, where Andrew made a sketch of the cathedral, La Seo and El Pilar. Their route to Barcelona took them "through the kingdom of Aragon, a desolate region," and then through beautiful valleys and picturesque villages." At Barcelona Mr. Van Rensselaer gave Andrew a Roman Catholic prayer book. On Sunday, October 20, Andrew "began a little book of meditations." The next day and a half were spent seeing local sights before taking the overnight steamer, Catalan, to Valencia. On landing, they had to take one of the "peculiar carriages." In his diary, Andrew made a tiny sketch of this strange vehicle (see note 1, below). They visited churches, the botanical gardens, the museum—and Andrew bought a Spanish dictionary. The next day they took the overnight train to Madrid (MS Diary, October 16-25, 1861).

Dear Jim,

Pardon me for beginning on a half sheet, but the size of my letter of descriptions to Eliza for the family compels me to it, as otherwise I should overstep the weight and so have double postage to pay, for I believe they won't take unpaid letters. The letters I do send are utterly unsatisfactory to myself and the way really to read them to give them even what little weight they have is to have some of the printed Guide books at hand at the time. There is a book of Starr's[?] in the library with fine illustrations on travels in Spain of which I am often reminded. Perhaps it would interest you to hunt it up and read it a little in connection with these scraps of mine. I am trying to keep fuller notes of this trip than I did in Italy last spring, and that with hours wasted now and then in bungling attempts at <u>sketching</u>, pretty well consumes the time I can take from the ordinary avocations of a traveller—for a traveller in earnest I begin to feel myself to be. If I learn nothing [p. 2] else of Spain, I shall know something of her different modes of conveyance from her nice little & still nicer big steamers to the funny Valentian one-horse carriage without springs, with the driver's seat on one of the shafts in close proximity to the horse's tail, whose motion on the rough roads of that famous old town can be better <u>felt</u> than described.[1] We are in Madrid, the <u>highest</u> capital in Europe, both above the level of the sea and above the level of <u>prices</u> in general and in particular. It is not like the rest of Spain, which is all <u>old</u>, either old Gothic or old Moorish, but like Barcelona, it is new and French with only Spanish modifyings in the application. The streets are gay, busy, of good width, and the air more like what Philadelphians would understand as the climate 40 [degrees] north latitude,[2] than the rest of Spain is. But further accounts by & by. I hope to have time to write up pretty well here as we make quite a halt after the hurry of the last ten days.

Yours faithfully,

Andrew

[*Written crosswise on p. 1*] Accept my best thanks for letters and papers which I found awaiting me at the Banker's when I called this morning. Surely letters have rarely been so welcome as these were. I began to feel that after all the old world is on the same globe as the new. What a strik-

Madrid
October 25, 1861

[LETTER 56]

ing coincidence that this thought should strike me in Spain—the country which started Columbus out in pursuance of the same bright thought and its results!!

I thought of the proud discoverer's return to Spain when I was at Barcelona, and I felt a thrill of pleasure in thinking that in the old cathedral & the church of Santa Maria del Mar I might be just where he had stood. You know he landed [written crosswise on p. 2] there and was received by Ferdinand and Isabella. How I felt on the Plaza de Inquisicione I need not say! Yours, if you can read—what I abominate—crossed-writing.

Andrew

My dear Jim,

Your letter of the 9th (I guess the date) was forwarded from Paris and reached me yesterday. You complain of my neglect in writing or, rather, in not writing to you. The simple fact of the case is this, that since the total change of my plans, all the regularity of my correspondence has been broken up. I think by this time you have had more satisfactory accounts from me, but I cannot promise much for the future. In travelling one must catch what time he can for such luxuries. The hurrying of a day, at any point, may put a week's letters out of place, postponing them indefinitely. Here at Madrid I am doing the best I can to fill up old gaps, but I do not count upon anything satisfactory in the letter line till our journey ends next Spring.

I am sure you will understand why I write my descriptive letters all to Eliza. It is, if possible, to keep them together, and she is the fittest person to receive them both because she is herself & because no one else can or will so [p. 2] readily give the rest the benefit of them. I have some wish that they should be kept, for tho' I make the effort, I find it is difficult to keep much private records of my journeyings, so I am depositing them with her for safe keeping & it may be for future reference.[1] My letters to her are really to all, and you must be good enough and forbearing enough to look out your portions generally in them. <u>Of course</u>, I shall write to you separately <u>when I can</u>, be sure of that.

We are getting on pretty well with our Spanish tour. At present we are making our chief halt this side of the Nile. Unfortunately, we are rather late in the season to find good weather in Madrid. The climate, as far as we can judge, is terrible. The morning air is damp, sharp & chilly and penetrates through & through one's poor lungs. Fires are unknown, at least <u>yet,</u> and all we can do is to "grin & bear it."

We feel it the more having come in a single night from the tropical atmosphere of Valencia, where oranges, figs, palms, & olives were growing [p. 3] luxuriantly, to this wintry mountain region. Madrid has not much of interest beside its gallery, and of that I have written enough both to Father and Sallie to show that it is a perfect mine of pleasure and profit, quite enough to atone for the loss of all other things.

We visited among other things yesterday, the <u>Armory</u>, a choice tho' not very large collection of arms & armor of much interest in themselves and for their history. We saw the swords of the Cid, of Boabdil, last king of the Moors, of Hernando[2] Cortez; the armor, shield, leather camp-bed & embossed plates used by the Emperor Charles V. But the object of greatest interest, as you may suppose, was the armor of Christopher Columbus, a really elegant suit engraved in black and silver. Near it was the full equipment for himself & his horse [and] of Cortez of plain polished steel. There were many beautiful shields and helmets of Moorish make, others superbly inlaid with gems and cameos, old fashioned guns, rich in gold & silver chasings, flags [p. 4] of different nations taken by Spain in the time of her glory when the armies of Charles V & Philip II ruled the world.

It was in those old days of glory that the rare collections of pictures was made. It was fortunate for Spain that there were monarchs of that old Austrian line of such taste as to turn their power in Europe to the gathering of such a collection that stands first among all the great galleries of the world.

I am surprised to find out how little I knew of Spain. In Italy my surprise was the other way, delight in recognizing so much which I had known. Here, all is new. Of all the pictures of this gallery, for instance, there are only a very few which I have seen engraved or copied. For that, I feel as if I wanted to enjoy them <u>all</u> I can <u>while</u> I can, so we go for the third time, again to the gallery today.

I think I shall enclose one to Sallie with this & some <u>stamps</u> for Saidee.[3]

Yours faithfully – *Semper Eadem*,

Andrew Longacre

Dear Jim,

Tho' I have just written one letter to you today, I feel like writing a little more, as I said nothing before on some points which seemed to weigh on your mind a good deal when you wrote your last letter.

You speak sadly of your circumstances and prospects.

Two or three things have come to mind in thinking about you (and I doubt if you know how much my thoughts are upon you), which I think may not come amiss to you, even from so far away. You must take them for what they are worth.

To begin. It is a bad time to begin (or to continue) to worry yourself about your small salary. When rich people are becoming poor, when poor ones grow poorer, when business generally is at a stand, when, in a word, the whole country is making an immense sacrifice for law and order, it is unfortunate that you undertake to deliberate on what a young man of eight and twenty ought to receive per annum. [p. 2]

In reference to other matters, it was once wisely said to me, "Never settle with the devil on a rainy day." To apply it to your case: don't settle with your Insurance Co. or with I. M. L. himself in a gloomy time. *Verbum sap &c.*[1]

Next, you fear you can never think of marrying without some change in your fortunes. I admit that is bad: but matters <u>might</u> be worse. Many a poor fellow now with young wife and little ones is living on a painfully reduced salary or even trying to bear to live on none at all. But you look at it wrongly. When you really want to marry any body, and the girl is worth having, you will see that it can be done <u>somehow</u>. The fact is, you are not in love. There is no one in the world you really want. You are calculating what sort of an establishment will or would tempt [you] into taking this or that individual on your hands. When you are so in love that you have to say so, and when you find that the saying so is not unpleasant to the other "party," you may begin to groan at the slow improvement of salaries. I am afraid, my dear Nephew, you are a long [p. 3] distance from that delightful consummation.

We are brothers, and both sons of our Pa. Don't be alarmed! Our time will come.[2]

Now a few words seriously.

Every life has its cares. Life always has. The future is secured to no one. There is not a man living but may be on the brink of changes more bitter than he ever dreamed of. The best schemes for success fail. The poorest often succeed. What can we do? Do you need that I reply?

The promises of God—old, forgotten, neglected as they are—are true. "The steps of a good man are ordered by the Lord."[3] "Godliness is profitable and all things having the promise of the life which now is and of that which is to come."[4]

God wants our whole hearts, our full service, and he will, if we are faithful to him, take the right care of us. I have tried it. In sadder & darker hours than you are ever likely to know, when put aside from active life, by a stroke that threatened to make me a life-long invalid, and that too when I had before renounced all hope of worldly wealth in consecrating myself to a [p. 4] profession to which I believed God had called me: in such a time I have put my cause into God's hands and I need not tell you how he has fulfilled his promise. He has not given me wealth, but he has given me all I needed, and even all that wealth itself could have gained for me, both of honor and of profit.

Of course, your way must be different from mine, but God is as willing to guide and order your life in its way as he is to guide mine. Only give it up faithfully to Him: "Casting all your care upon him for he careth for you."[5] Do simply your duty, to the full, every day & everywhere, and keep an eye thro' all, looking not to earthly chances but to his guidance, and He will care for you. Oh I wish you could know how absolutely true this is: how fully you may rely upon God for everything. "Be careful for nothing, but in every thing by prayer and supplication with thanksgiving, let your requests be made known unto God, and the peace of God" &c.[6]

May God lead you to that wonderful peace and abundantly bless you, prays

Your loving brother, Andrew

[El] Escorial, Nov. 1

I have seen the coffins of Charles V. and his gloomy son, Philip II.

Travel over the next three weeks included a side trip to Toledo before going to Alicante, then by sea to Malaga. After two days of sightseeing, Van Rensselaer and Andrew departed for Granada and its many sights, including the Alhambra which they visited several times during their stay.

On November 13, bound for Cordova, they began one of the most arduous portions of their entire trip. The first leg of the journey took them to Bailen. The mountainous terrain made progress difficult, and Andrew walked during the relays when the horses were changed because he

"suffered more than usual in riding." The picturesque descent in the moonlight reminded him of Mont Cenis. Passing through Jaen, they arrived at Bailen early the next morning.

Securing transportation out of Bailen was difficult. Both the mail coach and the diligence had no room, so they remained overnight only to find the early morning diligence had only one space available. Finally, they left Bailen "in a rude cart drawn by a poor mule and a worse horse." Andrew walked beside the cart almost the whole distance to Andujar, 16 miles, where they stopped for "a good dinner in a clean house." Onward they rode, slowly, often walking to keep warm, until they reached Villa del Rio in late afternoon. Here they found tolerable beds "at a genuine Spanish posada."

The next day they drove through Pedro Abad, the "country losing its hills," and trudged "footsore and weary" toward El Carpio until a diligence passed with two empty places. When they finally reached Cordova, Andrew's feet and ankles were in much pain from his tight-fitting gaiters. He was too lame the following day to leave the hotel, but by November 18, he was able to make a fast tour of the city before leaving in the late afternoon for Seville. From the train, he reported a "fine sunset, moonlight on the Guadalquivir."

The next morning, as had become their custom, they went to the cathedral, "but it was too dark to do any more than get an imperfect general impression of its immense size and grace." Andrew was surprised at how the Alcazar "nearly rivals the Alhambra." Two days were spent visiting museums, palaces, and gardens before departing for Cadiz. (MS Diary, October 29-November 21, 1861).

My dear Jim,

Once in a while you see a letter really does get your name at the beginning. If my thoughts were all letters, you might be surprised to find how often they came. In travelling more than at most other times I am apt to think of you. You seem in so many things the complement or finishing, the other half of myself that I feel a special need of you rather than of others. You are strong & I am weak; you are ready in accounts and money matters and I am bewildered by them. You seem to enjoy or at least to go over triumphantly the little troubles and strifes and pushings of travel while they appal[l] me from a distance. When they actually come, I work thro' them with a degree of equanimity. Then, and as important as any, you have always had a surprising patience and forbearance with your "big brother," and a loving sympathy for him and an esteem far beyond his deserving so that he cannot but feel upon travelling with others often and often how different Jim would act. If all these thoughts and others of the same kind could turn themselves into letters, you would be overwhelmed with postal favors. As it is, they come few and far between, few have tokens of a love to which paper & ink [p. 2, written crosswise against the page] are incapable of doing justice.

There is one thing in relation to my correspondence that I wish them to know at home. I shall trouble you with it. Letters directed as I have already said to Tod Rathbone & Co., Cairo, Egypt, will reach me until the middle or 20th of January: that is, I shall leave Cairo probably at that time. You can calculate on about four weeks transit from America to that place which will bring the time to about the 20th or 23rd of December as the latest date which it will be safe to send letters there. After that, you can send to J. DuChêne & Co., Beyrouth (as the French spell Beyrout). Whenever you feel in any doubt, just send to John Munroe & Co., Paris. Letters will always be forwarded to me by them, and I don't know but on the whole it would be best to send to them always. It will add a trifle to the expense for me (it will be less on your side, of course), but that is of small account. You can think the matter over and decide whichever way seems best to you.

I hope you have received my letters. I have been in some uncertainty with regard to some I wrote at Alicante[1] and which I particularly wished should carry safely. If when you write [p. 3] you would let me know the letters you have received, given by the names of the places where they were written, it would be a satisfaction. I have written very faithfully, indeed almost too much so for my limited time in the places we visit in Spain. In Madrid, for instance, I gave too much time to it and came away with regret leaving some things of moment unseen. We are likely to do the same here but from unavoidable want of time. I only begin my letter today and will conclude either at Cadiz or Gibraltar as I find time.

Cadiz
November 22nd

We are at last on the end of our Spanish tour. At this point the nearest to "dear home and native land" that I have occupied for some time. We bid "good-bye" to this kingdom for Gibraltar is rather a part of England than Spain. It is something of a relief to feel that so much of the journey is over. We have had our last of custom-houses and *octroi* searches at the entrance into every town. We have done with diligences and, except that short ride from Alexandria to Cairo, with rail-ways. The greater part of the travel that is before us must be by ourselves, independent of all the world in hired boats on the Nile and on horses in Syria. But I am more rejoiced that we are so near the end of our dull weather. For two [p. 4, written crosswise of the page] or three weeks, the weather has been gloomy enough, rainy and chilly at night. I have felt it a good deal, both in rheumatism and diarrhoea. I am hoping after this to be better every way. It is not a comfortable thing to be ill when travelling. Low spirits make but a poor *compagnon de voyage* and, besides, when one is as far from home as I am, it is very bad policy to become homesick, as I am sure to do when sick in other ways. It is yet too early to go to the Banker's or I should probably have to acknowledge the receipt of sundry letters from you and the rest of the family. Unfortunately, we have somewhat lengthened our time in Spain, so that there are probably your latest letters waiting me now at Cairo, where I ordered them to be sent after the 10th of this month. As I have not heard from home, however, for some three weeks, I shall not feel any extreme sadness in finding that my letters have not the latest possible date on them.

I cannot tell you how the sight of our own dear Atlantic once more draws me homewards; I look out on it from my window here spreading away to the West and almost forget the months that must elapse before I see it again. But, I hope that with improving health, the winter will pass rapidly away and that next May or at the latest June will see [me] with you all once more.

Your affectionate brother, Andrew

Andrew and Van Rensselaer left Seville on November 21 for Cadiz. "Fine views of the flat country of Andulusia, wet, rich, green but not picturesque." On November 22 Van Rensselaer gave Andrew "a Spanish copy of Don Quixote." *Two days later, before sunrise, they went on board the* San Servando *and sailed away from Cadiz. Through the day they passed Tangier and in late afternoon anchored off the coast of Algeria. The next morning, they crossed over to Gibraltar*

where they spent the day sightseeing and purchasing souvenirs. That night they went on board the Pera *bound for Alexandria, Egypt, by way of Malta.*

With calm seas, Andrew enjoyed the first part of the voyage, taking salt water baths, walking on deck, meeting pleasant company, reading. He liked Malta and its "fine Italian style of houses, clean and steep streets." On a ride into the countryside he found "the houses neatly built of stone, few trees, small fields divided by stone walls, old aqueducts."

Leaving Malta, "the weather became quite rough," which sent Andrew back to his berth for two days, quite ill "in a rough and rolling time." But when the steamer docked in Alexandria harbor, he had recovered his equilibrium and was back to normal. They checked in at the Hotel de l'Europe on the Grand Corniche and spent the day touring local sites, including Cleopatra's Needle and Pompey's Pillar, and enjoying the city and its "fine avenues of trees." The next morning, December 4, they left by train for Cairo (MS Diary, November 21-December 4, 1861).

Dear Jim,

I can't tell you how much I wish you were here. What I have seen today only <u>seeing</u> can show. Nothing I had read or seen in pictures had given me an idea of the reality nor will my words begin to impart it to you.

We left Alexandria this morning at 9 and had a long ride of seven hours to reach Cairo. How strange it seemed! and rushing over the rich and cultivated plains of the Delta, leaping over canals and the different mouth-branches of the Nile in a rail-way train. How the flocks of Abraham would have started off in fright! How Joseph would have stopped his chariot to gaze! How Pharaoh's daughter would have been terrified! And even Moses, fresh from the plagues of Egypt, might have thought the magicians had got ahead of him; and Ptolomy [sic] Philadelphus,[1] and Cleopatra, and even the conquering Amrou[2] himself would have stood aghast at such a spectacle. As it was, the simple Arabs only looked up from their donkeys or their heaps of corn husks with a grin, showing all their teeth at once, or indulged in some funny gestures like overgrown boys on a frolic. Over histories and memories, the dust of all ages since the [p. 2] the [sic] flood, on rushed our train; through cotton fields and rice fields and corn-fields, by mud villages and rude wells and groves of palms; keeping close by the common road for miles and miles, with all its picturesque groups of travellers, and then boldly leaping over a wide stream of the mighty Nile on a bridge of iron; on we came, an intense impersonation of the genius of this age of finished civilization, going on its work of human advancement, careless of the might or memory of the past.

There! I feel relieved. Now I shall settle down into a small amount of sober talk.

In the midst of all the amazing novelty of this really Oriental city, to find letters from home tho' so old as the 28th Oct., touched a spring of pleasure deeper than the things I saw. Having a little time this evening, I begin my letter which, however, will not go for several days.

As yet I have not seen much of Cairo; altho' as I had a pretty round about tramp to find my banker, I saw more than I had expected to do, so soon. As we were coming here on the train, I saw while we were at an hour's distance the lofty dome and slender minarets of the great Mosque,[3] and on the other side two dim triangles that I did not need to be told were the Pyramids. I did not think [p. 3] a great deal or look a great deal at the last. I felt as if they needed a special time of their own which I could not give them while so far off and with so many other things crowding into my eyes.

Tomorrow, the first business is to get a boat and a dragoman.[4] We may have several days here while these things are arranging, but we wish to start as soon as possible and shall leave the real sight-seeing here until our return.

And now, "Good-night"—but oh how I wish you were here!

Dec. 7th   Our letters must be finished tonight for the mail. What busy days these few have been since I began this letter! We have been chiefly occupied in getting ready for our sail up the Nile, and I believe are now pretty well prepared. It is a tremendously expensive business, but then, I do not carry the purse. The hire of the boat for six weeks, including the eight or ten Arabs that belong to it, is $450, and then there is to be hired the dragoman and cook and the expense of provisioning, which here is enormous. The many other items I have not begun to look at. Of course, people can do it all more cheaply. Boats can be hired for about half what we pay, but [p. 4] ours is the fastest on the Nile and one of the most complete. There is about as much difference between the different ones as there is between different houses in a city. We have the pleasantest boat we could find, tho' it is not the most luxurious, nor is it as large as some. It is amply large for us, and we are not sorry that it is not larger as there have not been wanting applicants for any spare room we may have. In my letter to Father I have given some little description of the boat.[5]

We have done but little in the way of sight-seeing as we think it will be better to defer that till we return. So the Pyramids are left to crown my Egypt instead of beginning it.

I am anticipating a great deal of pleasure in these six lazy weeks of enjoyment with nothing to do—plenty of books, pencils and colors, the climate and scenery of the Nile and the kindest friend possible to bear me company. A past act of his kindness is the gift of [a] handsome Turkish handkerchief or scarf that has cost between six or seven dollars.[6] He insists upon my taking the best state-room in the boat, but on that point I mean to be obstinate in declining. For some weeks you will not hear from me as I shall be away from the post office.

Your affectionate brother, Andrew

After making arrangements for leasing The Ibis, *hiring a crew, and putting in supplies, the travelers went on board on December 10. The crew immediately began "tracking" up river (i.e., dragging the boat against the current). The days passed leisurely. A week later Andrew wrote that he "walked on a bleak, sandy shore, treeless and bushless, picked up a few pretty pebbles." But the next day he had "the prettiest walk we have had—fine groves of acacias and a few palms, a village and stone yard where were many blocks of alabaster."*

There were occasional sightings of other boats on the river and the exchange of news with the passengers. Andrew did some sketching, noting on December 18 that he "painted a little sketch of The Ibis." *On December 23, he "began a picture in water colors of our boat" as a gift for Mr. Van Rensselaer, which he finished on Christmas Eve, the day they arrived at Thebes.*

Here they visited "the temple at Luxor, sunset from the top of the Pylon." On December 29 they arrived at "Assouan, the southern limit of our journey on the Nile." The next day, they "saw the cataract—two English boats were ascending. The scene was wild and rugged in extreme."

On New Year's day, 1862, the travelers began their return journey down the Nile. Although the current was in their favor and the crew could row instead of tracking, the cold wind was high and made for rough sailing. Andrew still took frequent walks on shore and read and sketched. On January 3, 1862, he made a sketch of the interior of the spacious cabin of The Ibis. *On January 4, a passing English boat informed them of the death of Queen Victoria's consort, Prince Albert. By January 6 they were back at Thebes, and the next day they crossed the river to visit the tombs of the kings and had lunch in the doorway of one of the royal tombs. January 8 they "visited the colossal statues." At Karnak on January 9 they spent the whole day sightseeing and "stayed until the moon rose"* (MS Diary, *December 7, 1861-January 9, 1862*).

My dear Jim,

I say it as short as usual, but I feel like a long piece of apostrophizing affection to relieve the surcharged feelings of nearly two years. We are fairly turned Northward and have completed one, and it the most important one, of the stages in our progress. We left <u>Thebes</u> this morning after a busy and fatiguing sojourn of three days. It is a great place but after all its wonders, I am prepared to say that the things which gave me the most intense pleasure there was a package of letters containing two from you, two from Father and one from Eliza. The date of your last one was Nov. 21st. In it you acknowledged the receipt of the little package by Mr. Evans and of my letter from Madrid, besides giving me a whole budget of cheerful news—for which I am very much obliged. Perhaps I have confused the contents of the two letters in this summary but never mind, they gave me more pleasure than you can easily imagine.

As to my own life for the last four weeks, a great deal might be said. Whether I shall be able to say it or any part of it with interest remains to be seen.[1]

To begin, we have the fastest boat on the river and on the journey <u>up</u> and so far <u>down</u> we have passed everything we came in sight of. The secret of our speed is that instead of a clumsy Egyptian body our boat is English [p. 2, written cross-wise against the page] of modern construction, with a bow that parts the waves instead of running butt up against them. Besides, we have three masts instead of two. A Nile boat is a long, low barge of light draft and generally with the cabin built on the hinder half: ours is the only one whose cabin is put in the middle, which gives us a very private deck in the rear to have a Reis (pronounced rice)[2] and ten men for our crew, besides a cook, a dragoman, and our courier—fifteen of us in all on board. The crew, in going up, often were compelled to "track"—that is, to drag the boat along against the current which of course always sets down. When we had wind, they had only to attend to the sails. Now, in descending they row, eight oars, a good part of the day. The wind at this time of the year is rarely from the South.

Our accommodations on board are very good—a saloon, about 12 by 10 [feet], two nice bedrooms, two others not so good for courier & dragoman, a pantry & water closet. Our bed-rooms are of course small, about 6 by 8 ½, but this is wider than is common. The table is sumptuous, as we have a good cook and an ample stock of provisions. I doubt if you sat down to better turkeys on Christmas and New Year's than we did.

Going up, the time passed very quickly. We read a good deal and took walks on shore which was easily done whenever the men were tracking as it is very slow work. I drew a little, and so the time passed. It was a luxury to be so quiet. It is somewhat the same now, except that as we have left all our sight-seeing for the return trip, we have been stopping almost every day to explore some old temple or quarry. The greater part of the ruins, however, are at and above Thebes so that hereafter we shall only stop two or three times in the whole descent, unless indeed we take in the Pyramids, &c, when we get near Cairo.[3] The climate for the most part has been like our early October. Occasionally, we have had it quite hot in the day time, but I have worn winter clothing without discomfort all the time. Of course, we have never felt the need of fires, but I fear I am saying again to you what you will find in others of my letters. The fact is Thebes has come in and made a complete overturning of all that preceded it, so that I feel as if I ought to begin and write all my letters over again.

I cannot give in a letter any idea of the ruins I have seen. The photographs are better than a thousand letters. Generally, I have not been disappointed, except at finding things greater & finer than I had anticipated. That I suppose will always be the case. The clearness and distinctness in the granites and even the sandstone sculptures of such immense antiquity is wonderful. Then to see in the shattered places the color remaining, for it appears that walls and columns and rooms were all painted, is startling. Such things can only be in Egypt; and it is a mistake to carry to Paris, or London, these preserved fragments, for they cannot stand the difference of climate. Already the obelisk which Louis Philippe took to Paris looks half a dozen times shabbier than its [p. 3] fellow at Luxor.[4] Perhaps the most interesting things are <u>the tombs</u>: they are in vast numbers and of great variety and travellers can only visit two or three of each kind, at the most. It is fatiguing business, too. One gets weary in the confined air much sooner than out of doors. We visited in all twelve or thirteen of them; and I recognised several times the originals of features I have seen taken from them.[5] I ought not to omit to mention that at Karnak I saw the famous cartouche of the king of Judah in the long list of princes conquered by or subject to Shishak or Sesonchis.[6] I did not discover the strong Jewish features which some travellers remark in the face over the cartouche.

No where I felt the influence of associations so strong as in Egypt. There is something in the completeness and perfections of these remains that annihilates time. I feel as if the life were yet in them and the glory and mystery of the past ages return to reassert their rights and resume their place.

Travelling is like everything else: it needs the digestion of after thought to turn it to profit; and I feel as if I were only now putting aside, laying up the material for future enjoyment and improvement. Part of that improvement and enjoyment I anticipate when I go over these scenes with you at home. I would value it all very little if it could not be shared in some way by others. I am much obliged for your <u>very good</u> sketch of Mr. Keen's house.[7]

Your affectionate <u>Uncle,</u>
Andrew
[P.S.] I enclose letters for Betsy & Irenee Pepper,[8] which you will please deliver.

On January 14, passing an American boat, they "heard there were reports of a peaceful termination to difficulties with England." Three days later an English boat reported the same news, a ref-

erence to the international diplomatic crisis which began the previous November when two officials of the Confederacy sailing toward England were seized by the United States Navy. England, the leading world power, demanded their release, threatening war. President Lincoln eventually gave in and ordered their release in December, with the remark, "One war at a time" (MS Diary, January 14-17, 1862).

[Written on both sides of a quarter sheet of paper]

Dear Jim,

Fearful of overloading my letter, I put on this scrap my best thanks for your kind letter of Dec. 17(?).

Our Alicante letters were under-paid,[1] as we learned afterwards, by a mistake of our courier. I sent on money to the care of the consul there, so you got yours without troubling your "<u>Spanish correspondent</u>."

I am ashamed of my ill-written and hasty letters when I read yours, but you don't have so many as I to write. Writing so much I am fast losing what little grace of penmanship I ever possessed.

With love and <u>daily prayers</u>,

Your loving Uncle Andrew

Back in Cairo, Andrew and Van Rensselaer checked in at the Shepherd's Hotel before calling at the banker's for mail that had been held for them. Sixteen letters from family and friends were waiting for Andrew. The next day they visited museums and mosques and, on Wednesday, January 22, made a day trip to Suez "in the cars." Although they had only a hour at Suez, this was time enough for a quick lunch and a walk on the beach of the Red Sea.

Back in Cairo, there were letters to write, courtesy calls to make, shopping to do. They rode out to see the tombs of the Caliphs, and one day they rode donkeys to "what is called the petrified forest; the ride was interesting, wild and desolate." Afterward, they made a trip to Heliopolis to see the obelisk.

On Sunday, they sought a Coptic church, "hoping to see their mass, but owing to the stupidity of our guides were too late." However, they were able to attend the service at the English church, as well as an afternoon service at the Mission Chapel, where Mr. Lansing, an American missionary, preached.

On Monday, January 27, they took the train from Cairo to Alexandria but, on arrival, were "thunderstruck to hear that the French boat for Jaffa had left." They were much relieved to learn this report was unfounded and that the boat would sail the next day. They went on board the Carmel that evening. "Elegant rooms, a good table, beautiful weather," and a ship's library of good books made the voyage a pleasant one.

Andrew's first view of Palestine was from the deck of the ship, "the low line of blue hills, from below Jaffa to Mount Carmel." At mid-morning, the Carmel cast anchor at Jaffa. Andrew and Van Rensselaer made a brief tour of the city before joining a caravan of four horses and six mules. Among others, "a German ecclesiastic (Roman) and a monk, both passengers on the Carmel" joined the party. And so began the journey through Palestine.

Cairo
January 20, 1862
⌈ LETTER 62 ⌉

The first night was spent in a Latin convent at Ramleh (through which passed the great caravan road between Egypt and Damascus). Early the next morning, with only a cup of coffee for breakfast, they started out, traveling over very muddy and then rocky roads and finally arrived at Jerusalem in late afternoon. (MS Diary, January 20-30, 1862).

Jerusalem
January 31, 1862
[LETTER 63]

My dear Jim,

I have not been here long enough to put the name at the beginning of my sheet without mingled feelings of gratitude and surprise. Whether I am really here or not, I have not been in a state to decide since my arrival. From a tour about the city this morning I think it likely I am, but from my feelings I should be disposed to say it was a dream. With this reservation implied, I date from Jerusalem.

We had a jolly ride from Ramla (the ancient Arimathea)[1] yesterday. Excuse the adjective, but no other word will suit. It was a fine day, after the passing of a little shower in the morning. The roads, no the paths (hardly worthy of that name even), were as muddy as possible, for it had done nothing but rain in Palestine for two months. Wherever mud could be made, we had it, for there is no <u>made road</u> at all. The way from Jaffa to Jerusalem is only a track made of camels & [p. 2] and donkeys and buses. When we got to the mountains, the mud almost ceased, but in place of it we found the bare rock, in many places, a slippery sheet washed clean by the rain, and in others, a perilous flight of steps over broken fragments tumbled down by the winter torrents. Even in a land of good roads, travelling in the rainy season is bad, but here it is something which must be seen to be believed.

On this road we were going, without once stopping to rest, from seven A.M. till 5 P.M. We lunched in the saddle, on hard boiled eggs, bread, cheese and oranges.

In spite of all these shadows to the picture, it was all bright to me. I enjoyed it beyond measure. The donkey riding in Egypt had been a good apprenticeship for the riding so that I am not a particle stiff or sore from it today. As for the rest, I enjoyed it all, except perhaps the <u>mud</u>. I say, perhaps, because I am not sure I did not rather enjoy that.

The weather is like our own in March. Men were plowing for the summer crops and the winter grain was up, giving some sort of verdure to the sterile looking land. [p. 3]

You wish to follow our route, so I will say to guide you that we passed the ancient Kirjath-Jearim where once the ark rested a number of years,[2] and we looked down upon Emmaus,[3] a little before arriving here. The first part of our journey was in the plain of <u>Sharon</u>[4] where the nearest approach we saw to roses was the white iris, blooming all over the ground and only an inch or two above it.

This and all the level country was once the country of the Philistines. The Israelites never could dispossess them of these rich plains, and were forced to make the best they could of the <u>hills</u>. These hills are very like Bartlett's[5] pictures of them, with that peculiar look of layers in lines around them, formed by terraces, sometimes natural & sometimes artificial. As we got near to Jerusalem, the hills became higher and more stony. The last one on whose declivity Emmaus is built is a mass of stones where it is difficult to imagine how the flocks of little black goats which were dropping down among them toward the village can get enough to live upon. [p. 4]

It is not the season to see Palestine in its beauty. It is cold and damp and the little verdure which the land has is now invisible. Olive trees and orange trees keep their leaves; the first grey and the others most beautiful fully grown. Fig trees have only their branches except the kind called sycamore[6] which does not lose its leaves. But the want of verdure is of far less moment than the want of warmth. It is really cold so that a little stove we have in our room is a very agreeable part of its furnishing.

We find quite a <u>party</u> of Americans here, two gentlemen and two ladies, who with the consul, also at this house, and ourselves and six others make quite a national circle here. I suppose Americans are the only people crazy enough to come to Syria in the winter, but necessity has no law. We could not come unless we did it now. After all, too, Palestine is a place which less than any other depends for its interest on such a thing as pleasant weather. All its seasons are consecrated like its soil.

Don't be troubled at my repeating some things I put in other letters. I <u>must</u> write fast and such mistakes are almost inevitable.

Your affec[tionate] brother,
Andrew

The first morning in Jerusalem was spent visiting major sites, the "Hospital of St. Helena (mills, copper caldrons, etc.), Chapel of Flagellation, Church of St. Anne (ruined), Via Dolorosa, the bazaars," and after lunch, the Church of the Holy Sepulchre, the Jews' quarter, and "the Wailing place." On Saturday, February 1, they went to the Garden of Gethsemene and the Mount of Olives. Franklin Olcott, the American Consul, went with the party to visit the American convent. On Sunday morning, they attended the English Church, and at 3 o'clock Andrew preached in the room of the Consulate to "half a dozen or eight people."

Early the next morning, they went to the Mosque of Omar, which had to be visited between seven and eight a.m. After breakfast, on "a cloudy and cold day," they set out for Hebron. In the late afternoon, they "encamped near the quarantine." The next day, "wet and dismal, [they] rode through two or three showers to the 'Pools of Solomon' and to Bethlehem," where they saw the church and chapels and went into the kitchen of the Latin convent "to dry our feet." Continuing through more showers, they finally arrived at the Convent of Mar Saba (MS Diary, January 31-February 4, 1862).

Convent of Mar Saba[1] Near the Dead Sea February 4, 1862

[LETTER 64]

Dear Jim,

Perhaps a letter from this place will be quite as acceptable as if dated from Jerusalem. I am sure it would be so if you could see the place. The buildings of this fortress-convent run up both sides of a narrow gorge in the mountains of Judea, not far from the Dead Sea, to the shores of which we are bound, and we stop here a night on the way. Before admitting us, a basket came down from an upper window, high aloft, which took up a letter we brought from the Greek patriarch in Jerusalem (perhaps he is only a bishop). After the missive had time to perform its mission, we had the satisfaction of seeing an iron door open for our horses and camp equipage, while one lower down opened for us. Entering this, we descended a good many flights of stone steps, with the precipitous face of the rock on one side and buildings of varied form, chapel and churches, &c, all around. At last crossing a little garden and ascending some more steps we were shown into [p. 2] this very comfortable and spacious lodging place. It has an arched ceiling, divans covered with

Turkey carpet all around the room, which now has also beds made in two of the corners, and everything is scrupulously clean. On our arrival one of the Greek brothers (it is a Greek convent) brought us water, *arrak* (a sort of spiced spiritous drink), and raisins, and afterwards coffee. Since then we have had a sufficiently good dinner, tho' no meat. Even some chickens which we brought were not allowed to be cooked. While guests of the convent, we must conform to its rules, and neither meat nor women are allowed within the walls.

The road from Hebron[2] to this place, or rather as far as Bethlehem, is very bad indeed. No words can convey to you an idea of its badness, especially at this inclement season of the year. Mud and rocks in the most appalling forms of each combine together in it. We lunched <u>standing</u> at the pools of Solomon, these grand reservoirs which are ancient enough to deserve their title and as good today as when first built.[3] We stopped at Bethlehem long enough [p. 3] to visit the Church of the Nativity with its caves and chapels, and to dry our feet in the Latin convent[4] connected with it. The town of Bethlehem is beautifully situated on the side of a hill near the summit, and even at this dull season it looks well. From Bethlehem to Mar Saba, we had, for a change, the only piece of decent road we have found in Palestine; and even this, no one in America would call a <u>road</u>. It is a mere bridle path, and in many places not worth calling by so fair a name as that.

The views it offers to the traveller, however, ought to be taken into account. I do not know that I have ever seen more magnificent pictures of wild desolation than lay about these rugged mountains and dark precipitous valleys. As we rode along, the Dead Sea rose before us, in its narrow bed, and the light of the sun, not far from the setting, fell in golden masses on the lofty mountains beyond. The wild and strange scene near at hand, and the grand distance, combined to make a grand picture, one I shall scarce forget.

But I must finish for tonight, leaving space for something further later. [p. 4]

Encamped near Jericho February 5th

We have had a glorious day—sky without a cloud, air warm, pure and invigorating, a total contrast with yesterday and fine enough to compensate for all its unpleasantness. We rose early and after a cup of coffee made the tour of the Convent, visiting the grottoes, cells, chapels, &c. We were five hours in reaching the Dead Sea, half the time among the lofty mountains and the rest getting down to the low shore which you know is some 1200 feet below the level of the Mediterranean. I did not care to take a boat, so I only drew off shoes & socks and went in barefoot. As far as I could perceive, there was not the slightest unpleasantness in the perfectly clear water. It produced no pricking and I half regretted I had not gone in for a complete bath. We were at the North end of the sea, near the mouth of the Jordan and in that locality I did not observe such utter desolation as travellers speak of. Down to within a very short distance of the water, bushes and especially great reeds with feathered tops were growing in abundance. The verdure such as it was, was much beyond what we had noticed in parts of our mountain travel.

From the Dead Sea, we rode on to the Jordan, striking it some considerable distance above its mouth. It was a perfect torrent. The banks are all overflowed, and it was difficult to find a place where we could get near the main stream. We did find a place, and I only of the party undressed and went in and enjoyed a bath in the muddy water very much.[5] Turning our backs on the river, we came on in two or three hours to this place, where there is really nothing to be seen but the worst Arab village I have seen in the country and a ruined fortress which, I believe, dates from the Middle Ages.

We are encamped back of the town toward the mountains of Judea. Tomorrow we cross those heights and return to Jerusalem, a journey of some six or seven hours.

Next Monday we go North to Naplouse,[6] Nazareth, the sea of Tiberius, [Mount] Carmel,[7] Tyre-Sidon and Beyrout, a journey of ten days, or eleven, with the Sunday. If the weather is not too bad, we shall go from Beyrout to Damascus and take in the Cedars and Ba[a]lbek,[8] perhaps(?) going to Antioch and Tripoli afterwards, instead of returning to Beyrout. We shall hardly reach Constantinople before the 25th of March.

Your loving brother,
Andrew

In superb weather, the caravan struck their tents and headed back toward Jerusalem, stopping at Bethany en route to visit the tomb of Lazarus. They entered the Holy City by St. Stephen's Gate in time to do some afternoon shopping. The next morning, after checking at the banker's for mail, they took a walk south of the city. The Valley of Gihon, Aceldama, Valley of Hinnom, En Rogel, Valley of Jehosephat, the Pools of Siloam, Tree of Isaiah, Grotto of Agony are some of the sites Andrew mentioned.

The next day there was time for a visit the Tower of David and a walk on the city walls. They saw the lepers' houses, the Dung Gate and, from the top of Nebi Samuel, they had a fine view of the Mediterranean and Dead Sea.

Sunday found them in the English Church. In the afternoon, in company with the consul and others, they had "a pleasant though long and too fatiguing walk" to Bethany and Bethphage.

On Monday, February 10, they left Jerusalem, passed several villages, including "Bethel, the place of Jacob's vision," and continued to Sinedjil where they camped. The next day they visited Seiloun, "the ancient Shiloh," before continuing to Naplouse [Nablus], where they camped just outside the town. They visited the Tomb of Joseph and Jacob's Well before going on to Samaria, where Andrew reported a "fine view of the plain of Esdraelon from the top of the hotel back of the town." The next day brought the travelers by Jezreel, Mount Gilboa, Mount Hermon, and "to the foot of Mount Tabor" (MS Diary, February 6-13, 1862).

Dear Jim,

Time is precious in these days of hard travel, so I begin at this early date my letter to you that I may be sure to have it done by the time I get to Beyrout, some two weeks from this time. You must not look at dates in letters from this land of few post-offices. I am travelling in Palestine in the approved style, which means on horseback all day, in front or in the rear of a small caravan, and under a tent at night. We are a little early in the season for this mode of life and consequently meet with some inconveniences—muddy roads, and damp evenings, &c. On our trip to the Dead Sea, we had quite an experience of these with the addition of rainy days, but this time, since

Encamped at the foot of Mt Tabor[1] February 13, 1862

[LETTER 65]

leaving Jerusalem last Monday, we have had magnificent weather and have only suffered from the heat of the sun. What that must be later I am glad I am not likely to be able to judge.

We form quite an imposing array in our march. Four pretty fair horses carry Mr. V[an] R[ensselaer], myself, the courier & the dragoman—nine other animals, horses, mules and donkeys carry our goods and four or five men are with them. Now and then we have in addition one, two [p. 2] or three mounted Arab guards furnished by the various agas or governors of the towns thro' which we pass. We start usually about eight o'clock in the morning. It takes us till that hour to get breakfast and to pack up tents and baggage. We travel on at a good walk till four or five in the afternoon. In half an hour after stopping, the two tents are up. Ours, which is the larger, is a very nice one; not exactly round but <u>polygonal</u> (if that is not too geometrical a title for a tent). It has one pole, a high one, in the center, and the top and sides are fastened with long cords and iron pins. Two light iron bed-steads with mattresses, &c, a light table, and two camp stools, constitute its furniture. The floor is carpeted, and by the door is spread a soft Turkey rug. (Turkey <u>carpet</u> is the name, but it sounds large for six feet by three and a half). We have a handsome blue and black table cover, two tasteful candlesticks and when we are all in order with books, ink and paper spread out before us, and trunks and carpet bags scattered around, we look really comfortable and cheery. Our living, too, is all that could be desired. Our dinner, which is served about two hours after our arrival at any place, is of five courses, beginning with soup and ending with fruit, and we have found few hotel tables so satisfactory. [p. 3] Our breakfast is eaten rather *sans cere-monie,* <u>but</u> is good and warm. Our lunch we take either in the saddle or under an olive tree near a roadside spring. It is simple enough: two hard-boiled eggs, bread and an orange, and rarely a slice of cold meat.

As well as I can judge, this strange life suits me very well. At first, on a cold ride to Hebron and afterwards to Mar Saba in the rain, I took cold which served me as colds usually do. Since then I have been working that attack off, and look forward to a decided increase of strength.

I cannot give you an idea of the pleasure of riding thro' this land where every hour brings up some new point of interest. The old Bible history seems re-enacted before me. Sacred things that have been mere thoughts all my life grow into solid facts. Today, for instance, we were in Jezreel and looked down the valley where Jehu drove furiously,[2] while on the right rose the beautiful Mountain of Gilboa,[3] where Saul and Jonathan were slain; to the east, was the distant ruins of Beth Shan[4] where their bodies were exposed on the wall, & to the north, the village of Nain[5] where the widow's son was restored to life by our Lord. This is just one instance.

February 14 (by the Sea of Galilee)

We have had a most de- [p. 4] lightful tho' a fatiguing day. We ascended [Mount] Tabor the first thing—the going up and coming down crucifying two hours and a half—and hard work. It is far more beautiful than I had imagined, and anything but like the stiff pictures I have often seen of it. The summit is very picturesque, covered with trees, flowers and fine old ruins. As we rode away from it, it took the regular shape so often remarked. The general outline is an arc of about the fifth of a circle, with the ends a little turned out, and the whole rising out of undulating ground. The view from the top, very fine. But we are in a far more charming spot now. I have never had an idea of the beauty of this lake. A placid sheet of water nearly oval, lying deep among hills, with the snowy top of [Mount] Hermon[6] presiding over the whole. This, seen in the golden light of a cloudless afternoon, with the hills green as spring can make them, and dotted with flowers, and all calm, still, serene, is something worth a long remembrance.

We had a delightful bath in the lake before dinner. The water was cool but not cold, tho' it is St. Valentine's day.

By a change in our plans, we are here a week or two sooner than I had expected, so I must finish my letters at once to be ready for the mail. [p. 5] We have got on very well so far. From Tiberias, we went to Nazareth, on a windy & showery day, and stayed there all day Sunday encamped outside of the town because the Latin convent was undergoing repairs. Monday, we went to Carmel and slept in the grand convent,[8] and from Carmel we have come up keeping close to the shore to this place, passing Khaiffa,[9] St. Jean d'Acre,[10] Tyre & Sidon, &c. We saw at a little distance, Sarepta[11] yesterday, and today we passed the place where Jonah was set on shore after his sojourn in the whale.[12]

This region of Ancient Phoenicia is very interesting. The whole way along the shore is strewn with ruins of all eras. I believe all these cities were part of the promised land, but in regard to none of them was the promise literally fulfilled. The Israelites gave up fighting too soon for the pleasures of possession so that the strong and prosperous places on the coast never came into their power, altho' I believe in the interior their sway went farther north. There is a white cape[13] jutting out into the sea some distance below Tyre, which is called the [p. 6] boundary of the coast of the Holy Land.

Of the land we have seen, and as you will see from the places we have visited that has been by far the greater part of the whole country, there is no comparison between the strong hills and contracted valleys of Judea and the fertile plains and round green cultivated hills and pretty views of Samaria and Galilee. The last is certainly the finest part and our Lord's home in Nazareth was in a garden spot within an easy day's journey of the Mediterranean or the Sea of Galilee—and three and a half or four days from Jerusalem. I can't help a feeling of pleasure to find so much beauty about the place of his early home. From the hill-top back of his father's house is one of the finest views in Palestine—with Tabor, Carmel, the Mediterranean, the vast plain of Esdraelon[14] and, far away to the North, the snow-capped Hermon all in sight, and a charming bit of a valley right down by the town for the near view. He lived in sight of these things which are the grandest nature has to show. The world was beautiful to him. I cannot doubt that he enjoyed its loveliness, but I must stop now. The rest, by and by.

Your loving Uncle Andrew

[P.S.] Have rec'd with much delight yours of January 10th.

[Written across the top of p. 1:] "Please send the enclosed to Sallie & oblige yours, &c."

The three weeks between the travelers' arrival at Beyrout on February 21 and at Smyrna on March 14 were filled with activities. As was their custom, Andrew and Van Rensselaer called on the American consul, who in Beyrout was J. A. Johnson. They also went to the French and Russian steamer offices to inquire about passage to Smyrna. On Sunday, February 23, Andrew preached in the Mission Chapel in the morning and attended "Arabic Sunday School and church service" in the afternoon.

On Tuesday, the February 25th, they left Beyrout, taking a "carriage to top of Lebanon." Here they changed to horses to continue to Zahléh, where they spent the night (and where Andrew made two sketches). "Passed villages in ruins, work of the Druses and saw many ruined houses in Zahléh."

The next day they had "a rather monotonous ride to Baalbek," where they "stayed in the house of some Latin sisters of charity." The day following they visited the ruins, rode out to the quarries, and "saw the enormous hewn stone there." On Friday, February 28, "A beautiful ride to [Az] Zabdani in the Anti-Lebanon," where they had "a good room and fire at night." The next day, "Another beautiful ride with continual interest along the Barada to Damascus. Wild mountain pass, cascade, rock-hermitages, pretty villages. Wonderfully magnificent view of Damascus and the Hauran from the hill an hour and a half before we reached the city." They stopped at the Hotel de Palmyre, "a good specimen of a Moorish house."

On Sunday, March 2, they attended the Arabic service of the United Presbyterian Mission, called on the American vice-consul, and caught up on reading American newspapers. The next day they rode through a "desolated Christian quarter [from the Druse massacre], out the old Roman gate, saw the tomb of St. George, place of Paul's conversion, tomb of victims of the [Druse] massacre, the Mosque of Dervishes, the bazaars." That evening they "went out to see the illuminations as it is the season of Ramadan."

Wednesday, March 5, they called on Abd-el-Kader, the famous Emir of Algiers, who had surrendered to the French in 1846 on condition that he would not be deprived of his freedom but who was promptly imprisoned by Louis Philippe. He languished in prison until December 1852 when Louis Napoleon set him at liberty, gave him a residence at Broussa, Syria, and everything necessary in keeping with his high rank and splendid military record. When the conflict between the Druses and the Maronites broke out in Syria in 1860, Abd-el-Kader used his powerful influence to prevent the massacre of Christians and preserve peace. It was said that the Maronites would have been exterminated but for his protection (cf. Evans, 1:34-37; and Letter 11, August 27, 1860, note 5). The travelers also called on the consuls of England, Belgium and Holland, saw the Great Tree of Damascus, the triumphal arch near the grand mosque, and the citadel.

On March 6 they left Damascus for the two-day trek across the Baka to Mekséh, where they pitched their tent for the last time (Andrew made a pencil sketch of Mekséh). Again, they saw a Druse village and ruined Christian houses. The next day from Mekséh they traveled "to the top of Lebanon," and then took a carriage back to Beyrout. Sunday found them attending services at the Mission Chapel and hearing "a high-Calvinistic sermon from Dr. Vandyke."

On Monday, March 10, they left Beyrout aboard the steamer, Stamboul, bound for Smyrna by way of Cyprus (where they went ashore briefly "to see a newly discovered statue they call a Venus, which seems rather a portrait, draped, life-size, the later Roman period, good face but stiff") and Rhodes (where they did not disembark). On March 14, they arrived at Smyrna (MS Diary, February 21-March 14, 1862).

Left:
"Cabin on the Ibis,
Jan. 2[, 1862]."
Longacre Portfolio.

Bottom:
The Ibis. "Our boat on the Nile,
Dec. [23-24, 18]61."
Longacre Portfolio.

"Zahléh[, Lebanon], Feb. 26[, 1862], Lebanon in the distance." Longacre Portfolio.

"Zahléh[, Lebanon], Feb. 26[, 1862], Hermon in the distance." Longacre Portfolio.

Left:
"Constantinople, March 26, 1862."
Longacre Portfolio.

Bottom:
"Santa Sophia and Santa Irene
from court of Seraglio,
March 25, 1862."
Longacre Portfolio.

Santa Sophia & Santa Irene. from court of Seraglio. March 25, 1862.

Top Left:
Andrew Longacre.
Constantinople. March, 1862.

Top Right:
Andrew Longacre,
Philadelphia, 1863.

Bottom:
"Room in Berlin, Apr. 21[, 18]62."
Longacre Portfolio.

My dear Jim,

Somehow, writing pretty full letters to Father and Eliza, when I think of writing to you, I often feel as if there were nothing left to say. This time, however, I shall at least begin with something fresh. We arrived in the fine bay or gulf, rather, of Smyrna this morning and, after changing our baggage from one steamer to another which sails for Constantinople to-morrow, we came on shore to spend the intervening time. To one just from Europe, this place with its mosques and bazaars might seem quite Oriental. To us, so lately from Damascus, it looks very European. I have not seen the twentieth part of the hats, coats and pantaloons I have seen today before since we left Spain. The town itself is not interesting. Around it are hills and the harbor is very pretty, but of the country, it is hard to judge so early in the season.

We called on our consul here, who has lately been appointed. His name is Byng,[1] and is a man of some intelligence and knowledge of the world. He appears to have seen a good deal of society in Washington. We dined with him, and this [p. 2] evening went with him to a National Italian festival given in honor of the king of Italy, whose anniversary it is.[2] The affair was very characteristic, a concert given at the Opera-house. The music was good for the place and quite a crowd were gathered to hear it. It was amusing to hear the *vivas* of the crowd and to see how they were received. The most popular was *viva* or *enviva Garibaldi* and *viva Vittorio Emanuele.* When they added *"a Roma,"* there were evident signs of disaffection in some parts. At different intervals quantities of printed papers were let loose from the upper boxes in clouds. One I picked up has on it *"Viva Vittorio Emanuele re d'Italia. Viva il Pontefice Romano. Abbasso il Papa Re."* The latter part may be rendered, "Long live the Roman pontiff, but down with the Pope-king." Some of the ladies into whose boxes these papers flew, threw them out with manifest indignation. Very often during the evening the cry was made, *"Viva Garibaldi in Grecia."* Poor Garibaldi. If he has to come to the relief of all distracted or turbulent nations, he will have a busy time of it. You have heard perhaps there has been some little stir of a revolutionary character in some of the Greek islands. [p. 3]

While at the festival, quite a number of people of various degrees of distinction came to call on our consul in his box. Among them the Persian consul in his funny dress and tall dog-skin hat. On the whole, it was a funny and amusing time, an exciting re-introduction to European life.

I shall leave my letter to be finished some other time, as it is high time now that your 'spected uncle was in bed. "Good-night." It won't be very long before I say that with my lips instead of my pen.[3]

We are here at last—Wednesday, instead of Monday morning. Our sail from Smyrna here was one of the most disagreeable I have ever had anywhere. A small steamer,[4] crowded with passengers, of whom only half a dozen or eight were first class. So great was the crowd of common Turks, Jews, Greeks, Armenians, Africans, Arabs and of all other sorts imaginable in as ridiculous and filthy garments as are often seen, that they filled not only their own quarters but had the whole promenade deck, leaving us room for a single foot-path for our walks. Below, the people in the cabin were all very polite, but at the same time continual smokers. [p. 4] Add to these the comforts of a bitter cold wind, a rough sea, and a poor table, and you can comprehend that the beauty of "the blue Egean Sea" was slightly wasted on one, at least, of the passengers. I hope

Smyrna
March 14, 1862
[LETTER 66]

Constantinople
March 19

to see it more favorably as we go to Athens & on down to the Mediterranean on our way to Trieste.

Constantinople is like a vision of beauty & grandeur, as a whole, seen from the fort. But a short stroll thro' the very best streets this afternoon has recalled the adage, "All is not gold that glitters." Many of the streets are quite impassable for carriages because they are mere flights of mostly paved steps to climb up or get down which is no easy task covered as they are with shiny mud.

In my next I hope to give you more pleasant accounts. Santa Sophia and all the wonders of this Turkey Elysium have yet to be seen. Of course, I shall be enchanted, though at this season of the year it is probable I shall take it all very <u>early</u> especially as I am shivering now in spite of the bright fire in my room.

You see, your uncle is actually getting funny. If it needs an apology, you have it in the fact that I have today received two very kind letters from you.

Your affect[ionate] bro[ther], Andrew

**Constantinople
March 24, 1862**

[LETTER 67]

Dear Jim,

Our week in this city draws to a close, to-morrow being our last whole day. Few places I have visited have so fully satisfied me. The weather, too, has been remarkably pleasant, so that everything has been as we could wish. Something with reference to the weather here, or the climate rather, may be as new to you as it was to me. I had the idea before coming to this part of the world, that Constantinople was warm, much warmer than our country, but March here is exceedingly like March at home with as little appearance of spring, and as cold and rainy. We have had the good fortune to find some soft, balmy days, but they have been just such summery days as occasionally fall in our own early spring.

We have not done much since I wrote to Eliza about our glimpse of the Sultan, and our ride round the walls. Saturday, we went over to Scutari,[1] had a noble prospect of the city, the sea of Marmara, and the Bosphorus, almost to the Black Sea, from the top of Mt Bulgurlu,[2] then we rode around and partly through the immense cemetery and a perfect forest of cypress. We stopped a moment to look at the [p. 2] pretty structure, on six columns, that covers a favorite <u>horse</u> of Sultan Mahmoud. He is not so much out of place as you might think, buried among Turks.

We were interested too in the English burying-ground, prettily situated on the brow of a hill overhanging the sea. Here lie their dead, from the Russian war, the men heaped in great graves, hundreds together, and the officers honored with more or less stately monuments. There is a fine tall obelisk as a memorial for all, granite, with an inscription in English, French, Italian, and Turkish.

Sunday went quietly, attending service at the chapel of the English Embassy in the morning and spending the afternoon in meditation at home.

To-day, to continue the journal, we have had a wet day, for the first time in a good while, and we have devoted it to a patient and laborious seeing of all the bazaars, which I need not attempt to describe. They are finer and at the same time more European than those of Cairo or Alexandria. Indeed, the whole city is so. No Eastern city I have seen compares in neatness of the streets or of architecture with the better parts even of the Turkish part of Stamboul.[3] The most striking of the bazaars were those of <u>shoes</u> and of <u>arms</u>. The latter an immense curiosity-shop of all sorts of antique things, a terribly <u>temptatious</u> place to [p. 3] visit. We have not yet seen Santa Sophia, or the Seraglio owing to the dilatoriness of our *valet-de-place*,[4] but he has just been in to tell us we are to go to-morrow after twelve o'clock. This arrangement will give us the crowning pleasure at the last.

After all, in a place like this, it is not so much the particular places or things one sees, that give the chief satisfaction; it is the whole, the <u>being here</u>. We see the position of things, the promontories crowned with buildings, the immense domes and lofty minarets, the sea, the Bosphorus, and the Golden Horn; this is the enjoyment. It gives life, motion and color to all the engravings of the place I have ever seen, at once; and hereafter, pictures of Constantinople will seem like portraits of people I know. A photograph, you know, never gives you a just idea of a person you have never seen, but when you have once known the original you know how to find the likeness.

We are to sail for Athens on Wednesday and hope to arrive there Friday morning. Our time there will be very short, as the boat we want to take for Trieste leaves Syra[5] on Sunday night, so that we shall have to leave Athens on Saturday evening. As we shall only attempt to see the ruins right at Athens, I think we [p. 4] shall have time, although, two days longer would be very pleasant. I am hoping that from Trieste we may go to Venice. From there, we shall go to Vienna, Dresden, Berlin, Cologne, & Paris: at least that is the present intention. It is a great comfort to feel that there is [sic] only about five weeks between me and Paris. If I knew the times of sailing of the Cunard steamers, I might give you a pretty definite idea of my time for coming home, but I do not. I suppose it will be early in June.

Just now I suppose the preachers are gathering in Philadelphia to attend Conference. How glad I should be to meet with them. I have some natural curiosity to know what will be done with me; but I suppose I shall find out in due time. From a remark in one of Father's recent letters I am glad to hear there is a probability of my finding an appointment ready for me on my arrival. A little quiet laziness at home would be most agreeable to be sure; but I feel that my play-time ought to be ended. I have had a long holiday and work now looks more desirable than play.

I forgot to say before, that I have no such dislike of finances as not to be thoroughly interested in your late letters. Money for itself or by itself I hope I never shall love, but the money-cares of those I love I am glad to share.

Your affectionate big brother, A. L.

In the late afternoon of Wednesday, March 26, Andrew and Van Rensselaer went on board the Alphic *and sailed out of the Golden Horn. Caught in a fog, they "only went around the point of Stamboul," but a pleasant company of fellow passengers made the voyage enjoyable. In the night, they passed Gallipoli and the Dardanelles, landed at Piraeus on Friday evening and drove immediately to Athens. The next day, with a hired carriage and a guide, they visited "the places of note" and "bought some coins, etc." On Saturday they left Athens for "a delightful evening sailing toward Syra."*

The next morning, when the Alphic *docked in the port of Syra, Andrew and Van Rensselaer went ashore to the "little English chapel," where they "heard imperfectly a poor sermon." Later in the day, they boarded the* Arciduca F. Massimiliano. *"A quiet sail but uninteresting company; going toward the end of Greece passed between Cerigo [i.e., Kithira, southernmost of the Ionian Isles] and the mainland." On April 1, they landed at Corfu and having a few hours took a drive with fellow passengers, leaving the island mid-afternoon.*

On the sail up the Adriatic, Andrew wrote letters, read Evelina *by Fanny Burney, and began* Guy Mannering *by Sir Walter Scott. Also, on April 2, he made a sketch of his "Bed on board Arciduca F. Massimiliano." The next morning the ship docked at Trieste. They drove around the city seeing some of the high points (Austrian Lloyd Steam Navigation Company, the cathedral, the old Roman arch, etc.) before taking the train that evening for Venice (MS Diary, March 26-April 3, 1862).*

Venice
April 4, 1862
[LETTER 68]

My dear Jim,

As my last lot of letters got off without one for you among them, much to my chagrin, I shall begin this time with yours to make sure of it.

How the changes of travel chase one another like shiftings of a painted panorama. Yesterday about noon, we landed at Trieste. We spent several hours in driving about the town, looking at churches, &c, called on our consul, Mr. Hildreth[1] for news, and in the evening took the train for this place. We got here about half past five this morning, and have spent six or seven hours today in visiting the Cathedral, Ducal palace and the Academy of the Fine Arts, besides acquiring a fair idea of this singular city. Now, after dinner, I am sitting down to chat over affairs with you. Out of my window I look over the broad expanse of the Canal San Marco, with the Scuola de San Georgio right in front, almost exactly the view you have in one of your stereoscopes taken from under the arches of the Ducal palace, which is on a line with our hotel and only separated from it by one or two interesting houses. [p. 2] There are no photographs that I have seen more perfect than those taken of Venice, yet, now I am here I feel how far below reality all mere pictures are. You must imagine what the impression is when one finds all preconceived notions gathered from books and pictures at once started into life, turned into a reality, and that reality surpassing the dreams of fancy. It is an intense pleasure to glide along these streets of water, to look at the old, half-decayed but still beautiful palaces rising out of the sea and to say to myself, I am really here. I find Europe no less interesting for coming after Egypt and the East. The treasures of art, the exquisite details of the florid architecture of this city in particular seem more than ever precious to me, coming as I do from lands which have so little to show of the same kind.

Then, there is a dreamy luxury in this warm spring evening, the calm hazy sky is reflected in the gently rippled water, and churches and towers lie there also, trembling quietly. Even the gondolas and the boats that flit about have a luxurious peacefulness about them. All is soft, clear, calm, delicious; Italy of the painters and poets. "Beautiful Venice, queen of the sea"! [p. 3]

Only one thought oppresses me: you & the others at home are not with me. I take in all these pleasant and beautiful things. I feel and enjoy them, but it is <u>alone</u>. I know I have a kind friend with me, but there are very few people in the world who can enter into one's joy or sorrow, can understand the character and depth of one's feelings like one's own "kith and kin." Besides, I know how much you all would enjoy these things, and since I find out how really worthy to be enjoyed they are, I feel your deprivation all the more.

Ah well! We don't have the ordering of these things. We are very wise and kind, and think we could do it so well, but One wiser and kinder than we acts just contrary to what we wish, and we have only to settle down to think it must be for the best.

It grows dark, and I must stop for a while, beloved. Oh that I had you here to take[2] a quiet cozy walk!

We have spent this day on the churches, only adding to the half dozen of these, one or two little odds and ends, as the gate of the arsenal and ascending to the Campanile of San Marco. [p. 4] The churches, at least those we saw, are generally of a correct style of architecture and large, but somehow they seem to me <u>cold</u>. Their bare white walls and ceilings mourn for frescoes since their style forbids the endless ornaments of Gothic art. Scattered among them are some magnificent pictures by Titian,[3] Paul Veronese[4] and Tintoretto.[5]

In one of the churches, called the <u>Frari</u>,[6] are the grand monuments of Canova[7] and Titian. They face each other and are of great size. Canova's they say was designed by himself tho' intended for Titian. As he died before it was erected, they adopted it as the plan for his own.

Several of the pictures I have seen today are copied in "Burnet's hints on Painting,"[8] which you know Father has. It is pleasant to recognise old friends on these walls which I now see for the first time. I have regretted frequently that I did not study the engravings of these famous pictures more thoroughly before I came to Europe. To be thoroughly prepared to enjoy the originals one should be well acquainted with such copies of them.

The Empress of Austria[9] is here. We saw the children in their gondola today & bowed to them as was <u>our duty.</u> Their governess, or the lady with them, made them return our salutation.

Yours affectionately,

Andrew

The ten days between these two letters were busy ones. In Venice on Sunday, April 6, Andrew and Van Rensselaer attended the church service in the English chapel and "heard a good sermon against loving the world; if we live in the Spirit, let us also walk in the Spirit." They rose early the next morning to take a train for Milan. "Rode around half of the city seeing the boulevards and the arch of Sempione." The next morning they visited the cathedral and "went to Santa Maria delle Grazie to see the Last Supper of Leonardo da Vinci," before boarding the train for the eleven-hour trip back to Venice. They spent their last day visiting churches and purchasing postcards and souvenirs, departing "after a charming sail by moonlight to the R. R. station."

In the early morning of April 10, at Nabesina, they had a forty-five minute lay-over waiting for the train from Trieste. "The country became very pretty about Laibach and increased in interest by Gratz and still more in passing the Semmering Alps." That evening they crossed the summit, the lowest of all the great passes across the Alps, through a mile-long tunnel. "Down a fine series of curves," they arrived at Vienna and drove directly to the Hotel of the Arch Duke Charles.

As was their custom, they began their visit to Vienna by going to the cathedral (St. Stephen's), where they saw "Canova's beautiful tomb of Archduchess Maria Christiana," and on to the

Imperial Gallery, where were "many good pictures, but some appear too bright not to have been very much <u>restored</u>. A <u>fine</u> Albrecht Dürer. Good modern pictures." They rode out to the Schönbrunn Palace. The walls of one of the private rooms were "covered with small pictures by members of the Imperial family; another in embroidery by Maria Theresa. Drove across the city and out to the Prater, pleasant driving in the cool air of the close of day and with the budding trees and green grass redolent of Spring."

On Saturday, April 12, the tourists visited the gallery of Prince Esterhazy where they saw "fine Rembrandts, Reubens, and a precious little gem called Bronzino but unlike all the Bronzinos I have seen." Next was the gallery of Count Harrach who politely showed them through the palace where they viewed "a fine Velasquez and some pretty modern pictures." (Among his souvenirs, Andrew kept the calling card of Count Harrach.) A tour of the gallery of Prince Lichtenstein revealed "a good Raffaela and Corregio, good Guidos and many good Vandykes, Reubens and other Dutch and Flemish painters."

Sunday morning found the travelers attending the service at the English Embassy. Andrew spent the afternoon and evening alone, reading. Although not feeling well the next day, he went to the Museum of Antiques and Coins to see "a good collection of jewels, antique bronzes, utensils of various sorts, coins, and medals." After an early dinner, Andrew and Van Rensselaer left Vienna on the night train for Dresden. The next day "about noon" they "came to the beautiful country called Swiss Saxony." They arrived at Dresden mid-afternoon and checked in to the Hotel Victoria where letters from home were awaiting them (MS Diary, April 6-15, 1862).

Dresden
April 16, 1862
[LETTER 69]

Dear Jim,

We had a very pleasant time in Vienna. The picture galleries are better than I had expected and there are two or three collections of armor, old prints, coins and carvings, which are finer than any I have seen. The city itself is somewhat stately, narrow streets, but clean, fine shops, and quite the air of a great capital. A great deal of building is going on which in time will make a great change in the appearance of the place. Formerly the <u>city</u> was just the central portion within the fortifications. Between this and the outer parts extends all around fortifications with quite a breadth of greensward and broad walks. Unlike other cities, it is in Vienna the central part where everybody lives. Even people who have a palace and grounds in the suburbs have also a residence in the courtly center. They are now pushing the city across the walks and open spaces that once kept off the suburbs [p. 2] and in a short time the old division will be pretty well obliterated, except as it is marked by the course of the Danube & the Wien which were so used as to form part of the defence of the central city.

After a long season of fine weather, there was a change on Sunday and we have since suffered a good deal from the cold. Here today we are in a snow storm.

We got here yesterday afternoon and I found among the letters at the banker's one from you. From the small number of letters here I fear some have miscarried. This seemed to me more probable, alas, from the fact that the letters contain no acknowledgement of those I sent from Cairo, when I came down from Upper Egypt, but only of the later ones I wrote at Jerusalem.

It is just possible that you did not get the Egyptian letters till after the Jerusalem ones. I should be sorry if you did not get them at all as [p. 3] they were more than usually full.

It feels much nearer Paris here than anywhere else we have been. The route is much travelled, and the time between the two cities comparatively short. We shall be in that good town probably either the last of next week or the first of the week after. It will be a great comfort to be once more in a place which will have something of a home-feeling.

Just now I am feeling a little flutter of excitement and expectation in looking forward an hour or two to my visit to the gallery of pictures here, which contains, as you know, the famous *Madonna del Sisto*, a picture which many people regard as the finest in the world. The whole gallery has the reputation of being one of the finest in Europe. I should wait to see it before sending of this letter, but I am anxious that Father should have this as soon as possible as I want to hear from him in [p. 4] reply by the middle of May.

I am continuing to get rid of nearly all the money I had of yours when I left Paris. How you will like the things I have turned it into remains to be seen. I shall not tell you what I have bought for fear you may not find the things themselves equal to the expectations you might form of them. They have been picked up in all sorts of places: Spain, Jerusalem, Damascus, and Constantinople.

Give my love to Orly and to Cline, but on no account whatever to Rev. Reese F. Alsop if you know any such person.[1]

Your affectionate bro[ther],

Andrew

Andrew did indeed visit "the gallery of pictures" where he saw Raphael's Madonna di San Sisto *and, over the next three days, he also went to the "rooms of Mr. Kaufmann where are fine harmoniums and other musical instruments," visited the porcelain shops where Mr. Van Rensselaer made purchases ("which occupied all the morning"), and bought a Madonna and Child for his brother Jim. But the most important event was the receipt of a letter from home informing him of "my appointment by the bishop to Hestonville, Philadelphia," after which he spent some time in prayer. On Good Friday, April 18, the travelers left Dresden in the afternoon for Berlin, arriving tn the evening and going directly to the Hotel du Nord. The next day Andrew wrote Dr. John McClintock that he would be returning to Paris within the week (MS Diary, April 16-19, 1862).*

[Letter from Andrew Longacre to John McClintock. Endorsed on verso by McClintock: "Mr. Longacre / April 1862 / to Pa."]

Dear Doctor McClintock,

Don't you think I am improving in the matter of diligent writing of letters? This is the third to you this week. But do not be alarmed. I think it will be the last for sometime, and I only write to say that if all goes as well as we hope, you may have Emory's bed made up for me next Friday evening, for by nine or half-past, your bell will be ring[ing] violently and your ex-assistant, bag and baggage will come in upon you.

The news from home (of which [p. 2] I have already informed you) has put wings to my feet. I have some thought of trying to get off in the *Persia* or some other boat due in New York as near the first of June as possible.

Berlin,[1]
April 19th, 1862

[LETTER 70]

You know enough of "the people called Methodists"[2] to be fully aware of the surmises and suspicions which must be engendered in the bosoms of my affectionate congregation at Hestonville by my undue delay in rushing to their arms, on my part. I do not intend that they shall have any just ground of complaint if I can help it. I am almost ready to [p. 3] give up going to London, but it is on the way, and I feel as if I must have a farewell look at Highbury Grove[3] and a passing glimpse of the Great Exhibition.[4]

There are many reasons why I should enjoy a little longer time in Paris, and I should be very glad indeed, were I free, to preach for you in June, but it does not seem possible.

Give my love to Madame and believe me always,

Yours faithfully,

Andrew Longacre

The next ten days were filled with activity. Upon arrival in Berlin, Andrew learned that his friend from Paris, Ed Emmett, was in town and invited him to church and Sunday dinner. In the meantime, he and Van Rensselaer visited the museum, looking at the "pictures, statues, antiquities and curiosities of all sorts." They attended the English Chapel on Sunday. Andrew remained behind to take communion, followed by "a quiet and profitable afternoon; mind occupied with thought of my new charge."

On Monday they drove out to Charlottenburg and the palace where "the queen dowager now resides; nothing remarkable [but] fine park and grounds." Next came the mausoleum of Frederick Wilhelm III and Queen Louisa, "in very good taste but it should not have been built in a park nor should the legs of the statue of the queen been crossed."

They left Berlin in the evening, passing through Potsdam, Magdeburg, and Hanover. The next morning, before arriving at Cologne, they caught "a passing glimpse of Duisburg and Dusseldorf." Checking in at the Hotel Royal on the Rhine, they had breakfast before driving to the cathedral which they "saw inside and out, the choir, fine windows given by the king of Bavaria, the treasures, coffer of the three kings, etc." They posed for photographs.

The next morning they took the train for Mayence [Mainz] with "views of the Rhine on the opposite side." Here, they ate lunch before going to the cathedral and walking "a good deal in the town. Saw statue of Gutenberg, etc., went into a few shops." English and French newspapers reported news of the battle of Corinth, the death of Confederate General Albert Sidney Johnston, and the taking of Island No. 10 in the Mississippi River. On Thursday, April 24, Andrew took an early walk alone to the cathedral, "the great street, St. Peter's Church, etc," before going onboard the steamer Prinz von Prushen for a trip down the Rhine to Cologne. "A lovely day, warm, clear and every way charming" was Andrew's comment. They arrived at Cologne in the evening. Andrew had time for devotions before dinner and, again, photographs were taken before they boarded the night train for the twelve-hour ride to Paris.

On arrival, Andrew went directly to Munroe's, his Paris banker, to pick up mail before going to the McClintocks'. There were callers and letters to be written. On Saturday he was "sick a little in the morning" but well enough to make pastoral calls in the afternoon. Sunday morning, in the

rain, he walked down to Meurice's (hotel) "hoping to see Mr. Van Rensselaer, who was not there."
At the Chapel he read the service while Mr. Calkins preached. There were many greetings from
members, and in the afternoon he heard Dr. McClintock preach a sermon "furnishing thought."
Later, he took a walk with Mr. Van Rensselaer.

Early on Monday morning, April 28, Andrew went downtown to see "about steamers and some
other things." He went to the Hotel de Bado but missed Van Rensselaer, "who called on me while
I was out." The next day, Tuesday, Van Rensselaer went with him to the steamer office, "where he
paid for my passage in the Scotia *the 10th of May" (MS Diary, April 19-29, 1862).*

Dear Jim,

I am coming home in the *Scotia*, the new Cunard steamer, which leaves Liverpool the tenth of
May—if nothing happens to prevent. My boxes go today, and on Friday I go on to London and
to spend a week there before sailing. This is two weeks sooner than I had anticipated, but I find I
can do it by making haste, and I am feeling as if it were high time I were at my work.

Can you meet me at Jersey City on my arrival? You can learn when to expect the steamer by
the telegrams from Halifax. I shall have quite a lot of baggage and boxes, a big trunk, a valise &
carpet bag. The boxes are heavy and I think they had better travel as freight from New York to
Philadelphia. Then there will be the stupid customs-house to pass, and I would really be very
thankful to have your [p. 2] clear head to help my dull one, for I am ashamed to say that after all
my travel I feel as shy about doing anything <u>alone</u> as I ever did. I won't add to these solicitations
what perhaps is at the bottom of them all, the wish to catch the earliest possible glimpse of a
beloved face upon my arrival after so long an absence.

I am sure you will come if you can.

I add a few last words before going to bed. Yet I have nothing to say. My heart is full of thoughts
of home. When you remember that tomorrow is the first of May, you can imagine something of
the sadness that blends with my pleasant hopes. To none of us can that day ever bring unmingled
pleasure. God's will <u>was</u> & <u>is</u> best; and it is a happiness to know that each anniversary of our loss
brings us nearer the <u>restoration</u>.[1]

God bless you, my dear Jim.

Your affectionate brother,

Andrew Longacre

⤬

The following days were spent in packing, shopping, and last minute calls, including one to his den-
tist, Dr. Thomas Evans. He had lunch with Alexander Van Rensselaer after which they went to the
Louvre. On his last Thursday in Paris, Andrew made his first and only visit to the cemetery of Père-
Lachaise, where many of the city's most famous (and infamous) citizens were buried. After lunch,
he returned, for the last time, to the Bois de Boulogne. That night, he led Prayer Meeting.

During his last day in Paris, Andrew called on friends, including Edward Harrison May, the
painter, and he baptized Richard Howland Hunt, the small son of Mr. and Mrs. Richard Hunt. At

11 P.M.

the end of the day, when all the company had departed, Andrew and John McClintock had one last conversation before retiring at midnight.

Andrew left Paris on May 3 for London, where he spent almost a week with the Lycetts before taking the night train for Liverpool on May 9. After a brief lay-over, he went on board the Scotia *and sailed "down the Mersey."*

By Monday, May 12, the weather had become "rough and disagreeable," and Andrew "most of the time took such meals as I eat at all in my berth." He passed some of the time reading and reported the weather as "fogs often during the day." By May 19 they were "in the Gulf Stream, air soft, warm and damp." The next night, walking on deck, he could see "lights on shore on both sides, passing up the bay of New York." On Wednesday morning, May 21, the Scotia *landed "at Cunard wharf in Jersey City."*

New York
May 21, 1862

[LETTER 72]

Dear Jim,

I write to let you know that Father and I will come on to-morrow in the 4 P.M. train, arriving at Walnut St. Wharf somewhere about 8 o'clock. I should have chosen an earlier one but Father prefers the later.

I have two awfully heavy boxes and a trunk, besides valise, carpet bag, &c, &c, so I shall need <u>a furniture car</u>. Secure one for me. Putting the baggage in that, I can very well go up home in the cars.

I was sorry to miss your face on my arrival; however Mr. Baker[1] was on the spot, and helped through with my baggage, custom-house, &c, in the kindest manner.

I can['t] say anything else but that it will seem a week till I can see you and the old pet.

It is like a dream to be really here again.

Your own big brother,

Andrew Longacre

It must have been disappointing to Andrew, after such a long-awaited and anticipated reunion, that his brother Jim was not at the dock when he arrived. Instead, Henry J. Baker, who had so often befriended him while in Paris, was there and "assisted me with my baggage at the Customhouse," after which they went to the Baker home in New York City. Two of Andrew's fellow ministers, H. B. Ridgaway (who was serving St. Paul's Methodist Episcopal Church in the city) and R. L. Dashiell (serving Trinity Methodist Episcopal Church, Jersey City), were on hand. Andrew's father, James Barton Longacre, arrived at the Baker home in the afternoon, and other friends called throughout the day.

The next morning, Mrs. Baker drove Andrew and his father "out to Central Park" before putting them on the afternoon train for Philadelphia. When they arrived at the depot, waiting were Andrew's sisters, Sallie and Eliza, and his beloved brother, Jim. One can imagine Andrew's intense emotions after such a long absence. His brief diary entry tells it all. "Home. Talked, played, sang, opened trunk and boxes, etc." After a time of rejoicing in being together again, they all retired at midnight, once again under the same roof at 1206 Spring Garden Street.

Epilogue

AFTER TWO YEARS ABROAD, Andrew quickly adjusted to life back home in Philadelphia. Although he still lived in his father's house through the week, he immediately took up his pastoral responsibilities at the Methodist Episcopal Church at Hestonville to which he had been appointed while still overseas. Hestonville was on the railway west of the city and could be reached in an hour. Andrew preached his first sermon there on Sunday morning, May 25, 1862, and preached again that evening. In the ensuing months, he would often take the train to Hestonville on Saturday in preparation for Sunday preaching, dividing his overnight stays between members of the congregation. He made pastoral calls, conducted meetings, studied, read—and when other duties did not call, he continued to paint. In town through the week, he renewed acquaintances with clergy, friends, and family.

In late August, Andrew made a trip to Newport, Rhode Island, where some of the former members of the American Chapel had gathered: Mr. and Mrs. Henry J. Baker, the Munroe boys, Nelson Dale, Miss Emmett, and Alexander Van Rensselaer. When he left Newport to return to New York by steamer, Andrew reported that there were "several hundred soldiers on board" as well as the Honorable J. C. Frémont who Andrew had last seen in Paris in May, 1861, at the breakfast held by the Americans at the Hotel du Louvre.

In September, 1862, Andrew held his first Quarterly Conference at Hestonville, "my salary fixed at $500.00." Also, in September, his brother Jim "came home and said he had enlisted for state service." Three days later, "Jim went as a volunteer to Harrisburg." With his younger brother, Orly, already in the United States Navy, the Civil War once more touched the Longacre household.

John McClintock remained at the American Chapel in Paris until the spring of 1864 when an invitation came from members of his former church in New York City, asking him to return to St. Paul's. He accepted, and he and his family arrived in New York on May 2, 1864. But after only a year, he resigned and retired, aged 51, to a farm in New Brunswick, New Jersey. In 1866, an invitation came to him to become the first president of Drew University, a new university being built in Madison, New Jersey. McClintock accepted and held the post until his death in March, 1870.

On November 23, 1865, Andrew's beloved brother, Jim, married Augusta McClintock, the daughter of John McClintock and his first wife, Caroline Augusta Wakeman. Augusta, who had been a part of the household in which Andrew lived during his years in Paris, was twenty-two; Jim was thirty-two. They became the parents of four children. In later years, Jim founded the insurance firm of Longacre and Ewing.

On January 1, 1869, Andrew's father, James Barton Longacre, died in Philadelphia. On October 6 of that year, Andrew married Lydia Anne Eastwick, daughter of Lydia Ann James and Andrew McCalla Eastwick of Philadelphia. Andrew's bride was nineteen; he was thirty-eight.[1] Five children were born to them: Lydia Eastwick, Henry Baker (who died in infancy); Sara Keen; Frederick Van Duzer; and Breta. Daughters Lydia and Breta, like their father and grandfather, were artists. Some of their works are in the Florence Griswold Museum in Old Lyme, Connecticut.

Following his return from Paris, Andrew served a number of prominent churches in Philadelphia, Wilmington, Baltimore, Newburgh, and New York City, reapponted to some of them over the years a second time. In 1882 Dickinson College, Carlisle, Pennsylvania, conferred an honorary Doctor of Divinity degree on Andrew. From 1892-96, he was Presiding Elder of the New York District (which, in 1895, became the New York and Hudson River District) in the New York Conference. In 1896 he was appointed to Madison Avenue Methodist Episcopal Church in New York City where he served until his retirement in 1902.[2]

Health failing, the doctors diagnosed "valvular irregularity of the heart," which brought on sharp attacks of pain. He could no longer preach but could still paint and in his last years executed over thirty miniatures of close friends. He died at his home in New York City on February 18, 1906, age seventy-four, preceded in death by his older sister, Sallie Longacre Keen, by only twenty-three days.

Not long before Andrew died, an old friend, Bishop Cyrus D. Foss, inquired of his health. Andrew reported on his condition and then wrote, "That will tell you about where I am in things visible. . . . The dear Lord keeps me in entire quietness and peace, so that this episode of my life comes as simply and naturally as any before. It does not occur to me that I have anything to be troubled about. I am taking no anxious thought for the morrow. And if the end is near, it is what I have lived for and hoped for, since I was a boy."[3]

Andrew Longacre was buried in historic Woodlands Cemetery in Philadelphia beside his parents. His beloved wife, Lydia Anne, all of his siblings, their spouses, and some of their children were also buried in the Longacre plot that is marked by a large red granite obelisk. Close during their lifetimes, they remain so in death.

Appendix A

Letter from Andrew Longacre to Mrs. Darlington, New York, May 3, 1860, just before he departs aboard the Vanderbilt *for Paris.*

My dear Mrs. Darlington

After so long a failure to fulfill my promise to write to you, I suppose you will be almost surprised to hear from me at all. Without attempting to apologize for fulfilling a duty, and a most pleasant one, even at a late hour, it is but fair that I should state why it is that I write just now. I am here (in N.Y.) until next Saturday, the day after tomorrow, when I leave for Europe in the Steamer Vanderbilt on my way to fulfil my newly appointed duty of assistant minister at the American Chapel in Paris. I feel unwilling to leave so long a distance between us without informing [p.2] you of the fact. Besides, the approaching separation from all my friends seems to bring a special & peculiar love to each, and I feel reluctant to go away without a last appeal to their sympathy and kind feeling. When this reaches you, I shall be on the ocean. It will cheer me a little to know that I have your thought and interest even there & tho' I cannot have any manifestation of it. Love, especially the love of Christian hearts is <u>real,</u> the changing circumstances, the nearness, the distance, are but the cloud & sunshine that chase each other over the unvarying landscape. Just now, it is a great comfort to know that the world of soul, of mind, of heart, is to be classed with "the things which are not seen, are eternal," while the vicissitudes of outward life are but the temporary conditions and accidents of our being. There is a grand truth [p. 3] as well as dear old poetry in these lines

> "Inseparably joined in heart
> The friends of Jesus are."

But I have gone away into these abstractions while you are wondering how came all this to pass. I cannot tell you. I am as much surprised as you can be that Dr. McClintock, who goes out as the Pastor of the American Chapel in June, should have selected me to precede him & after his arrival to remain as his assistant. It has come to me as the rain & the sunshine come to the fields, without request or even the dreaming of such a possibility.

To me, for considerations too numerous to tell, it seems simply "the Lord's doing." Even if I should never reach the coast of France, but should land in a "better country," I am quite confident that in going I am only following the divine ordering. "The voice behind me [p. 4] saying this is the way" has not often spoke more plainly than it seems to speak now.

Now, at last, will you pray for me. I go to a hard field, spiritually considered. I go alone, to a land of almost magical power to tempt & lead astray, at least to some extent, all sorts of men. I am sure I go <u>to do good</u>. This is the object, as far as motive is concerned the <u>sole</u> object of my going. (Perhaps I ought to include a desire for improved health.) I know I cannot do good without grace for my own preservation, & the baptism of the Spirit of God upon my ministry. May I hope to have your prayers?

New York
May 3rd, 1860

If you feel like writing to me, and I should be very glad indeed, if you would address—1206 Spring Garden at Phila. & the letters will be forwarded.

My very warm love—full and hearty—to Stephen.

Yours faithfully,

(He owes me a letter)

Andrew Longacre

[*Postscript written across the top of the letter above the inside address:*] Remember me to your brother Enoch when you have opportunity. Will he write to me?

Appendix B
Ministerial Record of Andrew Longacre

1852—Philadelphia Conference, admitted on trial, appointed to Chestnut Hill, Reading District
1853—Remained on trial, appointed to Waynesburgh, Reading District
1854—Admitted into full connection, ordained deacon, appointed to Pottsville, Second Church
1855—Appointed to Pottsville, Second Church
1856—Ordained elder, appointed to Scott Church, Wilmington, Wilmington District
1857—Appointed to Central Church (supernumerary), South Philadelphia District
1858—Ditto
1859—Appointed to Union Church (supernumerary), South Philadelphia District
1860—Ditto
1861—Appointed as Assistant Pastor, American Chapel in Paris
1862—Appointed to Hestonville, South Philadelphia District
1863—Appointed to Trinity Church, North Philadelphia District
1864—Ditto
1865—Ditto
1866—Transferred to Baltimore Conference and appointed to Charles Street, Baltimore
1867—Appointed to Charles Street, Baltimore
1868—Ditto
1869—Transferred to New York Conference and appointed to Central Church, NYC
1870—Appointed to Central Church, NYC
1871—Ditto
1872—Appointed to Trinity Church in Newburgh, New York
1873—Ditto
1874—Ditto
1875—Transferred to Philadelphia Conference and stationed at Greene Street
1876—Appointed to Greene Street
1877—Ditto
1878—Appointed to Tabernacle church, North Philadelphia
1879—Ditto
1880—Ditto
1881—Appointed to Trinity Church, Northwest Philadelphia District
1882—Ditto
1883—Appointed to Arch Street, Philadelphia
1884—Ditto
1885—Appointed to Arch Street and St Luke's, Philadelphia
1886—Transferred to Baltimore Conference and appointed to Mt Vernon Place, Baltimore
1887—Appointed to Mt Vernon Place, Baltimore

1888—Ditto

1889—Transferred to New York Conference and appointed to Trinity Church, Newburgh, New York

1890—Appointed to Trinity Church, Newburgh, New York

1891—Ditto

1892—Appointed as Presiding Elder, New York District at Yonkers

1893—Ditto

1894—Ditto

1895—Ditto [now New York and Hudson River District]

1896-1905—Appointed to Madison Avenue church, New York City

Appendix C

The Parson's Courtship

I know a tale of olden time,
And this, to fill an idle day,
I fashion into idle rhyme,
And all who care to read it may.

The autumn leaves were all aflame,
And so, in autumn time of life,
A parson's heart was tinged the same,
With holy fire to wed a wife.

He girt the saddle on his mare,
To go the way his heart inclined,
But wore a sober look and air,
As one who had a troubled mind.

As through the ranks of golden rod,
He wound his way up Prospect hill.
He humbly asked Almighty God
To grant a token of his will.

The parson's vision cleansed by prayer,
His duty grew as clear as light;
And duty never looks so fair
As seen by prayer's illumined sight.

Already had he fixt his choice:
For every Sunday in the choir
He heard the Lady Annie's voice
Until she grew his heart's desire.

The parson's passions unconfessed,
Like smouldered heat within him burned,
Which never once the lady guessed,
Or haply it had been returned.

With hazel whip the mare was switched,
And cantered up the rocky road,
And underneath a tree was hitched
At Mr Eastwick's old abode.

The damsel was busy sifting flour,
Nor heard the comer till he said,
"Be praise to that Almighty Power
Who giveth man his daily bread."

The damsel caught by such a guest
In just her linsey-woolsey gown,
Instead of in her Sunday best,
Dropped bashfully her eyelids down.

Then spake her suitor to her face,
"I have a solemn word to say,
Whereto is need of heavenly grace,
So Lady Eastwick let us pray."

Devoutly did the couple kneel,
The parson at the rocking chair,
The lady at the spinning wheel,
And this the burden of the prayer.

He mourned for uncommitted sin,
Implored a pardon on mankind,
And craved that grace would enter in
And sweetly move the lady's mind.

Then, rising from his prayerful knees,
"I yearn to take a wife," he said,
"And loving thee—if God shall please,
Nor thou refuse, we twain shall wed."

The Lady started with surprise
(For women young are women still)
But answered lifting not her head,
"I seek to know the heavenly will."

The heavenly will was plain indeed,
And pointed to the flowery yoke,
For love is not a human need
Of young alone, but aged folk.

While yet the hyacinths were in bloom
There came a throng from far and near,
To wish the joy of bride and groom,
And eat and drink the wedding cheer.

A hallowed honeymoon they passed,
And younger grew in growing old,
Till sweetly fading out at last,
They left the tale that I have told.

[An undated, quaint, and charming Valentine by Andrew Longacre to his wife, Lydia Anne East-wick, written some years after their marriage, October 6, 1869.]

Notes
Introduction

1. For the history of the Longacre family, see Marian Sykes Longacre, ed., *The Longacre Line in America Descended from a Member of the Old Swedish Colony on the Delaware, With Special Emphasis on the Descendants of James Barton Longacre (August 11, 1794-January 1, 1869)*. Fayetteville, New York: Privately Printed, 1971. See also, *Dictionary of American Biography*. Dumas Malone, ed. New York: Charles Scribner's Sons, 1932, 11:380-81 (hereafter cited as *DAB*); and *Cyclopaedia of Methodism* (rev. ed.). Matthew Simpson, ed. Philadelphia: Louis H. Everts, 1880, p. 990.

2. The image on the Indian Head penny was that of Sarah ("Sallie") Longacre, Andrew's older sister. When she was about ten years old (i.e., *ca.* 1838), she paid a visit to her father's office at the U. S. Mint. At the time, he was entertaining two native American Indians who were wearing feather headdresses. One of them removed his bonnet and placed it on young Sallie's head. Her father was so enchanted with the image that he sketched her profile. Years later, when James Barton Longacre was commissioned to design a new one-cent piece, he remembered his sketch of Sallie and engraved that image for the new coin. Issued in 1859, 1,800 million Indian Head pennies were issued over the next fifty years.

3. *In Memoriam, Andrew Longacre, 1831-1906*. New York: n. p., 1906, p. 9, quoting Bishop Cyrus D. Foss. The Tuesday meetings were continued after Eliza's death by her oldest daughter, Sarah Longacre Keen. See also a letter from Mary Boswell of Philadelphia to Phoebe Palmer, in New York City, December 27, 1848: "Sister Longacre has come out clear and bold in her profession of sanctification. She holds a meeting at her house like unto the one at 54 Rivington Street [the Palmer home in New York]. How pleasant to think at the same time in neighbouring cities the sisters are meeting at the same throne of grace, while their maternal vows are being offered up. Sister Longacre labours not in vain, having fruit of her toil. Sister Keen and brother Andrew still aid the cause of holiness by their testimony" (Bridwell Library Manuscript Collection).

4. Phoebe Palmer Longacre lived only eight weeks. Knowledge of this birth had not come down in the Longacre family of the present day. Only when a trip was made in February 2001 to historic Woodlands cemetery in Philadelphia by Andrew's great-grandson and namesake were her name and dates discovered incised on the side of the red granite obelisk that marked her parents' graves. This information was subsequently confirmed in the burial and baptismal records at St. George's Methodist Episcopal Church in Philadelphia and at the Historical Society of Pennsylvania. See Letter 4, June 25, 1860, and note 1.

5. Reported by an unnamed member of the class in *The Christian Advocate*, James M. Buckley, ed. New York: Eaton & Mains Publishers, 81 (March 1, 1906):9, pp. (5)285-(6)286.

6. See Letter 58, October 29, 1861.

7. In the Methodist Episcopal Church supernumerary preachers are those who by reason of impaired health are temporarily unable to perform effective work. They can receive an appointment or be left without one according to the judgment of the Annual Conference to which they

belong. Whenever supplying a charge, they are subject to the same limitations and discipline as effective ministers. *Cyclopaedia of Methodism*, p. 843.

8. *Cyclopaedia of Methodism*, p. 990.

9. Andrew Longacre, *Manuscript Diary*, January 31 and February 20, 1860 (hereafter cited as *MS Diary*).

10. *MS Diary,* March 27, 1860.

11. *MS Diary,* March 21, 27, 30; April 11, 12; May 1, 1860.

12. Letter to Mrs. Darlington, May 3, 1860 (quoted by permission of Dr. Andrew Longacre, Jr., Skaneateles, New York). For the complete text of this letter, see below, Appendix A. See also Longacre's *Journal of Religious Experience, September 1856-August 31, 1861* (hereafter cited as *MS Journal*), April 14, 1860.

13. *MS Diary*, May 1, 1860.

14. Letter to Mrs. Darlington, May 3, 1860.

15. Sources for this account of John McClintock, Jr., are George R. Crooks, *Life and Letters of Reverend John McClintock, D.D., LL.D., Late President of Drew Theological Seminary.* New York: Nelson & Phillips; Cincinnati: Hitchcock & Walden, 1876; *DAB*, 11:589-90; and *Cyclopaedia of Methodism,* p. 573.

16. Crooks, p. 199.

17. For the history of the American and Foreign Christian Union and the American Chapel in Paris, see Joseph Wilson Cochran, *Friendly Adventurers; A Chronicle of the American Church of Paris (1857-1931)*. Paris: Bretano's, 1931, and the website http://www.americanchurchparis.org/.

18. John McClintock reported that the congregations usually numbered around three hundred and never less than one hundred and fifty (Crooks, p. 281). Soon after his arrival in Paris, Andrew reported to Jim, "Our chapel is beautiful and must be seen to be enjoyed. A written description would be of no account" (Letter 1, May 21, 1860).

19. This arrangement lasted for seventy-one years. The last act in the farewell service of the American Chapel at 21, rue de Berri, on Easter Day, 1929, before it moved to the new location across the Seine at 65, quai d'Orsay, was the removal of the Book of Common Prayer from its stand in the front of the pulpit. See Crooks, p. 281; Cochran, pp. 77-78, and note.

20. *MS Diary,* May 20, 1860.

21. *MS Journal*, September 29, 1856. Andrew added, "Having been deprived of them makes me see more clearly than ever their value and my own particular need for them."

22. *MS Diary,* May 29, 31, 1860.

23. See S. C. Burchell, *Imperial Masquerade; The Paris of Napoleon III.* New York: Atheneum, 1971, pp. 17, 193, 286.

24. Crooks, pp. 346-47.

25. *MS Diary,* May 27, 1860.

26. *MS Diary,* June 7, 1860.

27. Letter 6, July 9, 1860.

28. Andrew Longacre, quoted in Crooks, pp. 346-47.

29. *MS Journal,* August 12, 1861.

30. Letter 18, November 5, 1860.

31. Crooks, p. 297.

32. See Letter 9, August 20, 1860, note 2.

33. Crooks, pp. 333-34.

34. McClintock, letter to C. C. North, January 7, 1861; Crooks, pp. 297-98.

35. See Letter 20, January 2, 1861, and notes 2, 3, and 4.

36. Letter 33, May 2, 1861.

37. Letter 27, March 27, 1861.

38. Letter 51, September 4, 1861.

39. *MS Journal,* October 11, 1857.

40. *MS Journal*, September 11, 1856.

41. Foss, *In Memoriam*, p. 14.

42. *MS Diary*, September 26, 1860.

43. *MS Diary*, July 22, 1861.

44. Edward Harrison May (1824-1887) was born in England but grew up in America. In the early 1850's he was working in Thomas Couture's studio in Paris. He made exceptionally good copies of works in the Louvre, and a number of his paintings are in the permanent collection of the Metropolitan Museum of Art in New York City. See *DAB*, 12:446-47, and E. Bénézit, *Dictionnaire critique et documentaire des Peintres, Scuplteurs, Dessinateurs et Graveurs. Nouvelle Édition*. [Paris] Librairie Gründ, 1961 6:15. For William P. Dana, who was born in Boston in 1833, see Bénézit, 3:25. See also, Letter 26, February 23, 1861, note 2.

45. See *Christian Advocate*, 81(March 1, 1906):9, pp. (5)285-(6)286; Foss, *In Memoriam*, p. 13.

46. *MS Journal*, January 17, 1857.

47. *MS Journal*, September 21, 1856.

48. *MS Journal*, October 23, 1859.

49. *MS Journal*, September 7, 1856.

50. Letter 36, May 20, 1861.

Letter 1, Paris, May 21, 1860

1. Andrew's younger sister, Eliza Huldah Longacre, born in Philadelphia, May 5, 1837.

2. He had made his passage on the *Vanderbilt*; see below, Letter 12, September 6, 1860.

3. There had been 136 suicides in Paris in 1859; see *Galignani's New Paris Guide for 1860*. Paris: A. and W. Galignani and Co., Rue de Rivoli, No. 224 [1860], p. 78, note 1.

4. This was Norris Castle, built by architect James Wyatt in 1799, which still exists. At the time of Andrew's visit, it was owned by Robert Bell, the publisher of *Bell's Life in London*, a sporting chronicle published from *ca.*1822-1886. As a child, Queen Victoria spent holidays at Norris Castle, and it was said that this influenced her eventually purchasing Osborne House nearby (some accounts even state that she had tried to purchase Norris Castle, but that the owner would not sell). Grateful appreciation for this information is herewith expressed to Roger Hewitt, Isle of Wight History Centre, Newport, Isle of Wight (http://www.iwhistory.org.uk).

5. Osborne House, Queen Victoria's residence in the Isle of Wight, was built in 1846. She died there in 1901. *The Encyclopaedia Britannica,* 11th ed. Chicago: Encyclopaedia Britannica, Inc., 1956, 16:947; 23:126 (hereafter cited as *EB*).

6. *The Great Eastern* had six masts. At the time of her launching in 1858, she was the largest ship in the world, with alternate methods of propulsion. Originally conceived by I. K. Brunel, her hull and paddle engines were built by J. Scott Russell, a London company, while James Watt of Birmingham built the screw engines. In addition, her six masts were set with 6,500 yards of canvas. After unsuccessful attempts to lay a transatlantic telegraph cable with smaller ships (e.g., the *Niagara* and the *Agamemnon*), success finally came in 1866 when *The Great Eastern* was put to the task. But a ship of such unprecedented size presented unprecedented problems to her backers in launching, operation, and financing. Although a technical marvel, she was an economic failure (which Andrew refers to in Letter 14, September 21, 1860). See *EB*, 4:286; 20:514, 544; 22:415, and *The New Encyclopaedia Britannica*, 15th edition. Chicago: Encyclopaedia Britannica, Inc., 1985, 5:444; 28:806 (hereafter cited as *NEB*).

7. A hackney-coach or four-wheeled carriage drawn by two horses and having room for four to six persons.

8. John M. Maris, a wholesale druggist, was a leading member of the Methodist Episcopal Church in Philadelphia. He was educated as a Friend but united with Trinity Church and was one of the chief founders of Arch Street Church. See *Cyclopaedia of Methodism*, p. 562.

9. No town in France bears this name. Longacre may have misheard "Mantes" as "Mayence." Mantes-la-Jolie is on the rail line between Rouen and Paris.

10. Trains from Havre, Rouen, Versailles, and St. Germain arrived in Paris at the Western railroad terminus, a large handsome building at No. 122, rue St. Lazare; see *Galignani's Guide for 1860*, pp. 209-10. For a short time after 1860, the station appeared on maps as Gare dé l'Ouest (as did also Gare Montparnasse), but it soon became known as Gare St. Lazare, remains so today, and still handles rail traffic to and from the west.

11. In his *MS Diary* for Friday, May 18, 1860, Andrew reported, "Called on J. W. Tucker and delivered my letter [of introduction]—not satisfied with the interview—went away sad." Andrew never spelled out the specific reasons for this unpleasant encounter at the beginning of his new position as Assistant Pastor. James W. Tucker was the Secretary and Treasurer of the Executive Committee of the American Chapel and had held that post since the first formal meeting on February 18, 1858. From this first visit until late October, 1860, Andrew records at least a dozen visits with the Tuckers, usually of a pastoral nature and often in the company of Dr. McClintock and/or Emory McClintock, but he never elaborates further on his initial interview.

12. The J. D. B. Curtises were prominent members of the American Chapel and Andrew paid many visits to their home. They befriended this young, often homesick, clergyman and took him into their family circle. Together they attended exhibitions, went sightseeing within the city, and made excursions to St. Germain-en-Laye and St. Cloud. Their conversations often concerned the American Chapel and its interests, the education of the Curtis children, and "the various points of the religious life" (*MS Diary*, June 3, 1860). In August when the Curtises left the city for their apartment at Versailles, Andrew was a welcome guest, going out on the train on Mondays and returning early on Sunday mornings in time for services at the Chapel. At Versailles they made numerous visits to the Palace and Trianons to see the paintings and statuary and to the gardens for concerts and walks among the exquisite plantings. It was during this time that Andrew sketched Mrs. Curtis's head in profile. In mid-October Andrew reported that

Mrs. Curtis was not well, although he never gives the nature of her illness. By early November, she was somewhat better but still not able to come to the table for dinner. It was with profound shock that, while in Rome on March 24, 1861, Andrew received the news that Mrs. Curtis had died. Back in Paris on April 1, he called on the grieving widower. Andrew's diary entry reads, "[Returned] home; very sad." For the remainder of his tenure at the Chapel, Andrew continued his association with Mr. Curtis, but news of the Curtis children and family affairs no longer appear in Andrew's diary (*MS Diary, passim*).

13. John Foster Keen, a banker in Philadelphia and New York, had married Andrew's older sister, Sarah, on May 6, 1847 (Marian Sykes Longacre, p. 8). In these letters and in Andrew's *MS Diary*, he is always referred to as Mr. Keen.

14. George L. Prentiss had been appointed in 1859 to fill the pulpit of the American Chapel until a permanent pastor could be secured; i.e., until John McClintock arrived. The Rev. R. H. Seeley was also listed as a minister serving this church; see *Galignani's Guide for 1860*, p. 122.

15. The Palais de l'Industrie was located on the Champs Élysées across the Seine from Les Invalides. At the end of the nineteenth century, it was demolished, and the Grand Palais and the Petit Palais were built in its place for the International Exhibition of 1900. A sketch of this Paris landmark that Andrew "picked up in a shop on the quai" shows the Seine curving to the left, the Rond-Point at right center, the Arc d'Triomphe at the upper right, and Mont Valérien in the distance. For another description of the Palais and its surroundings, see below, Letter 12, September 6, 1860.

16. The most recent failure of the transatlantic telegraph had been in July 1858; success did not come until 1866; see note 6, above, and below, Letter 29, April 4, 1861, note 1.

Letter 2, Paris, June 16, 1860

1. This and other items, including a map of Paris (see below, Letter 3, June 18, 1860), were carried back to the U.S. by Dr. Gould (*MS Diary*, June 18, 1860). Dr. Gould had been Andrew's fellow passenger on the *Vanderbilt*.

2. Longacre had mistakenly begun his letter on the fourth and last page of his stationery.

3. A fine essay could be written about the various ships mentioned in these letters, about the companies which built and operated them and the people who sailed in them. Schedules and notices of arrivals and departures from Havre, Southampton, Liverpool, New York, Baltimore, and Philadelphia appeared daily on the front pages of the London "*Times*" and other European and American newspapers. For Andrew these vessels were life-lines to home and family. When one arrived behind schedule or failed to bring mail for him, his disappointment was palpable.

4. The unification of Italy had been a concern for many years. After the French Revolution and the Napoleonic wars, Italy became a grouping of major and minor independent states, first as republics and then as satellite states of the French Empire. After Napoleon Bonaparte's defeat in 1815, these states were restored to their former rulers, most under Austria. In a sincere desire to help these neighboring territories, in 1859 Emperor Louis Napoleon took an active role in helping Italy free itself from Austrian tyranny. In the negotiations, France was promised Nice and Savoy. When Austria declared war in April 1859, Louis Napoleon led his armies across the Alps,

winning victories at Magenta and Soliferino. A preliminary peace was signed at Villafranca on July 11, 1859. The formal treaty was signed at Zurich on November 10, 1859. See Burchell, pp. 292-93; *NEB*, 6:434; 10:87; 19:510.

5. Military parades were a prominent feature of the Second Empire. "The whole régime was cast in a military mold. Not since the days of Napoleon Bonaparte had the streets of Paris been filled with so many uniforms. Officers strolled along the Grands Boulevards, there was regimental music in the garden of the Tuileries, and impressive parades were mounted on the least occasion. In keeping with Louis Napoleon's emphasis on splendor, the uniforms of officers and enlisted men alike were dazzling in their richness and variety. There were élite troops of the Cent Gardes, Zouaves in their tasseled hats, Saphis from the desert, all manner of lancers and hussars and cuirassiers, Chasseurs d'Afrique and elegant officers of the Guides in green and gold" (See Burchell, p. 286). Andrew witnessed a number of these events during his residence in Paris; e.g., see Letter 17, October 30, 1860.

6. Charles James Faulkner (1806-1884), lawyer, congressman, diplomat, soldier, had been appointed minister to France in 1859 by President James Buchanan. After the beginning of the Lincoln administration, Faulkner returned to the United States. In 1861 he entered the Confederate Army and served as assistant adjutant–general on the staff of General Stonewall Jackson. After the war he returned to his home in Berkeley County in what is now West Virginia and resumed his law practice. In 1833 he married Mary Wagner Boyd, daughter of General Elisha Boyd. They had two sons and six daughters. *DAB*, 6:298. From Andrew's *MS Diary* we know that Mr. and Mrs. Scott of St. Louis were the other guests present on this occasion. Mr. Butterworth of New York and Mrs. Conrad of Washington are also mentioned.

7. Alexander Van Rensselaer was born November 5, 1814, into a wealthy Albany, New York, family. His father, Stephen Van Rensselaer III (born in 1764 in New York, NY), had been a Major General in the War of 1812 and Lieutenant Governor of New York. His mother (his father's second wife) was Cornelia Patterson, born 1780. Andrew Longacre was not able to make this trip to Russia but, eventually, Van Rensselaer did become his patron and benefactor on a lengthy trip through Spain, Egypt, the Middle East, and Europe; see below, Letter 51, September 4, 1861, Letter 54, October 8, 1861, and those following.

8. Euphemia White Van Rensselaer (1816-1888) was Alexander's youngest sister. In 1843 she married John Church Cruger, grandson of Nicholas Cruger, the largest merchant in New York in 1770 and owner of Cruger's Island on the Hudson river.

9. See below, Letter 26, February 23, 1861, note 6.

10. All efforts to identify this person in the Longacre household have been unsuccessful. He does not appear on the U. S. Census Records for 1860 nor in the genealogy of the family prepared by Marian Sykes Longacre (see below, Letter 29, April 4, 1861; Letter 30, April 11, 1861; and Letter 69, April 16, 1862).

Letter 3, Paris, June 18, 1860

1. Unfortunately, this map has not remained with the letter. Andrew had purchased another map on June 14 for 3 francs (*MS Diary*). This was, most probably, Logerot's map of 1860, which

has survived among Andrew's archives. Although he wrote that he did not like this map as well as the one he sent to Jim, it is in fact a very important and historic artifact. The new streets and boulevards, which were a large part of the "Haussmannization" of Paris that was taking place at this time, are drawn across the face of the city with red (streets under construction) and blue (streets approved for construction) lines.

2. The American Chapel was located at No. 21, rue de Berri.

Letter 4, Paris, June 25, 1860

1. Dr. Walter C. Palmer, a prominent New York physician and evangelist, and his wife, Phoebe Palmer, noted for their evangelical labors, were long-time friends of the James Barton and Eliza Longacre. When Eliza's last child was born, April 6, 1850, she was named Phoebe Palmer Longacre. Tragically, the baby lived only a short time (see above, Introduction, note 4).

When Andrew visited in New York, he attended meetings held by the Palmers and on one occasion spent the night in the Palmer home (*MS Journal*, September 30, 1857; see also September 11, 1856). During 1859-1863, the Palmers traveled in Great Britain, holding services in many places. In June, 1860, Dr. Palmer "took their son," Walter C. Palmer, Jr., "and some other friends on a trip to the continent while Phoebe stayed behind in Gateshead to regain her strength through a total rest." See Charles Edward White, *The Beauty of Holiness; Phoebe Palmer as Theologian, Revivalist, Feminist, and Humanitarian.* Grand Rapids, Michigan: Francis Asbury Press, 1986, p. 68 and n. 12, and p. 75. Also *The National Cyclopedia of American Biography.* Clifton, New Jersey: James T. White & Company, 1979, 5:182; and *Cyclopaedia of Methodism*, pp. 691-92.

2. Walter C. Palmer, Junior, was seventeen years old at this time. Later in life he served as publisher for his mother's writings. See *Notable American Women, 1607-1950; A Biographical Dictionary.* Edward T. James, ed. Cambridge, MA: Belknap Press of Harvard University Press, 1971, *loc. cit.*

3. John Munroe & Company, bankers, at 5, rue de la Paix.

4. Francis Lycett (later knighted) was a distinguished Wesleyan layman of London. Few men did more for the extension of Methodism. He was deeply interested in the spiritual destitution of London and its environs and gave fifty thousand pounds toward the erection of fifty chapels, on condition that a similar sum was raised to meet it. Later he donated ten thousand pounds toward the extension of Methodism in country villages on the same terms. See *Cyclopaedia of Methodism*, p. 554. On more than one occasion, Andrew did accept Mr. Lycett's invitation to visit in London; see Letter 13, September 13, 1860; Letter 14, September 21, 1860; and Letter 44, July 25, 1861.

5. The McClintocks arrived on June 28; see below, Letter 5, note 1.

Letter 5, Paris, July 6, 1860

1. The McClintocks had been living at the Hotel de Lille et d'Albion since their arrival in Paris on Thursday, June 28. See Crooks, p. 292.

Letter 6, Paris, July 9th, 1860, No. 42, rue des Ecuries d'Artois

1. Mrs. J. D. B. Curtis accompanied Andrew to the photographer's on this occasion (*MS Diary*, July 10, 1860). The full-length portrait, which he kept in an album of photographs, shows him standing with his right hand resting on the back of an ornately carved and upholstered chair.

2. I.e., Andrew's first cousin, Huldah Stewart West; see below, Letter 32, April 23, 1861, and note 2.

3. Living on the Right Bank in the western part of the city, Andrew was enjoying the benefits of Baron Georges Eugène Haussmann's work in Paris. Begun seven years earlier, he turned narrow, congested streets into elegant new boulevards, constructed new buildings, public parks, and squares, and changed a medieval city into a modern metropolis. Louis Napoleon had appointed Haussmann prefect of the Seine in June 1853 and, in addition to demolition and rebuilding above ground, Haussmann was also engaged in major construction underground of the sewer system (remarkable even today), water supply, and gas mains. The American Chapel was also new, having only been completed in 1858. Except for a brief mention of the new Central Markets which he saw shortly after he arrived in Paris, Andrew does not mention any of this activity until the spring of 1861, when he walked out to Passy "to Boulevart de l'Empereur to see the progress of the excavations" (now avenues Henri Martin and Georges Mandel). He returned home "by way of avenue St. Cloud" (avenue Victor Hugo). See *MS Diary,* May 25, 1860, and April 10, 1861, and Letter 12, September 6, 1860, note 2.

4. I.e., on the ground floor. In addition to Andrew's graphic description of his new lodgings at No. 42, rue des Ecuries d'Artois, he enclosed a charming sketch, in minute detail, of the rooms on the second floor. He also made color sketches of his room, the gilt clock, a scene from his window, and the elegant hôtel across the street at No. 41, rue des Ecuries d'Artois (dated "August 1860"), which he preserved in a portfolio of his art work.

5. The Bois de Boulogne was one of Louis Napoleon's most splendid gifts to the people of Paris. He had long admired Hyde Park in London and with that in mind, in July 1852, he set to work providing a similar space at home. With engineers and landscape gardeners (notably Adolphe Alphand), he turned two thousand acres of an arid state-owned forest into a masterpiece of lakes, waterfalls, gardens, grottos, carriage roads, bridle and footpaths. Over four hundred thousand trees were planted; cafés and restaurants were built. Part of the Longchamp Plain was added on which a race course was built. By 1858 two million francs and twelve hundred workers had performed their miracle. The people of Paris flocked to this green wonderland, and afternoon drives and walks in the Bois became one of the spectacles of the Second Empire. See Burchell, pp. 16-17, 91-92; *Galignani's Guide for 1860*, pp. 202, 495.

Andrew's letters and manuscript diaries are filled with references to the Bois de Boulogne. He often took early morning walks there as well as evening strolls. Many of these were of a devotional nature in which he prayed and felt "a sweet communion with God."

6. The summer of 1860 in Paris continued to be unusually cool. John McClintock remarked on it in a letter to Mrs. Dr. A. S. Purdy, dated August 14, 1860: "We have not had a hot day: warm clothes, overcoats when driving, two blankets at night. On no day yet have we been able to keep a window in the house open or to wear summer clothes of any kind." Crooks, p. 294.

7. From the *MS Diary*, however, we learn that Andrew did not receive his own key to No. 42, rue des Ecuries d'Artois. On September 4, 1860, he moved with the McClintocks to No. 10, rue Balzac; not until December 30 did he record that he had paid 2 ½ francs for a *passe partout*, for which he received reimbursement from Dr. McClintock.

8. See George Gordon, Lord Byron, *The Dream*, sts. iii.-viii, first lines.

9. Emory McClintock, John McClintock's son by his first marriage and a brother to Augusta McClintock, was twenty years old.

Letter 7, Paris, July 23, 1860

1. Sunday services at the Chapel began with Morning Prayer at 11.15 a.m., the sermon at 12, and the afternoon service at 3 p.m.

2. Thursday night Prayer Meeting was at 7.30 p.m.

Letter 8, Paris, August 11th, 1860

1. Queen Victoria and her consort, Prince Albert, made their visit in August 1855. The queen was enchanted. "It was like a fairy tale," she said, " and everything so beautiful!" See Burchell, p. 54.

2. John A. Wright of Philadelphia was a civil engineer engaged with railroads, especially in the organization of the Pennsylvania Railroad. A member of the Methodist Episcopal Church since childhood, he was a liberal contributor to the Arch Street Methodist Episcopal Church in Philadelphia. *Cyclopaedia of Methodism*, p. 966.

3. Mr. Roland was from Milestown, Pennsylvania; his friend, Mr. Drake, was from Philadelphia (*MS Diary*, August 10, 1860).

4. James Neill entered the Pennsylvania Conference in 1836. After preaching for several years, Neill's health problems necessitated his taking a supernumerary relation. Although he became engaged in mining and the sale of anthracite coal, he continued to preach on occasion and assisted in the organization of Methodist churches in Philadelphia, including Spring Garden, the home district of the Longacre family. *Cyclopaedia of Methodism*, p. 640.

5. Pharamond was a legendary Frankish king of the fifth century.

6. Françoise d'Aubigné, Marquise de Maintenon (1635-1719), consort of Louis XIV.

7. August 15th, the fête-day of Napoleon I, was celebrated in grand style during the Second Empire and drew large numbers of strangers to the capital, not only from the provinces but from England and other neighboring countries. The Place de la Concorde and the Place du Trône were centers of festivities, while on the Champs Élysées rope-dancers, buffoons, orchestras for dancers, and stages for dramatic presentations entertained the crowds, notable for their gaiety and good humor. In the evening the avenues and walks were illuminated, as well as the garden of the Tuileries, and fireworks took place on a magnificent scale. Celebrations of this sort were greatly favored by the French people, who had brought the art of preparing for them to a high degree of perfection (see *Galignani's Guide for 1860*, p. 492). In his *MS Diary* for this day, Andrew reported that he and Dr. McClintock, and others in the family, went to the Esplanade of

des Invalides, which was crowded with people, to see tight-rope dancing, acrobatic feats, military pantomimes, and shows. In the evening he went out again with the young ladies and John Emory to see "a magnificent illumination and such fire works as I never before saw or imagined" (for the "young ladies and John Emory," see below, Letter 11, August 27, 1860, note 1). See also, Letter 47, August 7, 1861.

Letter 9, Paris, August 20, 1860

1. Joseph Albert Wright (1810-1867), Governor of Indiana, congressman, and diplomat, was born in Washington, Pennsylvania. President James Buchanan appointed him minister of the United States to Prussia, June 1, 1857. He was recalled in May 1861, but before he departed Berlin, he sought a proclamation by the Prussian government disapproving the course taken by the Confederate States. He was re-appointed minister to Germany on June 30, 1865, and served there until his death in Berlin. *DAB*, 20:559-60.

2. Finances were a perpetual challenge for both Andrew and McClintock, and the arrangements for Andrew's appointment as McClintock's assistant if not ill-defined from the start were certainly ever-shifting. Of these changes, Andrew was often notified after the fact, which kept him in a state of uncertainty as to his future and recompense for his work. The letters and diaries contain numerous accounts of these matters and, at times, surprising developments. McClintock, of course, dealt directly with the board of the American and Foreign Christian Union in New York, the governing agency of the American Chapel in Paris, and only afterward was Andrew partially apprised of what had transpired. Some of the other issues involved were McClintock's health and lameness, which on occasion kept him from performing his duties as he would have wished, his frequent travels to England and other parts of Europe to lecture on current political issues, and his writings (he was serving as corresponding editor of *The Methodist* published in New York). In May, 1861, he wrote Lemuel Bangs, "I suffer from the want of money. My correspondence and writings of every kind are heavy. I could do a great deal more if I had free command of money" (Crooks, p. 300). In addition, McClintock was responsible for a large household, which consisted of his wife, two step-children, two older children of his own, plus an infant, a nursemaid, and a servant or two. And, he provided room and board for Andrew as part of their original agreement.

Letter 10, Paris, August 23, 1860

1. In March 1860 Irenee D. Pepper had been ordained an elder in the Philadelphia Conference and appointed to Centennial Church in the South Philadelphia District. The Conference records also show that Andrew Longacre had been appointed to Union Church in the same district both in 1859 and 1860, albeit as a supernumerary due to health reasons; see below, Letter 29, April 4, 1861, note 3, and Letter 30, April 11, 1861, note 2.

2. I. e., the "Chambre of Deputies"; see *Galignani's Guide for 1860*, pp. 344-50.

3. John Keats, *Endymion*, bk. i. ln. 1.

4. According the *Galignani's Guide for 1860*, p. 399, these living artists whose finest works had

been purchased by the Government were Horace Vernet, Biard, Court, Deveria, Granet, Pierre Guérin, Le Tiers, Rioult, and Roqueplan.

5. Suetonius Tranquillus, *Claudius*, 21. See William F. H. King, *Classical and Foreign Quotations*. Detroit: Gale Research Company, 1968, p. 27.

6. See above, Letter 6, July 9, 1860.

Letter 11, Paris, August 27, 1860

1. The young ladies were Augusta McClintock and Maria Stevenson Emory. Augusta was the daughter of John McClintock and his first wife, Caroline Augusta Wakeman; Maria Emory was his step-daughter. Maria and John Emory were children of Robert Emory and his wife, Catharine Stevenson. After the deaths of Robert Emory and McClintock's wife, John McClintock married Catharine Emory. At the time of this letter, the girls were seventeen and fifteen years old (Augusta was born April 20, 1843, and Maria on February 9, 1845). John Emory (named almost certainly for Bishop John Emory, his grandfather) was in his early teens. (See Robert Emory, *MS Journal*, *passim*; see also, below, Letter 32, April 23, 1861.)

2. Francis I (1494-1547), King of France (1515-47).

3. Guiseppe Garibaldi (1807-1882), renowned Italian patriot and soldier. On August 18-19 he had landed on the Italian peninsula and on September 7, entered Naples, Italy's largest city. He then fought and won another battle on the Volturno River north of Naples after which he was able to hand over the whole of southern Italy to Victor Emmanuel. When the two met, Garibaldi was the first person to hail him as king of a united Italy. The king made a triumphal entry into Naples on November 7. But when a new kingdom of Italy came into existence in 1861, it found Garbaldi in opposition. He opposed Cavour in Parliament, he accused the government of shabby treatment of the volunteer soldiers who had conquered half the country and given it to the king, and he condemned the inefficient administration of the provinces that he had conquered and for which he felt especially responsible. Victor Emmanuel gave him other opportunities for military campaigns in which he distinguished himself, but many people considered him an embarrassment. His final campaign was in 1870-71 when he went to assist the French Republic against Prussia. Again, he distinguished himself and was subsequently elected a member of the French National Assembly at Bordeaux (*NEB*, 5:123-25).

4. Orig., "one doors".

5. By the early nineteenth century, much of Syria was in economic decay. The Ottoman hold on the country was at its weakest. In 1831, Ibraham Pasha (son of Muhammad Ali, the ruler of Egypt), with the help of Bashir (prince of Lebanon), conquered Palestine, and for almost ten years ruled Syria, controlling the entire country from Damascus. But, eventually, heavy taxes, disarmament, and conscription of the population made Ibraham hugely unpopular. The European powers (except France) also objected to Egyptian rule in Syria because it was a threat to the Ottoman Empire, the weakness or disintegration of which might cause a European crisis. In 1840 these powers intervened and a British, Turkish, and Austrian force landed on the Syrian coast. The Egyptians were forced to withdraw from Syria, which reverted to the Sultan's government. The next twenty years brought a series of mounting crises. Lebanon became the scene

of a struggle for power between the Druses, an ancient Muslim sect confined principally to the mountains, and their hereditary enemies, the Maronite Christians. There were undertones of social conflict. European goods flooded the market and replaced the products of local craftsmen. This influx diminished the prosperity of the artisan class, largely Muslim, but increased that of the import merchants, mainly Christians and Jews. European interference and the Sultan's efforts to protect Christian privileges caused much resentment among the Muslim majorities. Tensions thus generated erupted in 1860 when a civil war between the Druses and Maronites culminated in massacres of Maronite Christians and sacking of foreign consulates (July 9, 1860). French and British warships were already at Beyrout when news came of a three-days' massacre at Damascus, in which some 5,000 Christians were slaughtered. Again, the European powers intervened, and French troops occupied Lebanon for nearly a year. See *EB* 7:681-82; *NEB* 28:384; and James M. Thompson, *Louis Napoleon and the Second Empire.* Oxford: Blackwell, 1954, p. 213.

During the trek through Palestine that Andrew made with Alexander Van Rensselaer in early 1862, while traveling through Lebanon and Syria, they saw evidence of these conflicts. For example, leaving Beyrout, they traveled to the top of Lebanon and then took horses to Zahléh. "Passed villages in ruins, work of the Druses, and saw many ruined houses in Zahléh" (*MS Diary*, February 25, 1862). At Baalbek they walked around the ruins. Going back over the mountain and across the Baka Valley, they "pitched their tent for the last time" and "saw a Druse village and a ruined Christian house" (*MS Diary*, March 7, 1862).

6. During this visit to Versailles, Andrew made two sketches. One he labelled, "Column, Jardin de Roi à Versailles, August 29, 1860"; the second was a profile of "Mrs. J. D. B. Curtis, August 30, 1860."

Letter 12, Paris, September 6th, 1860

1. See below, Letter 39, June 7, 1861, note 1.

2. Rue de Faubourg St. Honoré was the major thoroughfare from the west into the heart of Paris and the Central Markets. Located on the Right Bank between the church of St. Eustache and rues St. Denis and de la Ferronneire, *Les Halles Centrales* had been on this site since the twelfth century (Emile Zola in his novel *Le Ventre de Paris* would refer to them as "the stomach of Paris"). At the time of Andrew's residence, a massive rebuilding of the markets was underway. The new halls were designed with iron girders and skylights and were soon recognized as models for covered marketplaces throughout France and Europe. A week after his arrival in Paris Andrew walked by these "new Market houses of iron," and pronounced them "very fine" (*MS Diary*, May 25, 1860). *Les Halles* remained on this site until the late 1960s when they were moved to Rungis south of the city. See David P. Jordan, *Transforming Paris: the Life and Labors of Baron Haussmann.* New York: The Free Press, 1995, pp. 362-64; Otto Friedrich, *Olympia; Paris in the Age of Manet.* New York: Simon & Schuster, 1992, p. 137; Beth Archer Brombert, *Edouard Manet, Rebel in a Frock Coat.* Chicago: University of Chicago Press, 1997, p. 76.

3. The avenue de Marigny. After the Palais de l'Industrie was demolished, the Grand Palais and Petit Palais were built in its place and were separated by a street—now Avenue Winston Churchill. See above, Letter 1, May 21, 1860, note 15.

4. Merry-go-rounds and carrousels had been a part of fêtes and festivals since the Middle Ages; therefore, it is interesting to note that Longacre did not use either term to describe this "circular machine."

5. Cafés Concerts or Chantants were establishments of rather recent date. In the summer of 1860 there were three on the Champs Élysées, the *Café Morel, Café des Ambassadeurs,* and the *Pavilion du Jeu de Boule.* The public could enjoy music with their dinner in the open air. No admission was charged, but the visitor was expected to order some refreshment. A small trifle was given to performers who passed at intervals among the tables to collect from the audience. These places were enormously popular among the Parisian *bourgeois,* who flocked to them in great numbers; see *Galignani's Guide for 1860,* pp. 482-83. The following spring Andrew made this entry in his diary: "In the evening walked with Mrs. Baker down the Champs Élysées; saw the Cafés Chantants" (*MS Diary,* May 26, 1861).

6. Named after Philippe Musard (1793-1859), the French violinist, conductor, composer. Until 1852 Musard was considered the best composer of dance music and conductor of promenade concerts in France. His son Alfred followed his father's profession and in 1856 was selected to conduct the Concerts des Champs-Élysées. See *Grove's Dictionary of Music and Musicians,* Eric Blom, ed. 5th ed. London: Macmillan & Co. Ltd.; New York: St. Martin's Press, 1954, 5:1010-11. On August 21, 1861, Andrew records that he went to the Concert Musard where he spent 1 franc (*MS Diary*).

7. Two years after Longacre wrote this letter, Edouard Manet painted his famous canvas, "*La Musique aux Tuileries,*" a contemporary depiction of Paris life during the Second Empire and a scene such as Andrew described on this day. Throughout the autumn of 1860, on his way to and from downtown, Andrew frequently walked through the Tuileries Gardens and stopped to enjoy the music (*MS Diary,* September-October, 1860, *passim*).

8. The Henry J. Bakers and their son Willie were family friends, and their names appear frequently in these letters as well as in Andrew's *MS Diary.* The Bakers did not arrive in Paris until November 23, bringing with them "a bundle of things for me from home" (*MS Diary,* November 23 and 24, 1860); see also, below, Letter 34, May 8, 1861, note 1.

9. This is the first of eight times in these letters to his brother, James, that Andrew refers to himself as "uncle" (see Letter 13, September 13, 1860; Letter 31, April 17, 1861; Letter 61, January 10, 1862; Letter 62, January 20, 1862; Letter 65, February 13, 1862; and Letter 66, March 14, 1862 [twice]). And, in Letter 58, October 29, 1861, Andrew addresses James as "my dear nephew." Whether this was a private joke between the two or used in the sense of a "Dutch uncle" to advise or admonish is not clear.

10. Andrew's younger brother, Orleans, was born June 10, 1840. In 1860 he was living in his father's house, working as a machinist. Always referred to in these letters as "Orly," he was christened "Orleans" because his father was in New Orleans at the time of his birth. In 1861 he enlisted in the U. S. Navy (see below, Letters 33 and 52). In the years following the Civil War, he was an engineer in charge of a blast furnace in West Virginia. Eventually, he moved west and became an early president (founder?) of the St. Joseph Lead Company. In 1868 he married Rachel Bartholomew. They had three children. See Marian Sykes Longacre, p. 69. See also *U. S. Census Records*, Philadelphia, Pennsylvania, 1860.

Letter 13, Paris, September 13, 1860

1. The city of Paris paid 114,000 francs per annum to water the streets; see *Galignani's Guide for 1860*, p. 33, note 1. For other references to Paris streets, see below, Letter 16, October 18, 1860; and Letter 23, January 31, 1861, and note 3.

2. John McClintock reported on this day that "Mr. Longacre read prayers and preached and he and I administered communion. . . . [He] has won golden opinions, as, indeed, I knew he could not fail to do." See Crooks, p. 292.

3. Woodbury Langdon was born *ca.* 1825 in New York City, the son of Walter Langdon and Dorothea Astor, daughter of John Jacob Astor and Sarah Todd. He married Helen Colford Jones. Their son, Woodbury Gersdorf Langdon, was born in New York City, April 9, 1849. Although Langdon's name does not appear in the printed version, he is the person mentioned in McClintock's letter of January 7, 1861, to C. C. North: "Mr. —— partook of his first communion on Christmas day. A great change has been going on in him for some months, and he is now living for the glory of God. This blessed result is due largely to Mr. Longacre, who has been greatly useful to him and his family," Crooks, p. 297. Andrew Longacre's *MS Diary* entry for Christmas Day is ecstatic: "Mr. Langdon communed to my inexpressible joy. Home, as happy as I could be."

4. Soon after he had agreed to go to Paris as the assistant pastor at the American Chapel Andrew called on the Misses Marino in Philadelphia about studying French—and bought a French Grammar (*MS Diary*, April 12, 1860). But he had time to take only two lessons before sailing for France. Once there, he contacted a Miss Beaumont about taking French lessons but took only a lesson or two. He then called on a Miss Poiret about lessons and for almost a year he studied under her tutelage (see *MS Diary,* May 28, 1860-May 31, 1861, *passim*).

Letter 14, London, September 21, 1860

1. A four-wheeled carriage with a driver's seat high in front, two double seats inside facing each other, and a folding top over the back seat. For Andrew's comments on other Parisian "equipages," see Letter 16, October 18, 1860.

2. Thomas Wentworth Strafford (1593-1641), English statesman and leading adviser of Charles I, went to the scaffold, May 12, 1641; Charles I was executed in 1649; Warren Hastings (1732-1818), first governor general of India, whose seven-year trial (1788-95) resulted in his acquittal. See *NEB*, 11:298-99; 3:112-13; 5:742-43.

3. The tunnel under the Thames from Rotherhite to Wapping was the first subaqueous tunnel in history. The work was begun in 1825 by I. K. Brunel (the great British civil and mechanical engineer who would later design the *Great Eastern*). In 1828 a sudden inundation seriously injured Brunel and brought the project to a standstill. Financial problems halted the work for seven years. Fifteen hundred and six feet in length, it is in regular use today as part of the Metropolitan Line of the London Underground. See *NEB,* 2:576; 11:671-72. In the *MS Diary* Andrew noted that in company with the Reverend Mr. Gibson of London, he visited the Thames tunnel on Tuesday, September 25, 1860. William Gibson was appointed to Islington in 1860.

4. In 1860 William Arthur was General Secretary of the Wesleyan Missionary Society in London, Samuel Coley was stationed at City Road Chapel, and Richard Roberts at Great Queen Street; see *Minutes of the Methodist Conferences, the first, held in London, by the late Rev. John Wesley, A.M., in the year 1744*. London: John Mason at the Wesleyan Conference Office, City-Road, and sold at 66, Paternoster-Row, 1862; XIV.413.

Letter 15, Paris, October 8, 1860

1. Orig., "of".

2. Princess Clotilde was the daughter of King Victor Emmanuel of Sardinia. When France acquired Savoy, her marriage to Louis Napoleon's cousin, Prince Napoleon-Jerome ("Plon-Plon") in 1859 was one of the terms of the treaty. Prince Napoleon was thirty-seven years old; Clotilde was fifteen; see Thompson, pp. 181, 184, 186. Andrew purchased a "card-portrait" of this couple during his time in Paris and kept it among his souvenirs.

The duchesse d'Alba, Paca (Maria Francisca de Sales), was the older sister of Empress Eugénie. Both the sisters had fallen in love with the duc d'Alba, but it was Paca who married him and duly became the duchesse d'Alba (see Friedrich, p. 47).

3. The Péreire brothers, Jacob-Émile (1800-75) and Isaac (1806-80), Parisian bankers, were the chief financial backers of the urban renewal going on in Paris in the mid-nineteenth century. Deficit spending to finance public projects had begun with the railroad boom in the 1840s and continued because public building on borrowed money provided thousands of jobs and economic stimulus. The Péreires created in 1852 the Société du Crédit Mobilier, a private investment bank, which tapped into the capital resources of small and large investors alike, selling shares to the public and making funds available for promising projects of an expanding industry. It was the Péreires who purchased a quarter mile along the north side of the new rue de Rivoli and built the arcades that ornament that street today. They also built the Hotel du Louvre and, eventually, the Grand Hotel across from the new Opera. Their house to which Longacre refers was on the rue Royal. And, though he suffered greatly from asthma, Émile Péreire lived fifteen more years. See David H. Pinkney, *Napoleon III and the Rebuilding of Paris*. Princeton, New Jersey: Princeton University Press, 1972, pp. 90-91, 179; Jordan, p. 230; Friedrich, pp. 140-41; and Burchell, pp. 179-80; 344, note 5.

Letter 16, Paris, October 18, 1860

1. Charles F. Deems, was born in Baltimore, December 4, 1820, and after graduating from Dickinson College, entered the ministry of the Methodist Episcopal Church, South. At the time of this visit to Paris, he was the Presiding Elder of the Wilmington District, North Carolina Conference.

2. Hiram Shaw, Jr., a native of Lexington, Kentucky, was born *ca*. 1836. He was brought up in the Methodist Episcopal Church, and his father and family remained faithful members of the mother church as long as it was possible—i.e., until the church divided over the slavery issue in 1844. At the first opportunity thereafter, however, they reunited with the M. E. Church. Shaw

served as a lay delegate from the Kentucky Conference to the General Conference of 1872. His name appears in the *MS Diary* several times during the last two weeks in October, 1860 (see *Cyclopaedia of Methodism*, p. 795).

3. The foundations for Hotel des Invalides were laid in 1670 during the reign of Louis XIV. The main building and the first church were completed about 1706 as an asylum for the veterans of various wars. At the time of Andrew's visit on this occasion, the Dome Church was open to the public only on Mondays and Thursdays (this visit was on a Thursday) between noon and 3 p.m. The body of Napoleon Bonaparte had been returned to France in 1840. His coffin lay under the cupola in St. Jerome's Chapel until the tomb, designed by Visconti, was completed. Finally, it was transferred to the crypt on April 2, 1861.

4. Located south of Les Invalides and east-southeast of the École Militaire in the court of the Abattoir de Grenelle, the Artesian well of Grenelle was begun in 1834 and completed in 1841. In 1858 the water was conveyed horizontally from this spot to the centre of the Place de Breteuil where an open-worked tower of bronzed cast-iron was constructed. It was 42 metres high and enclosed the ascension and distribution pipes, which were all encased in a main cylinder. A winding staircase, visible from the outside, lead to the top. The structure rested on a circular masonry base 14 metres in diameter, and 2½ metres high. Surrounded by a balustrade, the whole was crowned with a small cupola. The well provided 264 gallons of water per minute at a warm temperature of 84 degrees Fahrenheit. Newly completed when Andrew saw it on this day, "The Artesian well of Grenelle" was an impressive sight. See *Galignani's Guide for 1860, pp. 354-55.*

5. I.e., the rue Rousselet.

6. This was the first commercially successful internal-combustion engine. Made in Paris in 1859 by (Jean-Joseph-)Étienne Lenoir, a Belgian inventor, it was a converted double-action steam engine with slide valves to admit the air-fuel mixture to discharge exhaust products. Its two-stroke cycle engine used a mixture of coal ("illuminating") gas and air. Though only 4 percent efficient in fuel consumption, it was a smooth-running and durable machine. By 1865 more than 400 were in use in France and 1,000 in Britain, mainly for such low-power jobs as pumping and printing. In 1862 Lenoir built the first automobile with an internal combustion engine. See *NEB*, 7:268; 18:477; 28:467.

7. Of neo-Gothic design, the church of Ste. Clotilde, located at 23 bis, rue Las-Cases (just east of Les Invalides), had been completed three years prior to Longacre's visit. Construction had begun in 1846 by architect François-Christian Grau and was completed after his death in 1853 by Théodore Ballu. See Michel Poisson, *Paris Buildings and Monuments*. New York: Harry N. Abrams, 1999, p. 243.

8. A Paris landmark since 1791, the Pantheon, which replaced an old abbey church, was designed by Jacques-Germain Soufflot in the form of a Greek cross with an entrance marked by a monumental portico. The dome above the crossing was greatly influenced by the dome of St. Paul's Cathedral in London. After Soufflot's death in 1780, the construction was overseen by Maximilien Brébion and Jean-Baptiste Rondelet. At the time of Longacre's visit, the church, by a decree of December 6, 1851, had resumed its former name of church of Ste. Geneviéve. In 1885 it was once again declared the Pantheon. Poisson, pp. 172-73; *Galignani's New Paris Guide for*

1867. Paris: A. and W. Galignani and Co., Rue de Rivoli, No. 224 [1867], pp. 40-01.

9. The southern extension of the Boulevard Sebastopol became the Boulevard St. Michel.

10. Situated at Place St. Michel, this splendid fountain occupies the entire gable wall of the building behind it. Inaugurated on August 15, 1860, just two months before Andrew's visit, this project was part of the large scale urban renewal underway in Paris. The statue at the center of the composition, by Francisque-Joseph Duret, represents the archangel Michael crushing the demon. See *Galignani's Guide for* 1867, p. 389-90; and Poisson, p. 217. The construction site was so new that only a brief notice of the fountain appeared in *Galignani's Guide for 1860*; see p. 406.

11. "La Morgue" was a well-known tourist attraction listed in all the Paris guide books. In a plain Doric building on the Ile de la Cité, located where the Pont St. Michel joined the Quai Marché Neuf, bodies of unknown persons who had drowned or met with accidental death were exposed for three days, their clothes hung up near them as an additional means of identification. The bodies were laid upon inclined slabs of black marble behind glass screens. If not claimed, they were buried at public expense. At this period of time, the average number of bodies exposed annually was 300, most of them males. See *Galignani's Guide for 1860*, pp. 78, 311. By 1867, the morgue had been moved behind Notre Dame to the southeastern tip of the Ile de la Cité; *Galignani's Guide for 1867*, p. 73. See also, Katherine Fischer Taylor, *In the Theater of Criminal Justice*. Princeton, N.J.: Princeton University Press, 1993, pp. 3, 110, and her Illustration #7 showing cadavers displayed through the public vitrine at the Paris Morgue exactly as Longacre describes them down to the "stiff wide leather aprons over the loins."

12. Louis Napoleon was 52½ years old. Dr. Thomas W. Evans, the American dentist, who first attended Louis Napoleon shortly after Napoleon came to Paris in 1848 and became a life-long friend, gave the following description: "[He] was not a handsome man in the sense commonly given to these words. His head was large, usually slightly inclined to one side, and his features were strongly pronounced. The forehead was broad, and the nose prominent, the eyes small, greyish-blue in color, and generally expressionless, owing to a somnolent drooping of the lids. . . . His complexion was blonde, but rather sallow; the lower part of the face was lengthened by a short "goatee"—called in honor of his Majesty an "imperial"—and broadened by a very heavy, silky moustache, the ends of which were stiffly waxed. His hair was of a light brown color, and when I first knew him, was abundant and worn rather long; at a later period it was trimmed short, and was habitually brushed in the style made familiar by the effigy on the coinage of the Empire. . . . A little below the average height, . . . he was always carefully dressed, and in public, when in plain clothes, usually wore a black frock coat, tightly buttoned. . . . [He was] a fine rider. In fact, he never appeared to better advantage than when in the saddle; and during the years of his Presidency he was often seen on horseback in the parks and suburbs of Paris, accompanied by only one or two attendants. A little later, and after his marriage, he liked to go out in a carriage and to drive the horses himself. When staying at Saint Cloud, he was to be seen almost daily in the park or its neighbourhood, riding with the Empress in a phaeton, behind a span of fast trotters, handling the reins himself, and entirely unattended." Thomas W. Evans, *Memoirs*. Edward A. Crane, ed. 2 vols. London: T. Fisher Unwin, 1905, 1:40-42.

Letter 17, Paris, October 30, 1860

1. See above, Letter 16, October 18, 1860, note 2.

2. See above, Letter 2, June 16, 1860, note 5.

3. Albert Edward, son of Queen Victoria and Prince Albert, who would reign as Edward VII, was at this time nineteen years old.

Letter 18, Paris, November 5, 1860

1. "By Dr. Maris," was written above the date of this letter, indicating that the letter was hand-delivered.

2. John McClintock had voiced the same opinion a few weeks earlier in his letter of September 8, 1860, to Mrs. Dr. Purdy: "Our new friends here are kind and good, but are not Methodists and that is a great bond of union missing." Crooks, p. 295.

Letter 19, Paris, November 15, 1860

1. Unless this is a diminutive for his sister, Eliza, this person in the Longacre household, as Cline (see above, Letter 2, June 16, 1860), has not been identified. See also, below, Letter 22, January 23, 1861; Letter 51, September 4, 1861; and Letter 61, January 10, 1861.

2. Her Serene Highness the Princess Marie Amélie, daughter of Stéphanie Beauharnis, the Grand Duchess of Baden and a cousin of Louis Napoleon, became the Duchess of Hamilton on her marriage in 1843 to Douglas, William Alexander Anthony Archibald, the eleventh Duke of Hamilton. Brodick Castle in Scotland was one of his estates to which, when Louis was an exile in England, he made occasional visits. See *DNB* 5:1280; and Evans, 1:43, 85.

Letter 20, Paris, January 2, 1861

1. *Ultimo*, "of the last month." Andrew uses this abbreviation again in Letter 48, August 12, 1861; and Letter 54, October 8, 1861.

2. Lincoln's election on November 6, 1860, gave a "better prospect" to those back home who were opposed to slavery. News of South Carolina's secession from the Union on December 20 had already become a topic of great interest to Americans living in Paris and attending the Chapel.

3. McClintock was far more politically inclined than was Andrew, and discussions between them had become heated. The previous November Andrew reported one such conversation as "too much excited. Mem. Try not to allow myself such freedom again—not good for me or others" (*MS Diary*, November 17, 1860). Andrew strongly felt that politics were not a matter for the pulpit. McClintock thought otherwise. His understanding was, "I consider the Chapel my first duty; patriotism the next" (letter to C. C. North, June 19, 1861, in Crooks, p. 302). However, even his son Emory thought politics engaged too much of his father's time, to which McClintock responded, "I am amused, and at the same time pleased, by your anxiety that I should not give much time to politics. In the first place the preservation of the Government is not politics, in the

ordinary sense of the word. If the Government is lost, all is lost—family, Church, property—everything. In such a crisis as this I hold it the duty of every man who has any influence, to use it on the side of law and order. If not, the wicked will prevail: God's law and all justice will be trampled under foot. In the second place, I have not given so much time as you think, even to this great duty. I have never neglected my duty to the Chapel in any degree (letter of July 28, 1861, in Crooks, p. 304). In September 1861, Andrew wrote that McClintock had preached "a fine sermon—of course political" (*MS Diary*, September 26, 1861).

4. President James Buchanan had delivered his Fourth Annual Message at Washington City on December 3, 1860, addressed to "Fellow-Citizens of the Senate and House of Representatives." It began, "Throughout the year since our last meeting the country has been eminently prosperous in all its material interests. The general health has been excellent, our harvests have been abundant, and plenty smiles throughout the land. Our commerce and manufactures have been prosecuted with energy and industry, and have yielded fair and ample returns. In short, no nation in the tide of time has ever presented a spectacle of greater material prosperity than we have done until within a very recent period." He then asks, "Why is it, then, that discontent now so extensively prevails, and the Union of the States, which is the source of all these blessings, is threatened with destruction?" The President lays the blame on "the long-continued and intemperate interference of the Northern people with the question of slavery in the Southern States." Although Buchanan thought slavery was morally wrong, he tried to find a compromise that would preserve the Union. His strategy consisted in prevention of Northern anti-slavery agitation and the enforcement of the Fugitive Slave Act of 1850, but these measures failed to avert the Civil War. By February 1861 seven Southern states had seceded from the Union. Buchanan denounced the secession but admitted that he could find no means to stop it. The President's speech can be found in its entirety on the Web at http://www.intac.com/~rfrone/ history/1860-sou.htm; see also *NEB*, 2:595-96.

5. John McClintock's general health was not robust. When he accepted the pastorate of the American Chapel, he knew he would need help and requested Andrew Longacre to take the position of assistant pastor. By January of 1861, he was complaining of his lameness in a letter to C. C. North: "My knee continues to be bad. I cannot walk, but I am able to ride to church and preach while sitting on a stool." By the end of March, however, he could report to Lemuel Bangs, "My knee improves slowly. I can walk about half a mile, but still have to sit in preaching." Crooks, pp. 297-99.

6. The American and Foreign Christian Union; see above, Letter 9, August 20, 1860, note 2.

7. As it turned out, Andrew returned to the U. S. in 1862 while McClintock remained in Paris until 1864.

Letter 21, Paris, January 7th, 1861

1. The family of Ambassador Charles James Faulkner; see above, Letter 2, July 16, 1860, and note 6. Andrew made no entries in his 1861 *MS Diary* until February 20; therefore, we have no other first hand accounts from him of flooding in Paris at this time. The Seine, flowing through the middle of Paris, was subject to flooding and, despite Baron Haussmann's diligent efforts,

drainage problems still plagued the city. Many of the streets did not yet have underground drains, and some that did exist were too small and frequently over-flowed, flooding low-lying areas (see Pinkney, p. 127).

2. For McClintock's recurring health problems, see above, Letter 9, August 20, 1860, note 2; and Letter 20, January 1, 1861, note 5.

Letter 22, Paris, January 23, 1861

1. This brand of gloves took its name from Xavier Jouvin, a young French medical student from Grenoble, the center of French glove-making. Jouvin studied the hands of patients in the Grenoble hospital and eventually identified 320 different sizes. With this information, he invented a glove pattern which he patented in 1824. Later he developed a punch for stamping out gloves, with separate dies for the smaller pieces like thumbs, fourchettes, and gussets, which he patented in 1838. This new system was awarded a bronze medal at the Industrial Exposition in Paris in 1839. The system quickly spread to German, Swiss, and Italian manufacturers, but it was only in 1849 when the patents lapsed in France that Jouvin's system was widely adopted in his native land. All modern methods of glove-sizing and pattern cutting are based on Jouvin's system. See Valerie Cumming, *Gloves.* London: B.T. Batsford, Ltd., 1982, p. 17. From the *MS Diary* we know that the purchase of gloves was a frequent expenditure for Andrew.

2. Soon after his arrival in Paris Andrew resumed his painting. On May 31, 1860, he recorded that he had bought an easel, and purchases of paints, brushes, colored pencils and other art supplies appear frequently in the *MS Diary,* as well as accounts of the portraits on which he was working. Occasionally, instead of a portrait, he would make a sketch from his window, a scene in the Bois de Boulogne, a column in the garden at Versailles, the interior of churches, etc. He also made a number of exquisitely detailed sketches of the interiors of the various rooms he occupied. We are extremely fortunate that a number of these survived in his portfolio, some of which are reproduced in this work and included in the exhibition.

3. Louis Evans. Probably the son of either Dr. Thomas Evans or Dr. Theodore Evans, both of whom are mentioned frequently in Andrew's *MS Diary*, as are Louis and John Evans (although without any clues as to relationships). It is surprising that in his two-volume *Memoirs,* Dr. Thomas Evans makes no mention whatsoever of any family member except his wife. See below, Letter 25, February 19, 1861, note 4.

Letter 23, Paris, January 31, 1861

1. As a young man, Jerome Bonaparte (1784-1860), the youngest brother of Napoleon Bonaparte, traveled to the United States. In Baltimore he met and, on December 24, 1803, married Elizabeth Patterson, the beautiful daughter of William Patterson, a wealthy Baltimore merchant. Even though the marriage was valid according to American Law and the Roman Catholic Church, Napoleon refused to acknowledge it and ordered Elizabeth excluded from his states. Jerome's pleas fell on deaf ears. Forced to separate, Elizabeth sailed for England where she gave birth to their son in 1805. By an imperial decree, Napoleon annulled the Patterson

marriage, arranged another marriage for Jerome (to Princess Catherine of Wurtenberg), and made him King of Westphalia. Jerome spent the following years in Trieste, Italy, or Switzerland. His wife died in 1835, and he returned to France in 1847. After Louis Napoleon came to power, Jerome became successively governor of Les Invalides, marshal of France, and president of the senate. He died June 24, 1860. Andrew attended the funeral ceremonies in the Church of the Invalides "of Jerome Bonaparte, ex-king of Westphalia, last brother of the great Napoleon.... Had a good place in the gallery, saw and heard all. The display very magnificent, the music chiefly from *Dies Irae*—very fine. Service from 1 o'clock till after 2" (*MS Diary*, July 3, 1860).

Elizabeth Patterson remained in England for a time after her separation from Jerome, but eventually returned to Baltimore. Her son (also named Jerome) married Susan Williams. They founded a family and brightened society at Baltimore where Jerome settled into his grandfather's everyday business life. But Jerome remained on good terms with his father, and they occasionally met. After Jerome Bonaparte's death in 1860, Elizabeth Patterson returned to France to claim the family succession for her son. Andrew gives the verdict on this appeal in Letter 25, February 19, 1861. See *EB*, 3:838-40; Thompson, pp. 45f.

2. Dr. Thomas Evans reported the incident this way: "[When] Prince Napoleon having petulantly remarked to him [Louis Napoleon] that he had nothing of his uncle (the first Napoleon) about him, he replied, 'You are quite mistaken. I have his family'." Evans, 1:64.

3. The condition of Paris streets was notorious and often commented upon. Before Haussmann's time, many streets were paved with sandstone blocks that did not hold up under heavy traffic. Later some of the streets were macadamized, which had advantages, but they were dusty during dry weather and muddy when it rained. Asphalt had long been used for sidewalks and crossings but when wet gave little traction for horses' hooves. This problem was finally solved, however, by mixing the asphalt with sand. See Pinkney, pp. 70-71.

4. A Philadelphia photographer.

Letter 24, Paris, February 13, 1861

1. *Mardi gras,* "Fat Tuesday," in allusion to the fat ox (*boeuf-gras*) which is ceremoniously paraded through the streets. Carnival, which took place during the five or six weeks preceding Ash Wednesday, was a favorite season for all Paris (even though Longacre reports it as a small affair). The streets were filled with "costumed revelers (harlequins, pierrots and pierrettes, pantaloons and punchinellos). During the day singers and musicians performed along the boulevards. Bugles, trumpets and drums were heard everywhere, soldiers in garish uniforms added to the colorful scene. Immense crowds in carriages, on horseback, and on foot, assembled to witness the celebration. At night there were masked balls in private homes and theaters, the most notable being that at the Grand Opera." See Burchell, p. 268; and *Galignani's Guide for 1860*, pp. 483-86.

2. See above, Letter 15, October 8, 1860, note 2.

3. South Carolina's secession on December 20, 1860, was soon followed by Mississippi, Florida, Alabama, Georgia, Louisiana, and Texas. On February 9, 1861, the Confederate States of America was formed with Jefferson Davis as president.

4. Victor Emmanuel II, king of Sardinia-Piedmont, who became the first king of Italy. War with

Austria, which led to the acquisition of Venice, did not break out until 1866 (see *NEB*, 5:125; 12:349).

5. Longacre is alluding to a familiar aphorism, "The blood of the martyrs is the seed of the Church," based on Tertullian's, *Apology*, 50, par. 13.

Letter 25, Paris, February 19th, 1861

1. Mr. Thomas N. Dale, a prominent member of the American Chapel with houses of business in New York and Philadelphia. See below, Letter 28, April 1, 1861.

2. Mrs. Henry J. Baker, a family friend from New York; see above, Letter 12, September 6, 1860, note 8.

3. For the Bonaparte-Patterson case, see above, Letter 23, January 31, 1861, note 1.

4. Dr. Thomas Wiltberger Evans (1823-1897) of Philadelphia was a long-time Paris resident and a member and benefactor of the American Chapel. A prominent dentist with a high degree of professional skill, he had a large and prestigious clientele. He had also long tended Louis Napoleon and the imperial family and from that relationship a friendship (assiduously cultivated) developed that laid the foundations of a large private fortune and the most distinguished dental practice of the nineteenth century. On professional, pastoral, and social occasions, the names of the Drs. Thomas and Theodore Evans appear frequently in Andrew's letters and *MS Diary*.

Dr. Theodore Evans had first known the Empress as Marie Eugénie de Guzman, Countess de Téba, before her marriage to Louis Napoleon. When the Second Empire came crashing down in September, 1870, Dr. Evans played a prominent role in helping Empress Eugénie escape to England. See Evans, 2:317-460, *passim*.

5. Dr. Evans' report that the Emperor had emphatically denied ever having had a relationship with the Countess Castiglione seems odd in light of the fact that the liaison was common knowledge in the French capital, and Andrew's skepticism was well-founded. An Italian of remarkable beauty, the Countess de Castiglione had been sent from Turin to Paris by her cousin, Prime Minister of the Piedmont, Count Camillo Cavour, with a plan to seduce Louis Napoleon and encourage his support for the unification of Italy. She was eighteen years old when she arrived in Paris in 1856, and although her qualifications for the second part of her mission were probably non-existent, she quickly accomplished the first part. The Emperor was soon giving her extravagant jewels, and his carriage was often seen in the early morning hours outside her apartment on the avenue Montaigne. But there were dangers. At 3 a.m. one morning, as he was leaving her residence, three assassins emerged from the shadows and attempted to seize the imperial carriage. The coachman managed to flail them off with his whip and drove the Emperor to safety. When the attackers were apprehended, the police found that they were agents of the Italian radical leader, Guiseppe Mazzini. Although the Countess was not implicated in the plot, Napoleon's ministers insisted that he put an immediate end to this dangerously open liaison. This posed no hardship. Louis was not one to combine pleasure with politics. Besides, he had already tired of the once delectable Countess who was exceedingly stupid and interested only in herself. "She bores me to death," said Louis to his cousin, Princess Mathilde. Also, Louis had already discovered another Italian beauty, Marie-Anne de Ricci Walewska, the wife of the French Minister of Foreign Affairs. Incidentally, her husband, Alexandre Walewski, the illegiti-

mate son of Napoleon Bonaparte, was Louis Napoleon's first cousin. See Burchell, pp. 72-73; and Friedrich, pp. 44, 54-56.

6. *Pour prendre congé*, "to take leave"; that is, to say goodbye; see below, Letter 26, February 23, 1861.

7. Julius N. Proeschel served as John McClintock's secretary in Paris. He became a lifelong friend of Emory McClintock. Part of their correspondence is in the Manuscript Collection in the Archives at Dickinson College, Carlisle, Pennsylvania.

8. Andrew's *MS Diary* for this day fills in details nicely: "Mrs. Munroe took me to see pictures at the Portalis Gallery, rue Tronchet [north of the Madeleine], a private but very interesting collection. Fine originals of Guido, Titian, Murillo, &c, &c, with some modern—Delaroche, Ary Scheffer, etc."

Letter 26, Paris, February 23, 1861

1. Mrs. Mary Jones of Baltimore, the sister of Andrew's friends Charles J. and Henry J. Baker. Although Andrew and Nelson Dale did not stay with her while they were in Florence, they did call on her and on Thursday evening, March 7, 1861, they dined and spent the evening with her (see *MS Diary*, March 4-7, 1861). See also, below, Letter 34, May 8, 1861, where Andrew speaks of the sad division in this family between North and South.

2. Soon after Andrew's arrival in Paris, Dr. George L. Prentiss took him to meet Edward Harrison May and William P. Dana, American artists living and working in Paris. Thereafter, Andrew met them occasionally in the course of his pastoral and social activities. On November 7, 1860, at Mr. May's request, Andrew began sitting for his portrait. This work continued off and on through the following year. On the day before departing for home, May 2, 1862, Andrew called on Mr. May, but no mention is made in the *MS Diary* of the completion or the disposition of the portrait.

3. "To take leave"; that is, to say goodbye; see above, Letter 25, February 19, 1861.

4. Andrew and Nelson Dale did make a brief visit to the Italian Parliament where Andrew reported they "heard the music of the Italian tongue" (*MS Diary*, February 28, 1861). For the unification of Italy, see above, Letter 2, June 16, 1860, note 4.

5. As his *MS Diary* shows, Andrew did keep meticulous accounts of his expenditures on this trip.

6. Julia M. Lynch, the daughter of Judge James Lynch, married the Reverend Dr. Stephen Olin, president of Wesleyan University, Middletown, Connecticut, in 1843. Widowed in 1851, she edited her late husband's works with the help of literary friends. In 1855 she compiled a volume of poems. A Sunday School teacher all of her life, she wrote Sunday School books and contributed articles to *The Ladies Repository, Western Christian Advocate,* and *Methodist Quarterly Review.* Active in the Woman's Missionary Society and many other church organizations, she died in New York in 1879 (see *Cyclopaedia of Methodism,* pp. 679-80).

7. James Remington Fairlamb, was an American composer, born in Philadelphia, January 23, 1838; died Ingleside, New York, April 16, 1908. As a young man, he played organ at several Philadelphia churches. He went to Paris in 1858. *Baker's Biographical Dictionary of Musicians.* 5th ed. Completely revised by Nicolas Slonimsky. New York: G. Shermer, 1958, pp. 454-55.

Letter 27, Civita Vecchia, March 27, 1861

1. This letter was written on blue stationery.
2. See *MS Diary*, Monday, March 4, 1861.
3. See *MS Diary*, Tuesday, March 19, 1861.
4. I.e., Nelson Dale, his traveling companion, son of the Thomas N. Dales, often referred to in the *MS Diary* as "Nellie."

Letter 28, Paris, April 1, 1861

1. See below, Letter 32, April 23, 1861, note 3.

Letter 29, Paris, April 4, 1861

1. The *Niagara* was a well-known U. S. steamer having been used (along with the British steamers *Agamemnon*, *Gorgon*, and *Valorous*) in three much publicized attempts to lay a transatlantic telegraph cable from Valencia Bay, Ireland, to Trinity Bay, Newfoundland. The first attempt was made in August 1857, the second in June 1858, and a third in July 1858. This last attempt was initially successful, but the insulation soon failed and the line went dead. Not until 1866 was reliable transmission established. There are many accounts of the laying of the cable. One of the best, almost first hand, was written by the brother of Cyrus Field, Henry Martyn Field, *History of the Atlantic Telegraph*. New York: Scribner, 1867. A concise account of the work up until 1860 appeared in the *Manual of the Corporation of the City of New York*. D. T. Valentine. New York: New York (N.Y.) Common Council, 1861, pp. 637-38.

2. George W. Brindle was a fellow minister of Andrew Longacre in the Philadelphia Conference. He had been admitted into full connection in 1852 and served various appointments in that conference until 1857 when he transferred to the Upper Iowa Conference and was appointed to Maquoketa in the Davenport District. In 1860, he was appointed to Lyons in the Davenport District. See *Minutes of the Annual Conferences of the Methodist Episcopal Church*. New York: Carlton & Porter, 1852-1860 (hereafter cited as *Minutes*).

3. Andrew had a special interest in Union Church, South Philadelphia Conference. His sister Sallie had joined that church when only a girl and, at twelve years of age (*ca.* 1843), Andrew was converted and joined that church. In 1859 and 1860 he had been appointed to Union as a supernumerary (see above, Letter 10, August 23, 1860, note 1). Union had been organized in 1801, following a disagreement among members of St. George's Church and the subsequent withdrawal of some members. At first they rented the north end of George Whitefield's Academy on Fourth Street, and the next year bought the south end. In May 1802, they petitioned Bishop Francis Asbury to appoint a preacher, which he did. However, Union does not appear as a separate appointment in the conference *Minutes* until 1812. In 1833 a new church was built, "introducing the era of modern church arrangement with basement for weekly lectures, prayer and class meetings, Sunday school, etc." See Francis H. Tees, *The Ancient Landmark of American Methodism or Historic Old St. George's*. Philadelphia, Pa.: The Message Publishing Company, 1951, pp. 116-18; and

Tees, *et al., Pioneering in Penn's Woods.* Philadelphia: The Philadelphia Conference Tract Society of the Methodist Episcopal Church, 1937, p. 78. See also, below, Letter 30, April 11, 1861, note 2. When the Philadelphia Conference met March 20-30, 1861, A. Atwood was appointed to Union (see *Minutes,* 1861).

Letter 30, Paris, April 11th, 1861

1. John Whiteman, born in 1804, was a manufacturer in Philadelphia and a very influential layman in the Methodist Episcopal Church. In 1840 he became a trustee of the Centenary Fund of the Philadelphia Conference, acting first as secretary and then as treasurer, until 1864. He also was manager of the Philadelphia Conference Missionary Society, holding various offices in that organization. He served as a trustee of Dickinson College and was closely associated with the Educational Fund of the Philadelphia Annual Conference, serving for many years as treasurer and then as president of the board. *Cyclopaedia of Methodism,* p. 942.

2. It was not until 1888 that Union Church finally moved west and erected a beautiful new church on Diamond Street, corner of Woodstock; see Tees, *et al., Pioneering in Penn's Woods,* p. 78.

3. John Francis Chaplain was born in Maryland, October 16, 1824, graduated at Dickinson College in 1843, and admitted to the Philadelphia Conference of the Methodist Episcopal Church in 1852. At the Conference of 1861, as Longacre had been informed, Chaplain was appointed to Trinity Church in the North Philadelphia District. *Cyclopaedia of Methodism,* p. 197; and *Minutes,* 1852, 1861. See below, Letter 31, April 17, 1861.

4. The dried rhizome and roots of the dandelion, used as a diuretic, tonic, and laxative.

Letter 31, Paris, April 17, 1861

1. John Talbot Gracey was born in Delaware County, Pennsylvania, September 16, 1832. In 1850 he entered the ministry in the Virginia Conference of the Methodist Episcopal Church, South, but in 1852 he joined the Philadelphia Conference of the Methodist Episcopal Church, where he held several pastorates. On March 11, 1858, Andrew went to Christine, Delaware, to attend Gracey's wedding (*MS Journal).* In March, 1861, at the Philadelphia Conference, Gracey was appointed as missionary to India, where he served at Seetapoor, Bareilly, and Nynee Tal. In this letter Longacre refers to the health of Gracey's wife, and it was for this reason that Gracey returned home in 1868. *Cyclopaedia of Methodism,* p. 416; *Minutes, 1852-1868.*

2. Longacre's comment about the changes coming out of "our class" refers to the group of men admitted on trial to the Philadelphia Conference of 1852. See *Minutes,* 1852; and see above, Letter 30, April 11, 1861.

3. Augusta McClintock would become Andrew's sister-in-law, on October 23, 1865, when she married his brother, Jim. Augusta was twenty-two years old; Jim was thirty-two.

4. A. Ken, Photographe, Boulevart Montmartre, 10, Paris. The full-length photograph that was taken of Andrew on this day shows a tall, slender, handsome young man in dark trousers, a waistcoat, and knee-length topcoat. His right hand rests on the back of a chair and his right leg is slightly flexed at the knee.

Letter 32, Paris, April 23, 1861

1. Augusta McClintock (John McClintock's daughter by his first wife), Maria and John Emory, John McClintock's step-children by his marriage to the widow of Robert Emory (see above, Letter 11, August 27, 1860).

2. Andrew's first cousin, Huldah, was the daughter of Mary Stiles Stewart, an older sister of Andrew's mother, Eliza. See Letter 6, July 9, 1860; and Letter 33, May 2, 1861.

3. Will Maddock was the youngest of Andrew's Sunday School scholars in the last class that Andrew taught (at Union Church in Philadelphia) before he entered the ministry in 1851. Although Will's character and intelligence were outstanding, he was the only member of the class who was not converted and united with the church. This was a grave concern for Andrew, doubly so because Will did not have the religious home life of the other class members. In the years that followed, Will took a job in New York, where he advanced rapidly carrying the responsibilities of a man though still only a boy. On the rare occasions when they saw each other, Andrew was saddened to see in Will a "recklessness and disregard for the religious convictions of his earlier training" although "he had been preserved from some of the most detestable vices." In 1859, when business brought Will to Philadelphia for several weeks, he was a frequent visitor in the Longacre home which offered opportunities for religious conversation. Will showed a cheerful willingness and interest and soon "expressed his firm resolution to do what had long been on his mind—to give his heart to God." This gave Andrew inexpressible joy, but he still had a deep desire that Will would join the church where he had formerly been a Sunday School scholar.

Although this did not take place, they corresponded regularly during Andrew's tenure in Paris. On May 22, 1862, when Andrew returned to Philadelphia, Will Maddock was present at the Longacre home for the joyful reunion of the family at 1206 Spring Garden Street, and they saw each other regularly through the summer. On August 7, Andrew noted that he had seen Will off on the train, bound apparently for New York. Sometime later, Will traveled to St. Paul, Minnesota, possibly on business.

On September 23, Andrew received a telegram from Will in St. Paul, asking him to come at once. Although Andrew was serving a full-time appointment at Hestonville and had been bedridden for almost a week with a severe bout of rheumatism and his old enemy, dysentery, he nevertheless "determined" to go. Such a journey was no easy undertaking for a sick man. It took four days by train by way of Pittsburgh, Chicago, Milwaukee, and La Crosse, Wisconsin, and required frequent delays and transfers. At La Crosse, he had to take an overnight steamer up the Mississippi to St. Paul. On arrival he found his friend seriously ill. Andrew never identified the exact nature of the illness but wrote that Will had been hemorrhaging and was exceedingly weak. He remained in St. Paul for eleven days, visiting Will often, praying with him, and talking of "serious things." During this time, Maddock agreed to become a probationary member in Andrew's church. On October 7, when Andrew began the return journey to Philadelphia, Maddock, his sister, Ella, his physician (Dr. Caine), and Mrs. J. B. Stitt accompanied Andrew as far as Chicago. Three weeks later Andrew received word that Will had died in Chicago at midnight on October 25. His body arrived in Philadelphia on October 29, and Andrew conducted the funeral, followed by a graveside service at Woodlands Cemetery (cemetery records show that he was twenty-four years old). Some evidence suggests that Mrs. Stitt was Will's mother. She was with him in St. Paul, in Chicago when he died, and accompanied the body to Philadelphia. After the funeral Andrew and his sister Eliza called on her several times and when Andrew wrote verses on the death of his friend, he read them to Mrs. Stitt and, presumably, presented a copy of them to her. See *MS Journal*, May 7, 1859, and *MS Diary* entries, September 15-November 3, 1862.

    4. See above, Letter 31, September 17, 1861, and note 1.

Letter 33, Paris, May 2, 1861

    1. See above, Letter 32, April 23, 1861. Maddock worked for J. B. Stitt & Co., 42 Barclay Street, New York City, merchants in "Cloths, Cassimeres & Vestings" (*New York City Business Directory*, 1860; appreciation is herewith expressed to Isaac Gewirtz, Curator of the Henry W. and Albert A. Berg Collection of English and American Literature, and Ruth Carr, U. S. History, Local History, and Genealogy Division, New York Public Library).

    2. Thomas D. James became the principal of Union Academy when it was established in 1851. Prior to that time, it is probable that James had his own school which Andrew attended in his younger years. Grateful appreciation for this information is herewith expressed to Max Moeller, Reference Specialist at the Historical Society of Pennsylvania.

    3. Virginia had seceded on April 17.

Letter 34, Phila. [i.e., Paris], May 8, 1861

    1. As often happened in this tragic conflict, families (such as the Bakers in this instance) found themselves on opposing sides, North and South. Andrew's friends, Charles J. and Henry J. Baker, were prominent Baltimore businessmen with various mercantile, commercial, and manufacturing interests. Henry J. Baker eventually moved to New York, but his business enterprises required frequent and extensive travel abroad. The brothers were prominent Methodist laymen with an interest in missions (for many years Henry J. Baker was an active member of the Missionary Board). Because of "border" troubles in 1860, Charles Baker withdrew his official relations from the church and aided in the foundation and growth of several Independent Methodist churches. *Cyclopaedia of Methodism*, p. 77.

    2. Dr. McClintock and his wife had gone to London on April 22 and returned on May 7. "News very sad on all sides," was Andrew's comment (*MS Diary*, May 7, 1861). It was feared that England (and perhaps even France) would recognize the Confederate States and come to their aid. On April 30, before he returned to Paris, McClintock wrote Andrew that he had spoken "at 4 p.m. in Exeter Hall—more politics than missions in the speech" (Crooks, p. 300). Earlier, McClintock had written to his friend Lemuel Bangs, "We are very anxious here about ministers and consuls. London, Liverpool, Paris, and Havre should all be filled with vigorous men. Things will be left in a sad condition, I fear, by some of our present diplomatic and consular agents. The English and French Governments are willing to do right, but the American ambassadors, who talk to them, are either not Union men at all, or are very timid ones. I hope these posts will be promptly and well filled by Mr. Lincoln" (Crooks, pp. 298-99). See below, Letter 37, May 22, 1861.

3. The annual Salon in Paris was of supreme importance in the art world. Since there were few art dealers or galleries, even in the mid-nineteenth century, the Salons provided the only real opportunity for both public and private collectors to view current works of art. If an artist was refused this venue, his chance of recognition and financial success was doomed at the outset.

The annual Salon had been a fixture in the Paris art world since Louis XIV had established the Royal Academy of Painting and Sculpture in 1663. Until the Revolution, only members of the Academy could participate. In 1791 the National Assembly opened the Salon to everyone but named a government committee to decide which works could be shown. Many of the jurors, however, had ultraconservative tastes and many well-deserving works were barred from exhibition. Problems arose immediately, and each year different arrangements were tried. None worked to everyone's satisfaction. After Louis Napoleon's *coup d'état* in 1851, the jury system was once again put in place but, as before, any unconventional work was excluded. Such was still the case in 1861 when Andrew went to see this exhibition at the Palais de l'Industrie. He notes that about 4,000 paintings (about half of those submitted) had been rejected. Two years later (when Edouard Manet submitted *Le dejeuner sur l'herbe,* along with two other works to the Salon), the same number was again refused (including works by Pissarro, Whistler, Fantin-Latour, Braquemond, and Cézanne). This prompted the Emperor to create the Salon des Refusés where the rejected works of art could be mounted in another part of the Palais de l'Industrie so that the public could judge the legitimacy of the complaints. This experiment was never to be forgotten by the revolutionary artists of later years (see Friedrich, pp. 15-17).

4. The painter, James Joseph Jacques Tissot (1836-1902) was twenty-four years old. In his *MS Diary* (May 7, 1860), Andrew wrote, "Good orchestra and fine solos on piano (Mr. Tissot), hautbois and violin, comical songs."

Letter 35, May 14, 1861

1. See above, Letter 25, February 19, 1861, note 7.

Letter 36, Paris, May 20th, 1861

1. The Francis Lycetts. These plans were delayed until July; see below, Letter 40, June 20, 1861, and note 3; also Letter 38, May 30, 1861, and Letter 39, June 7, 1861.

2. Almost certainly, "to be a better boy" had been a frequent and loving admonition of their mother, Eliza Stiles Longacre, to her young sons. Recalled and repeated here, Jim would have fully understood Andrew's meaning.

3. An interesting commentary on life in the French capital which often cut across the grain of Andrew's Methodist upbringing and commitment where "doing good" was a tenet of the faith (see John Wesley's oft-quoted rule, "not only to do good, but to do all the good you possibly can," in his letter to Mrs. Johnson, October 27, 1784; John Telford, ed., *The Letters of the Rev. John Wesley, A.M.* 8 vols. London: Epworth Press, 1931, 7:245; hereafter cited as Telford). A few weeks

after penning this letter to James, Andrew expanded on life in Paris: "As a field of ministerial labor, Paris is not attractive. There are many and great drawbacks upon one's usefulness. Pastoral work in a chapel, constituted as this is, is not much more than a mere name. Earnest, <u>praying visits</u> are unknown, except in a very few instances. The people would not tolerate them. Of course, there are a few exceptions, but very few. I really long for a pastor's right and true place once more. Upon this point of religious visiting that is formally declaratively religious, I have had many exercises of mind. Hitherto, I have not felt it right to undertake such a thing. As far as I could, I have striven to bring in religion as a subject of conversation from time to time, have talked plainly and freely with many of our people, but the regular pastoral visiting which is expected in our churches at home, I have not thought it best to attempt for fear of doing harm instead of good." (*MS Journal*, August 12, 1861).

4. With these words Andrew was standing firmly in his Wesleyan tradition. John Wesley spoke often of saving souls and the care of souls. E.g., in 1745 he added a rule to his "Rules of an Assistant" (later known as "Rules of a Helper"): "You have nothing to do but to save souls. Therefore spend and be spent in this work" (*Minutes of the Methodist Conferences, from the first, held in London, by the Late Rev. John Wesley, A.M., in the Year 1744*. London: John Mason, 1862, 1:28; see also the *Large Minutes*, ibid, 1:494). Later, in a letter dated October 8, 1755, to Christopher Hopper, one of his preachers, Wesley wrote, "You have one business on earth—to save souls"; to his brother Charles Wesley, March 25, 1772, John wrote, "Oh what a thing it is to have *curam animarum* [the care of souls]. You and I are called to this; to save souls from death, to watch over them as those that must give an account"; a month later, April 26, 1772, in another letter to Charles, he reiterated, "Your business as well as mine is to save souls. When we took priests' orders, we undertook to make it our *one* business" (see Telford, 3:148; 5:314, 316).

5. John and Charles Wesley, "Come let us join our friends in death," Hymn I, vs. 2, ln. 4, in *Funeral Hymns*. Second Series. London: 1759, in George Osborn, *The Poetical Works of John and Charles Wesley: Reprinted from the Originals, with the last corrections of the authors; together with the Poems of Charles Wesley not before published*. London: Wesleyan-Methodist Conference Office, 2, Castle-Street, City-Road; sold at 66 Paternoster-Row, 1870, 6:215.

Letter 37, Paris, May 22nd, 1861

1. The Woodlands, on the western outskirts of Philadelphia, is the site of the magnificent mansion of Andrew Hamilton, inherited by his grandson William in 1747 who had a passion for architecture and landscape design. William embellished the gardens with exotic plants and built walks and pathways. Nearby is Woodlands Cemetery where many Philadelphian worthies are buried, including Andrew's mother, Eliza Stiles Longacre. In October 1862, after Andrew returned to Philadelphia, he would bury at Woodlands one of his first "Sunday School scholars," Will Maddock (see above Letter 32, April 23, 1861, note 3). Today, this area comprises the Woodlands Heritage National Recreation Trail, and the entire property is a National Historic Landmark. For the website, see http://www.fieldtrip.com/pa/53862181.htm.

2. See above, Letter 34, May 8, 1861, and note 2.

Letter 38, Paris, May 30th, 1861

1. This important meeting of prominent Americans gave McClintock an opportunity to speak on the current political situation in America. "His speech on this occasion was full of eloquence and courage, but indicated his opinion that the war would not come to a speedy end." He did "justice to the English people. 'I have no fear,' he said, 'of the grand English nation. Its voice has not yet been heard. When it shall be uttered, it will not be on the side of piracy and slavery'" (Crooks, p. 288). Although Andrew's account of the meeting in his letter is fulsome, his diary entry for the day makes no mention of it whatsoever.

2. Orig., "W. T. Dayton." William Lewis Dayton (1807-1864), born in Baskingridge, New Jersey, was a lawyer, politician, and diplomat. Graduating from Princeton in 1825, he was admitted to the bar in 1830. On July 2, 1842, Governor William Pennington appointed him United States senator for the unexpired term of S. L. Southard, and the legislature chose him for the full term to March 4, 1851. From 1857-61, he served as attorney-general of New Jersey. In 1861 he was appointed minister to France. Although he could not speak French and was unversed in diplomacy, he nevertheless had the best of relations with Louis Napoleon's government, with diplomatic colleagues, and with the press. He gained the entire confidence of the Emperor whom he had frequently met during Louis Napoleon's residence in New Jersey. See *DAB*, 5:166-67.

3. Orig., here and below, "Burlinghome." Anson Burlingame (1820-70) was, in fact, appointed as U.S. minister to China, not Austria, by President Lincoln in 1861. He had entered public life in 1853 as a Massachusetts state senator; then from 1855-61, he served in the U. S. House of Representatives. A member of the Know-Nothing Party he had helped found the Republican Party in the mid-1850s. *NEB* 2:655-56.

4. Jacob S. Haldeman, a native of Pennsylvania, was Minister Resident, Stockholm, Sweden, from 1861-64. See Walter Burges Smith, *America's diplomats and consuls of 1776-1865: a geographic and biographic directory of the Foreign Service from the Declaration of Independence to the end of the Civil War*. Washington, D. C.: Center for the Study of Foreign Affairs, Foreign Service Institute, U. S. Department of State, 1987, p. 170.

5. Cassius Marcellus Clay (1810-1903), a United States antislavery leader who served the Abolition Movement in spite of his southern background. He was U. S. minister to Russia (1861-62 and 1863-69) and helped to negotiate the purchase of Alaska in 1867. *NEB*, 3:363.

6. John C. Frémont (1813-1890), mapmaker and explorer of the American West, played an important role in the U. S. conquest and development of California. In 1850 he was elected one of that state's first two senators. His firm opposition to slavery, the popularity of his explorations, and his part in the conquest of California led to his nomination for the presidency in 1856 by the new Republican Party, but he was defeated by the Democratic candidate, James Buchanan. After the Civil War began, Frémont was appointed major general and placed in command of the western department, with headquarters in St. Louis, Missouri, but political and military enemies made the most of his various failures, which brought about his resignation. *NEB*, 4:972.

7. General Winfield Scott (1786-1866), a U.S. Army officer who held the rank of general in three wars (1812, Mexican, and Civil War). He commanded the U. S. Army at the outbreak of the Civil War (April 1861) until age forced his retirement the following November. *NEB*, 10:566.

Letter 39, Paris, June 7, 1861

1. Camp meetings had always been a special means of grace and spiritual renewal for Andrew, and he looked forward to them each summer. His anticipation is especially interesting since he did not consider himself a "revivalist or fitted to do much in a time of excitement" (*MS Journal,* October 23, 1859). Earlier (August 19, 1857), he had written, "I have a kind of natural repugnance to great excitement and very public labors for individual souls. . . . Sometimes I think God mercifully withholds from me the extreme and intense feelings which some appear to possess for dying souls because he sees I am physically unable to support it." Yet camp meetings were nothing but prolonged, emotionally-charged gatherings. Nevertheless, in his *MS Journal,* Sunday, August 9, 1857, Andrew wrote, "We are on the eve of our annual camp meeting. I am always benefitted there—and never was I more blessed than last year." This camp meeting in mid-August, 1857, was held at Camden, Delaware. The following year, Andrew attended camp meetings again at Camden as well as at Pennsgrove, New Jersey. "I was as usual much blessed" (*MS Journal,* October 24, 1858). In July, 1859, he attended the camp meeting at Pennsgrove and then, in August, "I went by invitation of Mr. Charles J. Baker of Baltimore to the camp meeting held at Water's ground, which many of the Baltimore Methodists attended" (*MS Journal*, July 31, and October 23, 1859). Soon after his arrival in Paris, he wrote, "Here in this spiritually cold city, my heart has been reaching forth toward home. Just at this season, this very day probably, dear friends are gathered in the hallowed woods at Pennsgrove, having a quiet Sunday before camp meeting fairly begins tomorrow. How gladly would I join them. I feel as tho' I were really hungry for such spiritual food as I have found peculiarly at such seasons" (*MS Journal*, July 29, 1860). See also, Letter 12, September 6, 1860, where Andrew speaks of "the fresh sweet air of camp-meeting."

One of the best accounts of early Methodist camp meetings can be found in Jesse Lee, *A Short History of the Methodists in the United States of America.* Baltimore: Magill and Clime, 1810, pp. 360-62. Especially interesting is Lee's description of the layout of the camp ground, the arrangement for tents, carriages, horses, camp fires and other illumination, security, platforms or stages erected for the preaching, the schedule for religious services, etc. In 1901, Adam Wallace gave an account of "The Preacher's Tent" at camp meetings. "Sometimes [it was] of canvas construction, filled with sleeping bunks, [where] we sat on the beds during our nocturnal discussions until the candle burned out. ['The Preacher's Tent'] became a 'Post Graduate' theological seminary, long before we dreamed of Evanston or Drew. Here, around that embodiment of doctrinal and disciplinary wisdom, the presiding elder, the younger men clustered, receiving his utterances with silent reverence" (quoted by John D. Herr, Ch. VII, "Camp Meetings of the Philadelphia Conference," in Francis H. Tees, *et al., Pioneering in Penn's Woods.* Philadelphia: The Philadelphia Conference Tract Society of the Methodist Episcopal Church, 1937, pp. 87-94).

Letter 40, Paris, June 20, 1861

1. Another example of the ever-changing arrangements in regard to Andrew's tenure in Paris and the last-minute efforts to keep the work of the Chapel afloat; see above, Letter 9, August 20, 1860, note 2.

2. *Deo Volente,* "God willing."

3. For this trip, see below, the Introduction to Letter 43, July 19, 1861.

4. Montmorency is a small town some nine miles north of Paris situated on a hill opposite Enghien. "The forest of Montmorency is extensive and highly picturesque. Horses and asses are to be hired in the market-places, at moderate prices. . . . The country round is celebrated for its cherries." See *Galignani's Guide for 1867*, p. 522.

Letter 41, Paris, June 25, 1861

1. The American and Foreign Christian Union; see above, Letter 9, August 20, 1860, note 2.

2. Less than a week before Andrew penned this letter, John McClintock had written to his friend, C. C. North, about his concerns for the Chapel, financial and otherwise: "In these times, the Chapel has caused me a great deal of anxiety. Many of our pewholders have gone to America, and few have come to take their places. Yet our congregations are as good as ever. This is caused by the number who come in from other parts of Europe, to be nearer the news from home, and to be ready to go home if necessary. These persons do not take pews, but it is a blessing the Chapel is there for them. Thus far the treasurer has been able to pay my salary punctually every month out of the receipts, but I have no idea this can last" (Crooks, p. 302).

Letter 42, Paris, July 4, 1861

1. Located nine miles northwest of Paris, St. Germain-en-Laye had long been a royal residence and hunting lodge. Louis VI had built a castle here in the twelfth century. Destroyed in the Hundred Years War, it was rebuilt by Charles V in 1368. Francis I rebuilt it entirely in 1539. Henry II, Charles IX, and Louis XIV were all born here and Louis XIII died here. Associations with Great Britain went back for centuries. Mary Stuart lived here in the fourteenth century; Henrietta, wife of Charles I, lived at St. Germain from 1645-48; and James II, deposed from the throne of England in 1689, lived out the last years of his life here, dying in 1701. It was a favorite tourist attraction in the nineteenth century and remains so today (*Michelin Tourist Guide Ile-de-France*, p. 157). Andrew reported on his earlier trip to St. Germain-en-Laye: "Took cars to St. Germain. Spent entire day there riding and dining at Pavillon Henry Quartre." At the bottom of the page, he pressed an "Ivy leaf and moss from forest of St. Germain" (*MS Diary*, July 13, 1860).

2. The American and Foreign Christian Union in New York; see above, Letter 9, August 20, 1860, note 2.

Letter 43, Liverpool, July 19, 1861

1. Calling or visiting cards.

Letter 44, London, July 25, 1861

1. See Ps. 55:6, "Oh, that I had wings like a dove! for then would I fly away, and be at rest."

2. Edmund Storer Janes was born April 27, 1807, in Sheffield, Massachusetts. He joined the Philadelphia Conference of the Methodist Episcopal Church in 1830. Elected bishop in 1844, he was one of the last two bishops to receive that vote in an undivided church. See *Cyclopaedia of Methodism*, p. 493.

3. Andrew modernized this bit of verse to refer to Queen Victoria's dog. But the poem, by Alexander Pope, "On the collar of a dog," referred to the dog of Frederick Louis (1707-1751), Prince of Wales, the eldest son of King George II of Great Britain:
   "I am his Highness' dog at Kew,
   Pray tell me, sir, whose dog are you?"

Letter 46, Ryde, Isle of Wight, August 1, 1861

1. Information about Andrew's friend, Reese Alsop, has not been forthcoming. If he were a clergyman (see below, Letter 69, April 16, 1862), he was not a Methodist since no one by this name appears in the *Minutes* during these years. He is also mentioned in Letter 49, August 17, 1861.

2. Legh Richmond (1772-1827), an English divine, ordained in 1799 to the curacy of the parishes of Brading and Yaverland, Isle of Wight, took up his residence at Brading. In 1809, he wrote three tales of village life: "The Dairyman's Daughter," "The Young Cottager," and "The Negro Servant." The cottage of "Little Jane," the heroine of the second tale, is still shown at Brading. See *Dictionary of National Biography*. Sir Leslie Stephen and Sir Sidney Lee, eds. 22 vols. Oxford: Oxford University Press, 1921-23, 16:1144.

3. Andrew's impressions were still fresh when he wrote this letter to Jim, but his first hand knowledge of Wales came only from the windows of the train during his visit to Ireland where he accompanied Mrs. Baker before her homeward voyage to America. From London to Chester, they crossed over into North Wales and through Anglesey to Holyhead, where they boarded ship for Kingstown (Dun Laoghaire). A week later, they retraced their route (*MS Diary*, July 9, and July 16, 1861).

Letter 47, Paris, August 7, 1861

1. The First Battle of Bull Run (or the Battle of Manassas Junction) was fought on July 21, 1861, near a small stream named Bull Run. The Union Army had been ordered to advance southwest from Washington toward Manassas, a strategic rail junction, in a move against Richmond. But the advance was repelled by the Confederate forces under Generals P. G. T. Beauregard and Joseph E. Johnston, giving military advantage to the South. *NEB*, 2:624-25.

2. August 15th was the fête-day of Napoleon I. In the *MS Diary*, across the top of the page for this date, Andrew wrote in large letters, which he underscored, "Fête Internationale." He reported, "In the evening walked out with the young ladies and several young gentlemen." For the celebration of the previous year, see above, Letter 8, August 11, 1860, and note 7. Andrew again mentions preparations for this holiday in Letter 48, August 12, 1861.

3. See below, Letter 49, August 17, 1861.

Letter 48, Paris, August 12, 1861

1. See above, Letter 47, August 7, 1861, note 1.

2. As it turned out, the North also lost the Second Battle of Bull Run which took place on August 29-30, 1862. See *NEB*, 2:625.

3. See above, Letter 47, August 7, 1861, note 2.

Letter 49, Paris, August 17, 1861

1. See above, Letter 46, August 1, 1861, note 1.

Letter 50, Paris, August 29, 1861

1. The Malakhoff, or Malakoff, was a fort which formed one of the central defenses of Sebastopol during the Crimean War. It was taken by General MacMahon and his Zouaves on September 8, 1855; see Burchell, p. 345.

Letter 51, Versailles, September 4, 1861

1. See above, Letter 2, June 16, 1860, note 7.

2. The water supply and sewage disposal for the city of Paris had been an ongoing problem for years. By the end of the eighteenth century the situation had become critical. The Seine was the principal supply for water, but it also served as the dumping ground for all the city sewage. Overcrowding in the medieval city within the walls eventually contaminated not only the river but much of the shallow underground water supply, making shallow private wells unsafe. To help alleviate the supply problem, at the beginning of the nineteenth century, Napoleon Bonaparte constructed the Canal de l'Ourcq which brought in water originating more than 109 kilometers from the city and which by the mid-1850s supplied three-quarters of all the water in Paris. At this time only one house in five had water piped in—and that only on the first floor. Others depended on fountains placed throughout the city where water could be drawn for individual households. If patrons were wealthy enough, water could be purchased and delivered house to house, floor by floor by watercarriers. As Paris continued to grow, there was an ever-increasing need for more water. An artesian well was drilled at Grenelle in 1834 (see above, Letter 16, October 18, 1860, note 4) and one at Passy in 1855, which brought minimal relief to the city. But an adequate supply was still in the future. Andrew noted at least twice that he could not bathe because no water was available in the house (*MS Diary*, May 27-28, 1861). See above, Letter 6, July 9, 1860, note 3; J. M. and Brian Chapman, *The Life and Times of Baron Haussmann*. London: Weidenfeld and Nicolson, 1957, pp. 105-06; and Burchell, p. 84.

3. Matt. 3:5; Mark 1:28, 6:55; Luke 4:14, 7:17 (all Scripture references in these letters are to the KJV).

4. In 1851 Van Rensselaer had married Mary Ann Howland (b. 1830), daughter of Samuel Shaw Howland (a shipping tycoon) and Joanna Hone; she died in 1853, leaving no children. He later married Louisa Barnwell. Alexander died in 1878.

5. Although the arrangements (financial and otherwise) between McClintock and Andrew seemed as variable as the wind and kept Andrew in a perpetual state of uncertainty, there is no mention of this particular understanding either in the letters or the *MS Diary*. One certainty was Andrew's continually strapped financial state. See above, Letter 9, August 20, 1860; Letter 20, January 2, 1861; and Letter 41, June 25, 1861.

6. After the morning service at the Chapel on Sunday, September 1, Andrew had baptised Minna Emmets Griswold, infant daughter of Mr. and Mrs. John Alsop Griswold, for which he received 125 francs (*MS Diary*).

7. Matt. 6:34.

Letter 52, Versailles, September 19, 1861

1. Andrew had received news of the first blow by the Federal Navy to enforce the blockade of the Confederate coastline issued the previous April by President Lincoln. In late August an expedition of fourteen Union vessels sailed from Hampton Roads to capture the two forts on either side of Hatteras Inlet. By August 29 both Fort Hatteras and Fort Clark were in Northern hands. See Shelby Foote, *The Civil War, A Narrative; Fort Sumter to Perryville*. New York: Vintage Books, 1986, pp. 112f.; and *EB*, 1:757.

Letter 53, Versailles, September 27, 1861

1. See Ps. 34:10.

2. The Chapelle Taitbout had a long history of French-American cooperation in providing Protestant worship in the French capital and was, in some sense, the mother church of the American Chapel in Paris. In 1858 the Americans moved into their new chapel at No. 21, rue de Berri. See Cochran, pp. 42-43, 48, 53-54.

Letter 54, Paris, October 8, 1861

1. See Isaac Watts, Hymn 81, "A Song for Morning or Evening, Lam. iii.23; Isa. xlv," vs. 3, lns. 3-4, in *Hymns and Spiritual Songs*, Book I, in *The Works of the Late Reverend & Learned Isaac Watts, D. D.* London: Printed for T. and T. Longman, J. Buckland, J. Oswald, J. Waugh, and J. Ward, 1753, 4:175.

2. See above, Letter 31, April 17, 1861, note 4.

3. See Introduction to Letter 56, October 25, 1861, below.

Letter 55, Biarritz, October 16, 1861

1. Cape May, New Jersey, at the entrance of Delaware Bay.

2. Orig. "wall," perhaps a confusion while writing "was" and thinking of the word to follow: "ill".

3. Before leaving Paris, Andrew had called on Dr. Beylord. The next day he reported, "Very well satisfied with the effect of Dr. Beylord's medicine," although he does not specify the treatment (see *MS Diary*, October 4-7, 1861).

4. I.e., stagecoach.

5. Now known as Pamplona.

Letter 56, Madrid, October 25, 1861

1. Andrew made a pencil sketch of these carriages on October 23, 1861, which he titled, "Carriages at Valencia."

2. Far from home and often homesick, Andrew is acutely aware that the city he has reached in his travels is in the same latitude as his hometown.

Letter 57, Madrid, October 29, 1861

1. The location of this archive, if extant, has not been located.

2. Orig., Fernando.

3. His niece, Sarah Ann (Saidee) Keen, daughter of Andrew's sister Sallie. Born October 31, 1849, Saidee was just two days shy of her twelfth birthday.

Letter 58, Madrid, October 29, 1861

1. I.e., *verbum sat sapienti est*, "a word to the wise is sufficient."

2. Andrew is reminding Jim that their own father did not marry until he was thirty-three (at this writing Jim was twenty-eight and Andrew thirty); therefore, he is saying that there was still plenty of time to take a wife. James Barton Longacre was thirteen years older than their mother; Jim, at thirty-two, would marry Augusta McClintock, ten years his junior; Andrew, at thirty-eight, would marry Lydia Anne Eastwick, nineteen years his junior.

3. Ps. 37:23 .

4. See 1 Tim. 4:8.

5. 1 Pet. 5:7.

6. Phil. 4:6-7.

Letter 59, Seville, November 20, 1861

1. They had arrived at Alicante on Saturday, November 2, intending to depart immediately for Malaga but finding their steamer was delayed, their visit extended until Tuesday, November 5 (*MS Diary*). See also, below, Letter 62, January 20, 1862.

Letter 60, Cairo, December 4, 1861

1. Ptolemy II Philadelphus (308-246 BC), king of Egypt and second king of the Ptolemaic dynasty.

2. Longacre is referring to Amr ibn al-As, who conquered Egypt in A.D. 640.

3. The Mohammed Ali Mosque, built in 1840 on a rocky eminence, was visible for miles around.

4. An interpreter, chiefly of Arabic, Turkish, or Persian.

5. Their boat, *The Ibis,* was owned by American missionaries, and the arrangements for leasing it were made with a Reverend Mr. Lansing (*MS Diary,* December 5, 1861).

6. Van Renssaeler purchased this gift at one of the bazaars in Cairo on December 7. Later, when the travelers reached Constantinople, Andrew, with a mustache and beard, would pose for a full-length photograph wearing a brimless cap and this handsome scarf draped about his shoulders (*MS Diary,* March 19-26, 1862).

Letter 61, On the Nile, January 10, 1862

1. Andrew's letters, marvelously illuminated by his diary entries, some of which are exquisitely descriptive and often poetic, give the reader more than an adequate account of this "eastern tour."

2. An Arabic word for captain of a boat or vessel (*OED*).

3. On Sunday morning, January 19, Andrew took a short walk on the island where *The Ibis* was moored and in the afternoon another walk on shore "along the road leading to the pyramids." The next morning he reported, "Sunrise on top of the Great Pyramid," but these are his only references in the *MS Diary* to visiting the pyramids at Giza, although he mentions they had seen the pyramids and tombs at Sakkarah the day before.

4. The obelisk of pink granite came from the ruins of the temple at Luxor. It is 3,300 years old, covered with hieroglyphics, stands seventy-five feet tall, and weighs more than 220 tons. It was offered to Charles X in 1829 by Mohammed Ali, the Viceroy of Egypt, but it took four years to transport and did not arrive in Paris until the reign of Louis Philippe, when in 1833 it was erected in the Place de la Concorde. See *Galignani's Guide for 1867,* p. 179; and *Michelin Tourist Guide to Paris,* 1985, p. 43.

5. It is interesting to remember that the discovery of King Tutankhamen's tomb was still far in the future.

6. Shishak (or Shesong I), Egyptian, founder of the 22nd Dynasty (*c.* 940-919 B.C.). He may have been the unnamed Pharaoh who became the father-in-law of Solomon; see 1 Kgs. 14:25; 2 Chron. 12:2.

7. Andrew's brother-in-law. See above, Letter 1, May 21, 1860, note 13.

8. See above, Letter 10, August 23, 1860, note 1.

Letter 62, Cairo, January 20, 1862

1. See above, Letter 59, November 20, 1861.

Letter 63, Jerusalem, January 31, 1862

1. In the *MS Diary* (January 29, 1862), Andrew used the more traditional spelling, "Ramleh." But his guides were mistaken in identifying this place as the ancient Arimathea since Ramleh was founded by Suleiman in the early part of the eighth century. The site of ancient Arimathea remains uncertain, having been identified with various places including Ramallah near

Jerusalem. The general consensus locates it some 20 miles east of Jaffa and 10 miles northeast of modern Lod (ancient Lydda). The town that Andrew's caravan reached is located some 20 miles east of Jaffa and 10 miles southwest of Lod. See Edward Robinson, *Biblical Researches in Palestine, and in the adjacent regions.* 2d ed. Boston: Crocker and Brewster; London: John Murray, 1860, 2:234-41; *Anchor Bible Dictionary.* New York: Doubleday, 1992, 1:378; *International Standard Bible Encyclopedia* (revised). Grand Rapids, Michigan: William B. Eerdmans Publishing Company, 1979, 1:290; *Interpreter's Dictionary of the Bible.* New York and Nashville: Abingdon Press, 1962, 1:219; J. A. Fitzmyer, *The Gospel According to Luke; Anchor Bible.* Garden City, New York: Doubleday & Company, Inc., 1985, 28A:1526. (I am deeply indebted to Victor P. Furnish, University Distinguished Professor Emeritus of New Testament, Perkins School of Theology, Southern Methodist University, Dallas, Texas, for his valued assistance in identifying the places in Palestine, Syria, and Turkey mentioned in these letters.)

2. See 1 Sam. 7:1; 1 Chron. 13:5-6; 2 Chron. 1:4.

3. Emmaus was on the road to Jaffa (now part of Tel Aviv) about twenty miles WNW of Jerusalem. See *Dictionary of the Bible.* James Hasting, ed.; rev. ed. by Frederick C. Grant and H. H. Rowley. New York: Charles Scribner's Sons, 1963, p. 246.

4. The great Maritime Plain extending from south of Jaffa to Mount Carmel in the north. Its soil is rich and deep and yields annually a magnificent crop of wild flowers. See *Dictionary of the Bible*, p. 901.

5. William Henry Bartlett. Longacre was referring most likely to *Syria, the Holy Land, Asia Minor…* illustrated …by W. H. Bartlett, W. Purser, &c. 3 v. in 2. London: Fisher, Son, & Co., 1838. But see also Bartlett's *Footsteps of Our Lord & his apostles in Syria, Greece & Italy; a succession of visits to the scenes of New Testament narrative.* 5th ed. New York: Scribner, n.d.

6. *Ficus sycamorus,* which often grows to a height of 50 feet and produces its fruit along its branches, should not be confused with the sycamore trees in the west (*acer pseudo-platanus*). See *Dictionary of the Bible*, p. 943.

Letter 64, Convent of Mar Saba Near the Dead Sea, February 4, 1862

1. A Greek monastery founded in A. D. 483 in the Judean desert southeast of Jerusalem, located on the southern high cliff of the canyon at Kidron River. See Joseph Patrich, *Sabas, leader of Palestinian monasticism: a comparative study in Eastern monasticism, fourth to seventh centuries.* Washington, D. C.: Dunbarton Oaks Research Library and Collection, 1995.

2. Hebron, a very ancient city about 20 miles SSW from Jerusalem. See *Dictionary of the Bible*, p. 375.

3. Gihon, a spring near Jerusalem selected as the scene of Solomon's coronation (see 1 Kgs. 1:33, 38, 45). Hezekiah made an aqueduct from it (2 Chron. 32:30). See also Neh. 2:14; 3:15. *Dictionary of the Bible*, pp. 330; 914-15; and Robinson, 1:341, 311, 337.

4. This was a Franciscan convent. When the Crusaders arrived in Bethlehem in 1099, little remained of the Church of the Nativity. "Around the north side of the church, therefore, they built a cloister and monastery which was given to the Canons of St. Augustine." When the Latins lost

Jerusalem to the Egyptians in 1244, their situation in Bethlehem also deteriorated. In 1263, the Egyptian Sultan, Bibars, newly come to power, ordered Bethlehem destroyed, yet the church somehow survived. Although the Augustinians had at some point abandoned (or been evicted from?) their monastery there, the Franciscans subsequently moved in. "In 1347 the Franciscans were given the Basilica; some time earlier they had established themselves in Bethlehem in the deserted Augustinian monastery, where they still reside. . . ." See Fr. Eugene Hoade, O. F. M., *Guide to the Holy Land.* 4th ed. Jerusalem: Franciscan Press, 1962, pp. 365-67.

5. After he returned home, Andrew baptized his young nephew, John Foster Keen, Jr., born June 6, 1860, with water from the River Jordan (*MS Diary*, December 25, 1862).

6. A variant spelling for Nablus, which was on their projected route toward the north.

7. A hilly promontory rising over 1800 feet by which the sea-coast of Palestine is broken, forming the south side of the Bay of Acre. See *Dictionary of the Bible*, p. 128.

8. A town in east Lebanon north of Damascus on the site of the ancient city of Heliopolis.

Letter 65, Encamped at the foot of Mt Tabor, February 13, 1862

1. Mount Tabor, east of Nazareth, rises 1929 feet.

2. See 2 Kgs. 9:16.

3. See 1 Sam. 31:8; 1 Chron. 10: 1, 8. Mount Gilboa, 1696 feet, lies west of the Jordan and south of the Valley of Jezreel.

4. See 2 Sam. 21:12.

5. A village six miles southeast of Nazareth; see Luke 7:11-15.

6. Mount Hermon, a mountain 9232 feet high on the border between Syria and Lebanon.

7. "From Sidon to Beyrout [Beirut]," Andrew "rode in advance of the caravan and made the journey in eight hours." They stopped at the Hotel Bellevue "<u>outside</u>" and called at the Banker's for letters from home (*MS Diary*, February 21, 1862).

8. The travelers found their accommodations "a palace in comparison with any others we have seen. Have a suite of rooms, fine view from the terrace, the grand bay of Acre, with Acre itself lying on the further edge." The day before, Sunday, while at Nazareth, Andrew walked to the top of the hill north of the town where is the Weli Nebi Ismail, a poor little mosque, "touching in its poverty. In the afternoon walked by the fine meadow where all the boys and men of the town seemed gathered to play." The next day, a fine day, the caravan traveled over good roads from Nazareth to Mount Carmel until they reached the plain of Kidron, passing "pretty little villages among the hills," which were "covered with oaks, quite a forest for Palestine." In the plain they found the road wet and encountered sheets of water and mud (*MS Diary*, February 16-17, 1862).

9. Haifa, a city and port on the Bay of Acre at the foot of Mount Carmel.

10. Acre (Akko) on modern maps is some 20 miles north of Haifa. The name St. Jean d'Acre was given to this important and historic port by the Crusaders (the name was taken from the Order of St. John). The ancient Canaanite name was Acco (it appears in Judg. 1:31 as Accho). In the third century B.C. Acco received the name Ptolemais (probably in honor of Ptolemy II; see Acts 21:7) by which it was known for many centuries until the decline of Greek influence. See

Hoade; and *Dictionary of the Bible*, p. 824. Andrew and his party had a "delightful ride on the beach around the bay of Acre, past Acre to Ez Zib. On the way, a little out of Haifa crossed the Kishon in a rude ferry boat, the horses swimming" (*MS Diary*, February 18, 1862).

11. Sarepta, the city of Sidon; see Luke 4:26.

12. See Jonah 2:10.

13. The promontory Râs el Baiyada; see *Hachette World Guides, Lebanon*, 1955, p. 199, where it is identified as "the white rock," which drops sheer into the sea, mentioned in Pliny (*Natural History*, V.xvii.14). Edward Robinson (2:473) transliterates the name "Râs el-Beyâd or el-Abyad" and identifies it as "the *Promontorium album* of the ancients."

14. I.e., the Plain of Jezreel.

Letter 66, Smyrna, March 14, 1862

1. Julius Bing, a native of Frankfurt am Main, was a naturalized American citizen. Appointed out of Washington, D. C., he served as consul to Smyrna from 1861-1864. See Smith, p. 139.

2. Victor Emmanuel II, king of Sardinia and the first king of Italy, was born March 14, 1820.

3. On March 15, before leaving the city, Andrew sketched a Smyrna street scene.

4. The *Persia*, but "on account of high north wind" they anchored in a bay only a few hours from Smyrna where they remained all the next day; "a dull time," reported Andrew. The next day they sailed almost up to the Dardanelles but stopped again until the next day when they went through the straits and anchored below the Bosphorus. They rose early the next morning to see the entrance of the Golden Horn and a general view of Constantinople (*MS Diary*, March 15-19, 1862).

Letter 67, Constantinople, March 24, 1862

1. I.e., "Uskudar, the ancient Chrysopolis, known more commonly in Europe as Scutari, an important Asiatic suburb of Istanbul, is built in an amphitheatre around the old town on the western ridge of Mount Bulgurlu, which forms a headland facing the entrance to the Golden Horn"; see *The Hachette World Guides, Turkey*, 1970, p. 289. Andrew concluded his diary entry for this day, "After dinner read debate in Parliament on breaking American blockade" (*MS Diary*, March 22, 1862).

2. Orig., "Boulgourlou."

3. The old part of Istanbul south of the Golden Horn.

4. Their hired guide. The next day, "after long waiting," they were able to see Santa Sophia and Santa Irene, and Andrew made a sketch from the Seraglio. On Wednesday, March 26, before sailing, Andrew "spent the morning painting" a superb view of the harbor at Constantinople (*MS Diary*, March 25-26, 1862).

5. An alternative name for Syros or Siros, Syra is one of the islands in the Cyclades about 83 nautical miles southeast of Athens. In the nineteenth century it was an important industrial, shipping, and commercial center. The coming of railway networks and the rise of Piraeus closer to Athens brought about its decline. See Robert Nicholson, *Guide to the Greek Islands*. London: Robert Nicholson Publications, Ltd., 1986, p. 88.

Letter 68, Venice, April 4, 1862

1. Richard Hildreth (1807-1865), writer, editor, lawyer, was born in Deerfield, MA. In 1861 he was appointed consul at Trieste where he served until ill health forced him to resign in 1864. He died in Florence and was buried in the Protestant cemetery there. See *DAB*, 9:19-20.

2. Orig., "talk".

3. Titian (Tiziano Vecelli), 1477-1576; Venetian; pupil of the Bellini; formed by Giorgione; influenced slightly first by Raphael and later by Michelangelo. See Bernard Berenson, *Italian Pictures of the Renaissance*. Oxford: Clarendon Press, 1932, p. 568.

4. Paolo Veronese, 1528-1588; Venetian School; pupil of Antonio Badile (of Verona); strongly influenced by Brusasorci, Parmigianino, and Primaticcio; less, yet noticeably, by Lotto, Moretto, Romanino, and later by Titian. See Berenson, p. 419.

5. Tintoretto (Jacopo Robusti), 1518-1594; Venetian; may have been a pupil of Bonifazio Veronese; influenced by Titian, Michelangelo, Parmigianino and Lotto. See Berenson, p. 557.

6. *S. Maria Gloriosa dei Frari*, a cruciform church, one of the largest and most beautiful in Venice, in the Gothic style with peculiar Italian modifications, was built between 1250-1338. After Canova's death in 1822, his monument from his own design for Titian's monument was erected in 1827 by his pupils. Karl Baedeker, *Italy; Handbook for Travelers. First Part: Northern Italy*. 10th ed. Leipsic: Karl Baedeker, 1895, pp. 281-82.

7. Antonio Canova, 1757-1822, an Italian sculptor instrumental in the development of Neoclassicism (*NEB*, 2:811-12).

8. John Burnet (1784-1868), *Practical hints in light and shade in painting. Illustrated by examples from the Italian, Flemish, & Dutch schools*. London: J. Carpenter & Sons, 1826.

9. Elizabeth, empress consort of Austria, was regarded as the most beautiful princess in Europe. She married her cousin Francis Joseph I, April 24, 1854. Her life was tragic. Her son Rudolf, the crown prince, committed suicide in 1889, from which she never fully recovered. During a visit to Switzerland in 1898, she was assassinated by an Italian anarchist, Luigi Luccheni (*NEB*, 4:455).

Letter 69, Dresden, April 16, 1862

1. See above, Letters 46, August 1, 1861, note 1.

Letter 70, Berlin, April 19th, 1862

1. On April 21, 1862, before leaving Berlin, Andrew finished a detailed sketch of his room (No. 36) in the Hotel du Nord. "Funny feather coverlet" was his comment on arrival (see *MS Diary*, April 19-21, 1862).

2. This phrase denoting the followers of John Wesley first appeared in print in 1745 when Wesley published his *Advice to the People Called Methodists*. He had used it as early as 1742 in his Journal, but this was not published until 1749. (Grateful appreciation is herewith expressed to Richard P. Heitzenrater, William Kellon Quick Professor of Church History and Wesley Studies, Duke Divinity School, Durham, North Carolina.)

3. I. e., to bid farewell to his friends, the Lycetts.

4. Andrew spent part of three days at London's International Exhibition. The first day, May 7, he gave "attention only to the pictures, a very full display of British pictures and very fair of French." The next day, "Again visited the pictures (the foreign ones)," William Wetmore Story's statue of "Cleopatra," and the Libyan Sibyl, and other displays of "lace, silverware, furniture, porcelain, and bronzes." Before leaving London the next day, he "went with the ladies to see [William Powell] Frith's pictures of "The Railway Station" and "Derby Day" (*MS Diary*, May 7-9, 1862).

Letter 71, Paris, April 30, 1862

1. A poignant reference to the untimely death of their mother, Eliza Stiles Longacre, on May 1, 1850, shortly before her forty-third birthday. For Andrew, the traumatic experience left an indelible mark. Every anniversary of this event was noted in his diary, sometimes with a plain cross, sometimes an illuminated cross, sometimes a cross topped by a crown, drawn at the top of the page and accompanied by tender words of admiration, love, and loss.

Letter 72, New York, May 21, 1862

1. It is noteworthy that Andrew named his first son Henry Baker Longacre in honor of his friend. Sadly, the baby, born November 18, 1871, lived only seven months.

Epilogue

1. For a quaint and charming poem, "The Parson's Courtship," written by the older Andrew for his beloved wife, see Appendix C.

2. A complete record of Andrew's ministerial appointments can be found in Appendix B.

3. *In Memoriam*, pp. 15-16.

Bibliography

Manuscripts

Emory, Robert. *Journal, 1839-1847*. Bishop Frederick D. Leete Collection, Bridwell Library, Perkins School of Theology, Southern Methodist University, Dallas, Texas.

Longacre, Andrew. *Diaries, 1860-1862* (loaned by Dr. Andrew Longacre, Jr., Skaneateles, New York).

_____. *Journal of Religious Experience, September 1856-August 31, 1861* (loaned by Dr. Andrew Longacre, Jr., Skaneateles, New York).

_____. *Letter to Mrs Darlington, May 3, 1860* (loaned by Dr. Andrew Longacre, Jr., Skaneateles, New York).

_____. *Letter to John McClintock, April 19, 1862*. Manuscript Collection, Bridwell Library, Perkins School of Theology, Southern Methodist University, Dallas, Texas.

_____. *Letters to James Madison Longacre*. Bishop Frederick D. Leete Collection. Bridwell Library, Perkins School of Theology, Southern Methodist University, Dallas, Texas.

Guidebooks

Baedeker, Karl. *Italy; Handbook for Travellers. First Part: Northern Italy*. 10th ed. Leipzig: Karl Baedeker, 1895.

_____. *Italy; Handbook for Travellers. Second Part: Central Italy and Rome*. 12th ed. rev. Leipzig: Karl Baedeker; London: Dulau & Co., 1897.

_____. *Italy; Handbook for Travellers. Third Part: Southern Italy and Sicily*. Leipzig: Karl Baedeker; London: Dulau & Co., 1896.

Galignani's New Paris Guide for 1860. Paris: A. and W. Galignani and Co., Rue de Rivoli, No. 224 [1860].

Galignani's New Paris Guide for 1867. Paris: A. and W. Galignani and Co., Rue de Rivoli, No. 224 [1867].

Hachette World Guides, Italy. Paris: Hachette, 1956.

Hachette World Guides, Lebanon. Paris: Hachette, 1955.

Hachette World Guides, Turkey. Paris: Hachette, 1970.

Michelin Tourist Guide Paris. New Edition. London: Michelin Tyre Public Limited Company, 1985.

Michelin Tourist Guide Ile-de-France. Harrow, Middlesex: Michelin Tyre Public Limited Company, 1989.

Nicholson, Robert. *Guide to the Greek Islands*. London: Robert Nicholson Publications, Ltd., 1986.

Williamson-Serra, Herbert William, ed. *Tourist Guide-Book of Spain*. Madrid; New York: Times of Spain, 1952.

Periodicals

Christian Advocate. James M. Buckley, ed. New York: Eaton & Mains Publishers. 81 (March 1, 1906).

Times (London, England). [London Times Newspapers, Ltd.], 1788-.

Other Sources

Anchor Bible Dictionary. New York: Doubleday, 1992.

Baker's Biographical Dictionary of Musicians. 5th ed. Completely revised by Nicolas Slonimsky. New York: G. Shermer, 1958.

Bartlett, William Henry. *Footsteps of Our Lord & His Apostles in Syria, Greece & Italy; A Succession of Visits to the Scenes of New Testament Narrative.* 5th ed. New York: Scribner, n.d.

_____. *Syria, the Holy Land, Asia Minor… illustrated …by W. H. Bartlett, W. Purser, &c.* 3 v. in 2. London: Fisher, Son, & Co., 1838.

Bell, Robert. *Bell's Life in London, and Sporting Chronicle.* London: R. Bell, 1822-1886.

Bénézit, E., *Dictionnaire critique et documentaire des Peinteres, Sculpteurs, Dessinateurs et Graveurs.* Nouvelle Édition. [Paris:] Librairie Gründ, 1961.

Berenson, Bernard. *Italian Pictures of the Renaissance.* Oxford: Clarendon Press, 1932.

Brombert, Beth Archer. *Edouard Manet, Rebel in a Frock Coat.* Chicago: University of Chicago Press, 1997.

Burchell, S. C. *Imperial Masquerade; The Paris of Napoleon III.* New York: Atheneum, 1971.

Burnet, John. *Practical Hints in Light and Shade in Painting. Illustrated by Examples from the Italian, Flemish, & Dutch schools.* London: J. Carpenter & Sons, 1826.

Chapman, J. M. and Brian. *The Life and Times of Baron Haussmann.* London: Weidenfeld and Nicolson, 1957.

Cochran, Joseph Wilson. *Friendly Adventurers; A Chronicle of the American Church of Paris (1857-1931).* Paris: Bretano's, 1931.

Crooks, George R. *Life and Letters of Reverend John McClintock, D.D., LL.D., Late President of Drew Theological Seminary.* New York: Nelson & Phillips; Cincinnati: Hitchcock & Walden, 1876.

Cumming, Valerie. *Gloves.* London: B.T. Batsford, Ltd., 1982.

Cyclopaedia of Methodism (rev. ed.). Matthew Simpson, ed. Philadelphia: Louis H. Everts, 1880.

Dictionary of American Biography. Dumas Malone, ed. 22 vols. New York: Charles Scribner's Sons, 1932.

Dictionary of National Biography. Sir Leslie Stephen and Sir Sidney Lee, eds. 22 vols. Oxford: Oxford University Press, 1921-23.

Dictionary of the Bible. James Hasting, ed.; rev. ed. by Frederick C. Grant and H. H. Rowley. New York: Charles Scribner's Sons, 1963.

Encyclopaedia Britannica. 11th ed. 24 vols. Chicago: Encyclopaedia Britannica, Inc., 1956.

Evans, Thomas W. *Memoirs.* Edward A. Crane, ed. 2 vols. London: T. Fisher Unwin, 1905.

Field, Henry Martyn. *History of the Atlantic Telegraph.* New York: Scribner, 1867.

Fitzmyer, J. A. *The Gospel According to Luke; Anchor Bible.* Garden City, New York: Doubleday & Company, Inc., 1985.

Foote, Shelby. *The Civil War, A Narrative; Fort Sumter to Perryville.* New York: Vintage Books, 1986.

Friedrich, Otto. *Olympia; Paris in the Age of Manet.* New York: Simon & Schuster, 1992.

Grove's Dictionary of Music and Musicians. Eric Blom, ed. 5th ed. 9 vols. London: Macmillan & Co. Ltd.; New York: St Martin's Press, 1954.

Hoade, Eugene, O. F. M. *Guide to the Holy Land.* 4th ed. Jerusalem: Franciscan Press, 1962.

In Memoriam, Andrew Longacre, 1831-1906. New York: n.p.,1906.

International Standard Bible Encyclopedia (revised). Grand Rapids, Michigan: William B. Eerdmans Publishing Company, 1979.

Interpreter's Dictionary of the Bible. New York and Nashville: Abingdon Press, 1962.

Jordan, David P. *Transforming Paris: The Life and Labors of Baron Haussmann.* New York: The Free Press, 1995.

Keats, John. *Endymion.* Edited by Stephen Steinhoff. Troy, NY: Whitson, 1987.

Lee, Jesse. *A Short History of the Methodists in the United States of America.* Baltimore: Magill and Clime, 1810.

Longacre, Marian Sykes, ed. *The Longacre Line in America Descended from a Member of the Old Swedish Colony on the Delaware.* Fayetteville, New York: Privately printed, 1971.

Manual of the Corporation of the City of New York. D. T. Valentine. New York: New York (N.Y.) Common Council, 1861.

Minutes of the Methodist Conferences, the first, held in London, by the late Rev. John Wesley, A.M., in the year 1744. London: John Mason at the Wesleyan Conference Office, City-Road, and sold at 66, Paternoster-Row, 1862.

Minutes of the Annual Conferences of the Methodist Episcopal Church. New York: Carlton & Porter, 1852-1860.

National Cyclopedia of American Biography. Clifton, New Jersey: James T. White & Company, 1979.

New Encyclopaedia Britannica. 15th edition. 32 vols. Chicago: Encyclopaedia Britannica, Inc., 1985.

New York City Business Directory. 1860.

Notable American Women, 1607-1950; A Biographical Dictionary. Edward T. James, ed. Cambridge, MA: Belknap Press of Harvard University Press, 1971.

Patrich, Joseph. *Sabas, Leader of Palestinian Monasticism: A Comparative Study in Eastern Monasticism, Fourth to Seventh Centuries.* Washington, D. C.: Dunbarton Oaks Research Library and Collection, 1995.

Pinkney, David H. *Napoleon III and the Rebuilding of Paris.* Princeton, New Jersey: Princeton University Press, 1972.

Pliny. *Natural History* (Loeb Classical Library).

Poisson, Michel. *Paris Buildings and Monuments.* New York: Harry N. Abrams, 1999.

Robinson, Edward. *Biblical Researches in Palestine, and in the adjacent regions.* 2 vols. 2d ed. Boston: Crocker and Brewster; London: John Murray, 1860.

Smith, Walter Burges. *America's Diplomats and Consuls of 1776-1865: A Geographic and Biographic Directory of the Foreign Service from the Declaration of Independence to the End of the Civil War.* Washington, D. C.: Center for the Study of Foreign Affairs, Foreign Service Institute, U. S. Department of State, 1987.

Taylor, Katherine Fischer. *In the Theater of Criminal Justice.* Princeton, N. J. Princeton University Press, 1993.

Tees, Francis H. Tees. *The Ancient Landmark of American Methodism or Historic Old St. George's.* Philadelphia, Pa.: The Message Publishing Company, 1951.

_____, et al. *Pioneering in Penn's Woods.* Philadelphia: The Philadelphia Conference Tract Society of the Methodist Episcopal Church, 1937.

Thompson, James M. *Louis Napoleon and the Second Empire.* Oxford: Blackwell, 1954.

United States Census Records. Philadelphia, Pennsylvania. 1850, 1860, 1870. Microfilm.

Watts, Isaac. *Hymns and Spiritual Songs,* Book I, in *The Works of the Late Reverend & Learned Isaac Watts, D. D.* London: Printed for T. and T. Longman, J. Buckland, J. Oswald, J. Waugh, and J. Ward, 1753.

Wesley, John. *Advice to the People Called Methodists.* [Newcastle: Gooding,] 1745.

_____. *The Letters of the Rev. John Wesley, A.M.* John Telford, ed. 8 vols. London: Epworth Press, 1931.

Wesley, John and Charles. *Funeral Hymns.* Second Series. London: 1759, in Osborn, George, *The Poetical Works of John and Charles Wesley: Reprinted from the Originals, with the last corrections of the authors; together with the Poems of Charles Wesley not before published.* 13 v. London: Wesleyan-Methodist Conference Office, 2, Castle-Street, City-Road; sold at 66 Paternoster-Row, 1870.

White, Charles Edward. *The Beauty of Holiness; Phoebe Palmer as Theologian, Revivalist, Feminist, and Humanitarian.* Grand Rapids, Michigan: Francis Asbury Press, 1986.

Websites

Isle of Wight History Centre, Newport, Isle of Wight: http://www.iwhistory.org.uk.

Buchanan, James, president of the United States, presidential address: http://www.intac.com/~rfrone/history/1860-sou.htm.

American Church in Paris: http://www.americanchurchparis.org/

Index

[Numbers refer to the Letters not pages]

DATE DUE
